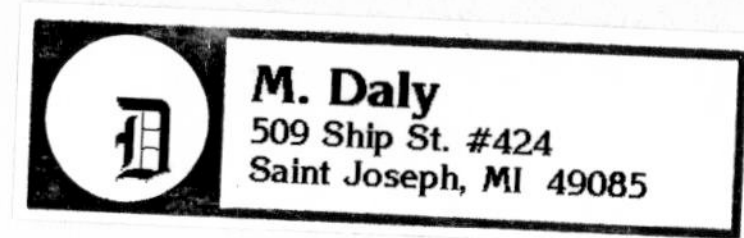

When Youth Was Mine

A Memoir of Kerry 1902-1925

Jeremiah Murphy
(1902-1990)

First Published in 1998 by
MENTOR Press
43 Furze Road,
Sandyford Industrial Estate,
Dublin 18, Republic of Ireland.

Tel: (353)-1- 295 2112 / 3 Fax: (353)-1- 295 2114

ISBN 0 947548 88 2

A catalogue record for this book is available from the British Library

Cover Illustration:	Jonathan Barry
Cover Design:	Design Image
Edited by:	John McCormack
Design and Layout:	Kathryn McKinney

The publishers are grateful to the following for their assistance in the preparation of this book: Michael F. Murphy (author's brother), Kilquane, Co. Kerry; Bill Mitchell, North Carolina, USA; Patricia (Murphy) Doran (author's daughter), Florida, USA; Pádraig O'Dineen; Ryle Dwyer; Timmy McCarthy; Michelle Cooper Galvin; Colin Vard; Cumann Sliabh Luachra; Una, Michael, Moira and Brendan Murphy (author's children) and finally, most of all Angela (Radile) Murphy (author's widow) who left us to be with Jeremiah, shortly before his story was published.

Printed in Ireland by ColourBooks Ltd.

3 5 7 9 10 8 6 4 2

Contents

Publisher's Note

The manuscript of *When Youth Was Mine* was discovered in an attic in Swiftwater, Pennsylvania, shortly after the author's death in 1990.

It is reproduced here in its entirety with only minor editorial modifications. The accuracy and detail displayed is a wonderful tribute to the author's phenomenal powers of recall. His brother, Michael, has corroborated the details of the events described and we are deeply grateful for his generous assistance in producing this book. The historical accuracy of the manuscript has been checked and endorsed by a number of local and national historians.

We, the publishers, believe this work to be an important social and historical record offering an unusual insight into social and political life in Ireland in the early 1900's. As such it needs to be preserved for future generations.

The views and opinions expressed throughout this book are entirely those of the author. The expression of these views sometimes reflects the tension, animosity and even the romance with which the events of the 1920's were viewed at the time and in later years.

The Editor

Map A
Co. Kerry

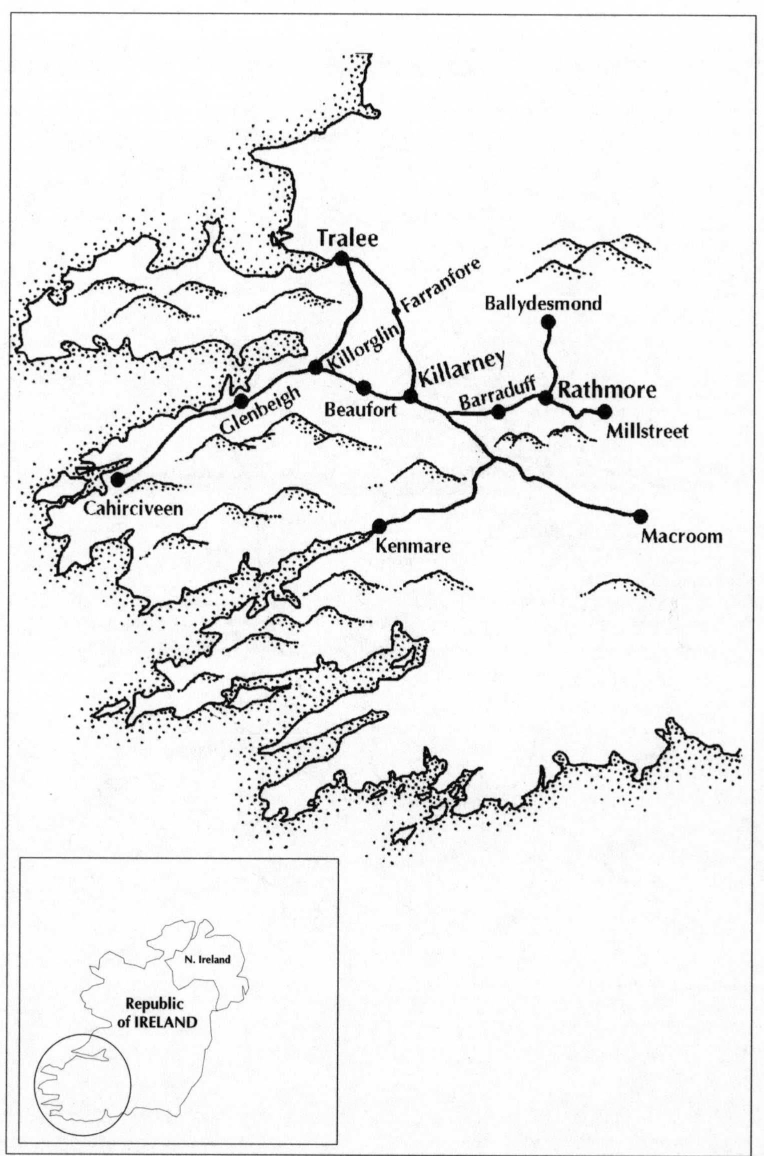

Map B
Co. Kerry (East)

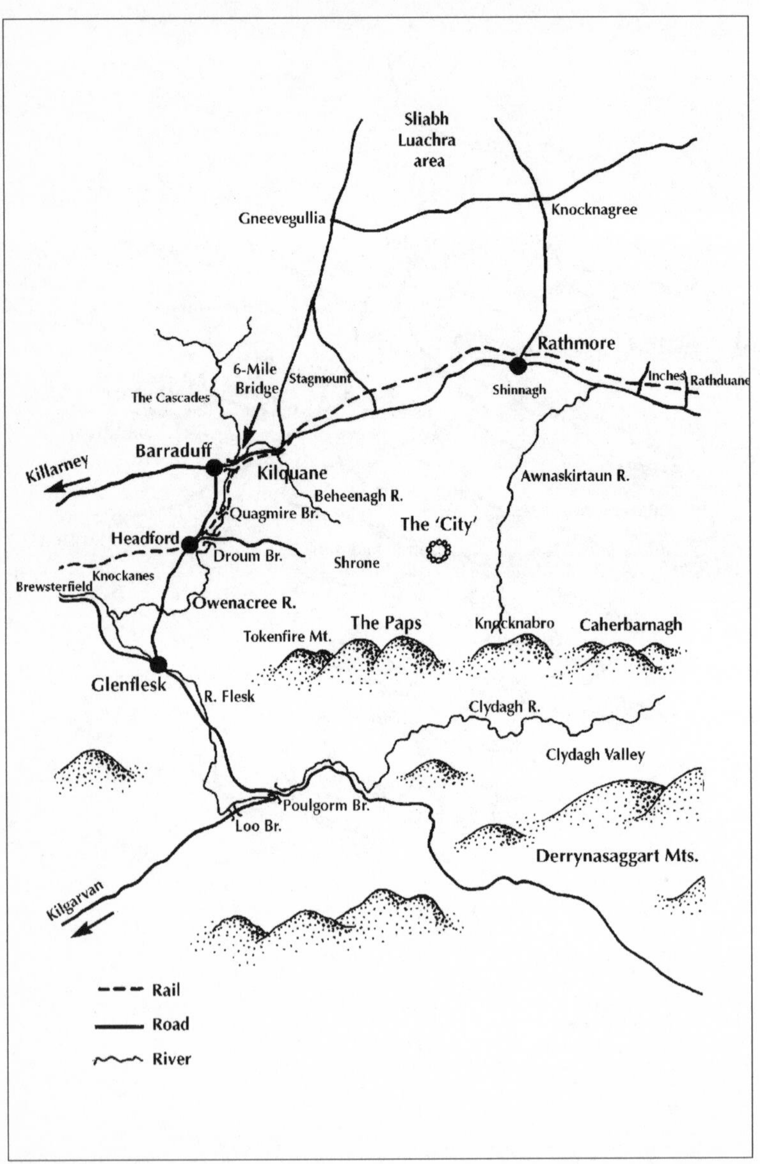

Map C
Kilquane area, Co. Kerry

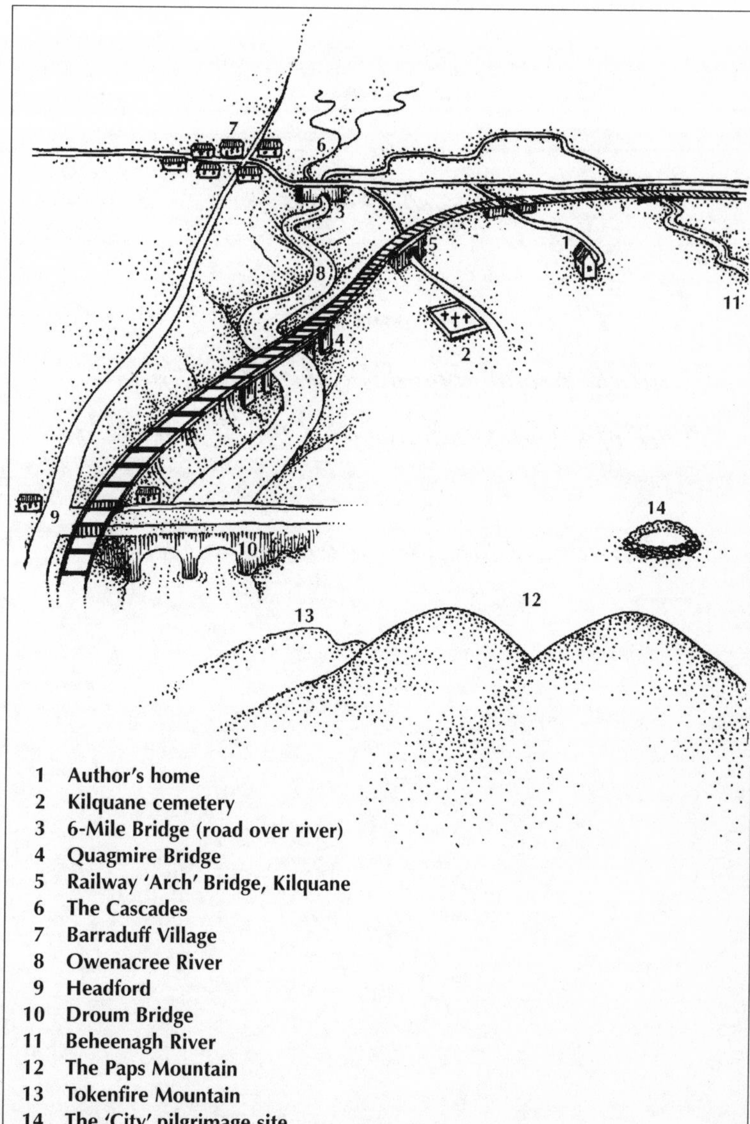

Dedicated
to
Angela Murphy

and
all the people who gave their lives in the
War of Independence and the Civil War,

regardless of the side on which they fought.

Prologue

Swiftwater, Pennsylvania, USA
31st July 1990

The cortège made its way slowly from Clark's funeral home in Stroudsburg to the nearby church of Our Lady of Victory. The warm summer sunshine illuminated the line of black limousines as they wound their way through the streets of the Pennsylvania town. He was making his final journey, over three thousand miles from the place where he had been born.

If he could have spoken to us that day he would probably have said, 'It's a grand day for a funeral!' These were the familiar words he had often uttered on such solemn occasions in the past. He usually delivered the words with a subdued eloquence, accompanied with a slight squint of his eyes which provided welcome relief and an assurance that life would go on.

Inside the church his son Brendan and his daughter Moira read from the scriptures. His granddaughter read the simple moving eulogy that she had written for the sad occasion. His widow, Angela, was deeply moved by this loving tribute.

As the mourners left the church a soft rain began to fall for just a few minutes. It was as if Stroudsburg had borrowed some of the light drizzle that fell regularly on his birthplace far away. The dead man's brother John, standing among the mourners outside the church, reckoned the angels were crying. Within a few minutes brilliant sunshine bathed the churchyard but it failed to lighten the dreariness of hearts heavy from the emptiness. He was gone.

The cortège resumed the last leg of its journey to Prospect Cemetery in East Stroudsburg. At the graveside his son Brendan read a passage from scripture about the promise of eternal life. In the warm sunshine Father Zabotocki led the group of mourners in prayers. The flag of his native country which had been draped over the casket, was removed, folded and presented to Angela. As the sad group stood silently beneath the trees, a lone piper started up the plaintive notes of *Danny Boy*. The lonesome sound wafted over the mourners and it seemed as if the notes were beseeching the 'old country' to finally let go of him. For eighty-eight years the 'old country' had had a firm grasp on the most vibrant part of the dead man's spirit and held it for her own. As the final notes of the pipes died away, the grave was covered.

There he rests in East Stroudsburg by the side of a busy highway. No doubt he will keep a constant watch for travellers in distress. In life he never missed an opportunity to help anyone stranded on the road. It was a habit often rewarded by disappointed looks on the faces of his children for having missed an eagerly awaited picnic or swim in the lake.

Over a hundred relatives and friends returned to the family home in nearby Swiftwater to share their grief. A cousin of Angela's, Bill Mitchell, had travelled from North Carolina for the funeral. Bill had always been close to Angela and had a great regard for her late husband.

Later that afternoon at the house, Angela asked Bill to fetch a treasured family photo album from the attic. Bill climbed the ladder to the dark attic. His eyes took a few minutes to grow accustomed to the darkness. The only illumination came from a small skylight window. As he searched among the items in the attic he eyes came to rest on a cardboard box abandoned in a corner. Thinking that it might contain the photo album, he dragged it over under the skylight window to search it. He peered into the box. Inside lay sheets of paper, yellow and faded with age. Bill immediately recognised the handwriting on the pages. It was the familiar style of the man they had just laid to rest.

He took the faded pages carefully from the box and sat down on the attic floor.

He began to read . . .

Introduction

The Attic

. . . AN ATTIC can be a wonderful place. It can be the hideout of a dangerous criminal or the refuge of a hard-pressed patriot. One has been the setting of a famous opera. Many famous masterpieces of art and literature were brought to perfection in humble attics. Rare old paintings have lain there gathering dust only to be discovered by accident. Some of the precious violins of Cremona have been hidden away in attics, their perishable wood and imperishable tones almost lost to posterity. A piece of furniture, once the idol of the master craftsman, can be dilapidated and consigned to an attic only to be thrown away or burned by a succeeding generation.

As the flowers and leaves of a summer sparkle for a while and fade away unnoticed, so too our precious belongings become less important until the time comes when they are cast aside and relegated to the least accessible part of the house. Too old to be in style, too good to be thrown away, many objects of sentimental value are put away in an attic, never to be admired again. The flowers bloom and are appreciated on each recurring summer for they are God's handiwork, but all things mortal must come to an end some day.

An attic can be a mysterious place. To a casual observer its contents are rather uninviting — a collection of discarded material of various ages and sometimes unrelated origin. It is just a pile of junk. However, a closer examination will reveal some articles that shed light on the lives and customs of its owners or occupants as well as their tastes in literature and dress and their refinement in manners and education. A picture, a piece of broken furniture or worn clothing can be a clue to a past personality and set minds to work reconstructing a haphazard existence or a faded glory.

I suddenly became aware of this some years ago while engaged in construction of a room in my attic to supplement the needs of an expanding family. In the process, many old pictures and books were disturbed from their long rest. The younger members of my family asked a great many questions about the mementos and I was forced to embark on a long and tedious explanation of various articles — especially the faces in some of the photographs. I too learned a few things at the same time. One was that my children knew very little about their ancestors and another, that it would be much easier to make a catalogue of the many relatives for purposes of clarification. It occurred to me also to write a description of the various people who were my relatives and associates during my early life. These thoughts took up some of my untidy brain but were crowded out by the business at hand, only to come back again in moments of relaxation, during some sleepless nights or at some family gatherings such as weddings and funerals.

I do not suppose that my meagre possessions will ever be the subject of a quarrel or that any of them will become museum pieces. Yet, I have a fervent desire that my family will respect my existence by remembering where I originated and why I came here. So many people don't know where their parents came from that it distresses me no end. Even first generation Americans are so ignorant of their ancestors that it borders on disrespect. Not that it matters much in our way of life, but the lack of sentiment shows lack of appreciation. Some people trace relatives back to the *Mayflower*, the Revolution or the Civil War, but the majority of us are content with more recent connections. Yet we are all part of the big stew that is America and whether we are the bone, the meat or the vegetable, we blend together to enhance the passing hour. Much of our country's greatness is due to the diversity of moods, ideals and ideas, customs and entertainment of the lowly immigrant. Whether our contribution is great or small, it matters not. Some things come easy to some people, others get everything the hard way. The effect may be as great in one instance as the other.

Before my memory becomes dim with time and while there are still around some of my contemporaries to verify many of the tales and jokes, I had better collect them between two covers if for no better reason than my own satisfaction. If anybody is interested, he is welcome to read them — if not, they can be relegated to some attic or the realm of forgotten things. The tales are not intended to be a story of my life, but rather an account of the people and events I came in contact with in the first quarter of this century. In a way, the world moved on, but many of us stood still. This may or may not be our own fault, but we lacked the leadership and initiative to move along at the right pace so we were left behind with only our memories to console us. The pleasant memories, in my opinion, outweigh the sad ones and the results justify the risks involved. Looking back over the bridge of fifty years is a long way back and like the "Vision of Mirza" we can never recross it. So many have fallen through, on the way across, and a lot of water has passed under that bridge. The accounts of some of the incidents may not be perfectly correct or may be overlapped and the chronology of events is not strictly adhered to, but these inaccuracies are not intentional. Neither are the omissions. Let me apologise by adding that details get very dim in that space of time.

Some of my old pals have long since passed away and laid to rest in many parts of the world. Others are still very active. A new generation has moved onto the scene. To all my erstwhile companions, I dedicate this humble attempt with apology for my inability to do justice to the characters. During the revolutionary period, pictures or written accounts of engagements were prohibited, obviously for reasons of security. There were no press correspondents to record or preserve an accurate description of the action during the periods of fighting in the war of independence against the British or the civil war. The mention of a name or publication of a picture could well turn out to be the issue of a death warrant. Perhaps history will treat the matter kindly. Action was often swift and sudden and there was little use for a swagger or strut during the dark days of fighting an uneven battle against a crafty, resourceful and powerful enemy. The little jokes and whims of some of the people are thick on my mind but somehow elude description. However, they evoked many a laugh in their time and often bear repetition. Some of the lighter moments will only be forgotten when those who made them are around no more. Association with them was one of the greatest satisfactions and among my most cherished memories. For friendship cultivated in adversity can be more lasting than that experienced in joy. Patriotism was the only incentive that moved them into circulation, otherwise they were simple folks. They were an unselfish lot and their failure to achieve complete success was only made more bitter by the lives that were lost and the emigration of some of the survivors. Every gateway has its toll.

So we all move closer to the attic of our generation. With these sentiments I am impelled to write an account of our fun and frolics, our woes and tears. I have a penchant for looking back. This is a personal as well as a racial drawback. However, history teaches us some useful, if expensive, lessons. Reasonably aware of my limited ability, I prefer to treat the side effects rather than the main events. So I will endeavour to give the reader as clear an account as possible of the period 1902 to 1925 — the way of life around me, the political and economic scene and the incidents that affected those people I knew "when youth was mine".

1
New Century, New Life (1900-07)

In the spring of 1902, two women were talking about the outlook for the current year. One was about 25 years old, the other about 60 years. They were discussing farm business because that was their way of living. The younger woman, a returned Yank, had gone to the U.S. seven years before and having saved enough money to pay the dowry or "fortune" (as it was referred to in that part of the country), had married a 'small farmer' (owner of a small holding) the previous year. Owing to the peculiar marriage arrangements which were the custom and the law, the older people could retain the ownership of the farm by agreement, for a year or two after the young couple got married. The purpose was to try to save some money to tide them over their declining years. Old age pensions and social security as we know them now, did not exist in those days and people, especially the elderly, were forced to make their own arrangements. In this particular case, the older woman was deploring the fact that the previous year had not been very profitable and in a few weeks she and her husband would be turning over the farm to the young couple with very little on which to retire. The younger woman countered by remarking that she had very little too, but during the past month she had a son born who would be very little help with the spring work. She added, "He and ten shillings and the clothes on my back are all I possess but he will be a man some day." This was absolute optimism but it was typical of the people in that part of Ireland. They trusted Divine Providence that each succeeding year would be better than the one gone by. These two women, as you may suspect, were my mother and grandmother.

Hannah Moynihan Murphy (author's mother) originally from Caherbarnagh.

Mrs Margaret Houlihan Murphy (author's paternal grandmother) from Stagmount.

The century was new and economic conditions were improving in many parts of the world. People who had emigrated from Ireland to the United States, England or Australia frequently sent money home to their aged parents and it was interesting to hear the old people boast about the gifts. Naturally, the ones with the largest families in America had the most reason to boast.

Twenty years earlier, Ireland had been witnessing few expressions of nationalistic fervour and had been experiencing the worst economic recession since the Great Famine of 1845-49. The big exodus had started during that national calamity and was stepped up after the Civil War in the United

States. Every train at every station along the railways of the country during the 1880's and 90's picked up emigrants and took them to Belfast, Dublin or Cork to embark for Canada, England, Australia and the U.S. The Cobh of Cork, then called Queenstown, had the biggest traffic as most people preferred to go to the United States even though the cost was greater. The British government by this time had come around to the idea of scattering the Irish people instead of fighting them and were in favour of emigration. Emigrants were encouraged to go to Canada or Australia with substantial grants of free land. The great ocean liners were kept busy in their transportation. Some of those who went to the United States earlier, now had enough money for a return trip or to buy a farm or marry somebody who had one. This traffic was also catered for by British shipping who advertised at length the glories of a holiday in Ireland while the government, by the political and economic squeeze, was making life almost futile for its natives. They had them literally going and coming. The returning Yank by his dress, manners and spending of money was also one of the best advertisements in favour of emigration. However, a few of these remained and went back to the old ways of farming while entertaining the neighbours with stories of the wonders of other lands.

The early Irish emigrants to the U.S. were people of some means, education and adventure, who wished to see the new continent and having settled there, rarely returned. The emigrants during the famine period were the broken and starving victims who abandoned even large farms and small businesses to escape its terrible effects. Those who left Ireland during the 1880's and 90's were largely a work force which otherwise would only increase the ranks of the unemployed. Since there was little or no industry in Ireland, and these people were willing and able to work, they went in large numbers to the U.S., Canada or Australia. In the States they were less likely to be discriminated against and even with a limited elementary education, at least they spoke the language and had a decided advantage over other non-English speaking immigrants. Many of them saved some money and returned for a trip or desired to settle down on a farm in their native land. The girls, especially, were prime targets of the young farmers contemplating matrimony and they provided almost unfair competition for other girls who never left home. They were smart looking, well dressed and their manners and speech were a distinct asset. However, when asked if they were going to marry a farmer some retorted, "I guess I'm too wise for that."

There was also another valve whereby the population of the towns and cities could blow off steam. The ever present unemployed who were dependent in part on some form of public relief were recruited into the British army by the thousands and made first class material to uphold the empire in many parts of the world. They served from Khartoum to the Khyber Pass. It was a nine year term, a combination of line and reserve with not less than three years in active line service. When these soldiers returned they were not the most popular members of the community but their tales of far-off lands inspired other idle young men whom they came in contact with, to go and do likewise. Thus, the public house became the unofficial recruiting station. In the following paragraphs, I will relate three stories which are typical of the recruiting technique. They were told to me first-hand by the principals.

My grandfather spent several years in England. Among other jobs he worked at in London, was the building of the famous steamship *The Great Eastern*, launched in 1858.

Sometime during the Crimean War, he was in a saloon in London. He struck up a conversation with a stranger at the bar. They had a few drinks together and when they felt merry, my grandfather became aware of something gliding up and down inside his glass of ale. With his tongue and lips he judged it was a coin, probably a shilling. He heard many tales of "taking the shilling", a favourite expression for enlistment at the time. The army recruiting fellows gave a shilling to the new recruit as sort of binder to clinch the deal. Acceptance of the coin in hand made the decision irrevocable. No doubt, the war had been a topic of conversation and enlistment was mentioned as England was desperate for men at that time. Obviously, this recruiter was desperate too, and he didn't care how he got the shilling into his prospect's hand. The trick was that when my grandfather wondered what was in his glass he would retrieve the coin by hand and thereby fulfil his part of the obligation. He sensed the plot and at an opportune moment, smashed his glass on the recruiter's face and left the saloon by a side door. The following day he took a train to Wales where he worked in a steel mill and a fertiliser plant in turn. But more about that later on.

The next story was told to me many years ago in New York. It seems two neighbouring farmers in Ireland took some cattle to the market. Each farmer took his son with him to help with the driving but not the selling. The latter was the father's province and dared not be encroached on by anybody as immature and inexperienced as a twenty-year old "boy". The demand for cattle was very low that day and after several attempts to sell at a rock bottom price failed, the two older men repaired to some saloon to drink and talk over the bad state of the market. The younger men were left to tend the cattle, in the hope that a buyer taking advantage of the slow market might turn up. And turn up he did! He bought the cattle for what he no doubt considered a bargain. The two young men had made a sale without telling their fathers and contrary to orders at that. This was an unpardonable error, if not a crime, and the more they thought about it, the more grievous their actions seemed. Both young fellows decided to run away rather than face their irate fathers. This was easy as they now had plenty of money. They took the boat to England the following day. Failing to find employment in England, they soon spent all the money and were reduced to begging. They decided to enlist in the army as an alternative to being jailed for vagrancy. The two got separated somewhere along the line but one of them served fourteen years in an English cavalry regiment, most of it in Rawalpindi in Northwest India. At the end of his term he emigrated to New York where he told me the story.

Anybody who cares to read Charles J. Kickham's ballad about "Patrick Sheehan" can get a pretty good picture of the fate of many of the Irish in the British army. Of course they were not all bums, but rarely, except in the case of the nobility, did they ever get beyond the rank of sergeant. There were only a few of note including the Duke of Wellington, Lord Kitchener and Lord Roberts and these were typical aristocrats.

Another average recruit was a cousin of mine, who after obtaining a job on the railways as an apprentice fireman, got fed up one day and quit. Two older brothers, one an engineer and the other a construction worker had got him a job when jobs were hard to get. He joined the Royal Garrison Artillery and served in Gibraltar and Malta. When his active service was over, he came back to Ireland and worked as a blacksmith's helper. His reserve time would terminate in September, 1914, but World War I broke out in August and he was called up immediately. He spent the next year and a half in Yorkshire training recruits in gunnery and discouraging the Germans from making a landing there. After two weeks leave in Ireland he went to France and engaged in the major battles, including the siege of Antwerp and the defence of Verdun where his regiment was sent to bolster up the Allied lines. After spending some time with the occupation forces in Germany, he retired to Ireland and worked as a postman.

There were about ten Irish regiments in the British army, all first class troops, highly disciplined and very tough. These were rarely stationed in Ireland as their allegiance was less of a problem when sent to India, Egypt or Singapore. The top officers were rarely Irish — another safeguard. All were disbanded later (except the Irish Guards) at an appropriate time which will be described in a later chapter.

The political scene was lively in Ireland during the last quarter of the 19th century. The principal and immediate aim of the Irish representatives who sat in the House of Commons was to get rid of an infernal system of landlordism which had reduced the Irish tenant farmers to poverty. There was very little money in circulation and one of its few sources was the sale of farm produce to England. In doing so, the farmer had to compete with the farmers in Britain as well as those in Europe. As no Irish shipping company existed, freight was at the mercy of British companies. Now and again, an occurrence of foot-and-mouth disease was conveniently 'discovered' which prevented the cattle from being exported. There was no inspection service in those days and very little grading or control. But that did not worry the landlord, who demanded his rent, whatever the prevailing economic conditions. When the tenant farmer couldn't pay his rent he was evicted by the sheriff who was always backed up by some members of the Royal Irish Constabulary (R.I.C.), who in turn were backed up in extreme cases by a company of British soldiers. What chance did a lowly farmer with his wife and a few small children have against such an array of force? If he could scrape the fare together, he emigrated, if not he became a public charge. His farm was taken over by the landlord or given to another tenant for a fee. The taker was called a 'grabber' and in all cases he was 'boycotted', whether he was landlord or tenant. This led to many atrocities and several paid with their lives for the farms they took over. A dispossessed farmer often got even with his successor before emigrating. Many were convicted of various acts of revenge. The boycotted people always had police protection. In several areas, temporary huts were built to accommodate the police and some of these were killed. Dispossessed farmers accused of acts of revenge were often convicted on flimsy evidence especially in cases where the authorities knew the accused person was nationally minded. Long jail sentences were very common even when the victim was innocent. Spies and informers were common and the R.I.C. were the eyes and ears of the authorities.

In some cases those who were dispossessed from their farms were aided by a secret organisation known as the 'Moonlighters'. This name refers to the fact that most of the organisation's activities took place under cover of darkness. The members of this organisation were local people, secretly belonging to the Fenian movement who had enough patriotism and backbone to resist the unjust evictions, but their effectiveness was hampered by secrecy, informers and the Coercion Acts. Riding at night, across the country, they visited 'grabbers', suspected informers and landlords, destroying their property and injuring or killing them on occasions. Barns were burned, cattle were driven off lands onto gardens and lawns, and meadows were ploughed up. Such scenes of destruction were a common sight to an early-rising landlord who had been marked for boycott. Some retired judges, ex-army officers and British civil servants augmented the police and supplied them with information. These were also the target of the 'Moonlighters'. Sometimes when a farmer went to use his horse, he found the animal completely exhausted after a rough cross-country midnight ride, but no questions were asked and no explanation was needed.

One incident which comes to mind is the trial and conviction of a man named John Twiss who lived in northeast Kerry near the border with Co. Limerick. This incident was a frequent topic of conversation with a great many of the old-timers when I was a small lad. It seems some 'grabber' was shot to death in that area and Twiss was charged with the crime. He was a very prominent Nationalist and this fact had been known to the local police. There was no direct evidence on which to convict him yet the authorities went to great lengths to establish a case against him. When it was proved he was in a certain place at a certain time, it was doubtful that he could be at the scene of the crime when it was committed. However, it would be possible to ride a horse or use other means of travel and get back to the point of alibi in the elapsed time. The prosecution for the crown seized this slim possibility and got two R.I.C. policemen to run the route over which the accused would have travelled. Needless to say, they did not select the laziest ones. Having accomplished the feat with a short time to spare, Twiss was convicted on purely circumstantial evidence, even though he did not use a horse, nor was he placed at or near the scene of the crime. The popular belief by those who were in a position to know was that the job was done by somebody else but that Twiss knew all about it. Be that as it may, Twiss was hanged.

One of these old-timers told me of another incident. He seemed to be well acquainted with the particulars. A landlord's agent while travelling between Rathmore and Killarney was to be shot by a special sniper who had been brought into the area for that specific purpose. The agent invariably rode on a certain side of the jaunting car, so the sniper took up a position on the same side of the road. However, on this particular occasion the agent rode on the opposite side, making a poor target and endangering the other occupants. Pure chance or good information, who knows? No shots, no story, nobody was any wiser, but a repeat performance was never tried. According to the story, "He was a dead shot and was using a new kind of rifle (the Martini Henri rifle) with a screw inside the barrel and it could carry a mile".

The movements of certain individuals were always recorded by the R.I.C. Once when Denny Lynch of Clydagh was seen on horseback in Barraduff on a Sunday morning, his time of arrival and departure was entered in a notebook by the local police sergeant named Bowsey. Lynch was a prominent 'Moonlighter' and the notation might come in useful in case anything unusual occurred.

The land question was seized on by two leaders whose names are well known, Charles S. Parnell and Michael Davitt. The former was the leader of the Irish Party in the British House of Commons and the latter a man of the people, pledged to direct action. Parnell held the balance of power in the Commons between the Liberals and the Tories while Davitt organised the Land League among the Irish peasants. While evictions were legal under the law, there was another canker that plagued the farmer which was outside any kind of law. This was the practice of taking over a farm whether the tenant paid his rent or not and giving it to some friend or well-wisher. In cases of this kind, the farmer was turned out after thirty days' notice, any time of the year. Is it any wonder the Irish farmers never improved their land or their homes? Taxes were based on arbitrary factors, such as the size of the panes of glass in the windows, thus denying the occupants even necessary sunlight. Parnell and Davitt forced a bill through the Commons which changed these conditions and which guaranteed 'permanency of tenure' to everybody as long as they paid their rent. This was the first economic relief the tenant farmers got since the Act of Union in 1801. Many English landlords rarely visited Ireland but sublet their interests to middlemen or agents and these raised the original rents to make more profit. This nefarious practice engendered corruption and broke the spirit of the poor farmers. A new Coercion Act was passed but in spite of its impact, the people won the struggle.

Parnell and Davitt were now the most popular leaders of the Irish people in the nineteenth century and inspired by success they pressed on for further relief for the peasantry. Under the law, farmers had no title to the land they occupied. Then who had, and how did they get it? This involved many different reigns and different expeditions. Land and titles were bestowed by English rulers on officers and leaders who led expeditions against the Irish since 1169. Most of them were granted in the reigns of Elizabeth I and Oliver Cromwell. Entire towns or districts were parcelled out to these adventurers for a royalty to be paid to the crown and administered at will. To these tyrants, their descendants or their agents, the peasant farmer had to plead, cap in hand, for the right to settle and eke out a bare existence. It was lower than a form of slavery because the landlords assumed no responsibility whatsoever. Any change must be an improvement, for conditions could not be much worse. Any landlord with any sense of decency grew sick of the stagnation and also sought reform called Land Purchase Acts. Laws were passed in the British parliament whereby a tenant farmer could purchase his land by a system of deferred payments. There were Acts passed at different sessions containing different provisions allowing farmers to purchase their land. The Bank of England advanced the purchase price to the landlords and the instalment payments were collected from the farmers in the form of rent through the Local Government Board. Stability had been established by the beginning of the twentieth century and it had a sobering effect on both sides of the issue. Davitt and Parnell were dead but they had achieved reform and immortality.

In order to give the reader a clear picture of life in the country in Ireland around the turn of the century, it is necessary to make a few more observations. So far, we have only touched on the political and farm life of the country. There was little industrial life except for the shipbuilding and linen in the North. Social life was confined to the aristocracy. The professional sector was something else again. Except in rare cases it was an aloof, arrogant and snobbish element, whose members believed themselves to be so much better than the farmers. They had no land problems and could afford to rub shoulders now and again with the forces and representatives of the government. The clergy were at least educated and neutral but only a few were very patriotic. Some teachers, lawyers, bankers, storekeepers and government representatives were unsympathetic and indifferent to the Irish language, culture and political independence. They could have been a powerful force in their country's destiny but they worked in reverse and helped only to anglicise it. Only the bare remnants of Irish language, music and dance survived in the remote parts of the poor and mountainous districts.

Such was the picture at the beginning of the 20th century when I came into the world. It was not dark and it was getting a little brighter each year. Prices of farm commodities were rising slowly and steadily and ploughs, mowing machines and threshers were starting to appear on the scene. The people were better fed and dressed a little more stylishly. The Department of Agriculture was sending out circulars intended to improve the crops and cattle. Creameries were being built and farmers co-operative societies were formed; spraying and fertilising were introduced. The Gaelic Athletic Association was staging regular events and concerts and dances were becoming common. Schools and churches were being improved and the Gaelic League had been formed to foster the language, drama and traditional music and dance. Irishmen in the USA had dominated the Olympics in 1904 and 1908 and there was a generous sprinkling of 'returned Yanks' in summer to liven the scene. Crossroad dances were in full swing on Sunday afternoons, weather permitting, and house dancing in the winter nights was very popular, especially around Christmas when people came home on holidays from other lands. The land purchase was under way and it was only natural that such a renaissance should produce an optimistic outlook. There was even talk about Home Rule. It was a big bite and England was slow to allow it. It occupied the major business of the Irish National Party in the House of Commons during the first decade of this century.

The people of the neighbouring church held a concert to raise funds for its renovation. The building itself was used to accommodate the big attendance. A prior collection and subscriptions from emigrants in many parts of the world had helped to launch the drive and already the floor and seats were in place. A temporary stage was erected in front of the incomplete altar and sanctuary and the place was jammed to the doors. Before the programme commenced a gallery on the right wing partly sagged with a crash. It was not completed but the local O'Sullivan carpenters shored it up and there was no damage. Jeremiah Cronin and Johnny Moynihan, a blind fiddle player, gave a few selections on their favourite instruments and various people danced and sang. Two of these I remember; Thady Sullivan (nicknamed 'the Clerk') danced a hornpipe and Margaret Lynch, then from Headford, sang some Irish songs. She later became a nun and is still hale and hearty at this writing. My mother, though quite a nice singer, did not contribute on this occasion. It was the first public function I can remember attending but I had been to Mass a few times in the old church.

The roof leaked then and the floor was mud and sand. Father John Browne had been assigned to the parish in 1906 and he proved to be very progressive, a stern man and a firm believer in higher education. The local talent proved worthy of the occasion and it was only the beginning. Father Browne got all the farmers to contribute stone, sand, lime and labour and the project was completed speedily. A choir and altar boys were organised.

Fr. Browne, though coming from a wealthy family in North Kerry, was very quick to recognise the inadequacy of housing in part of his parish of Barraduff. He advised the people to take advantage of loans and free grants made available to farmers in small holdings and congested districts. Many of them built new houses between 1910-1915. Others renovated their homes and many labourers' cottages were approved and built. Some removed large rocks from their land by blasting and we youngsters liked to hear the big noise. A rearrangement of estates in Headford and Barraduff made the land more convenient to the homes and the locality took on an air of general improvement. One incident during these operations is remembered. A cowhouse was built and the roof was applied on Saturday. During the weekend, a sudden storm raised the whole roof of timber and galvanised iron off the walls and deposited it across the road close by the railway tracks. It was completely wrecked.

My first brush with civilisation came in March, 1907 when I started school. It was a two-room building then, but another room was added in 1912. There were four teachers and the principal was a tall, serious man named Mr. Donoghue who glorified in good poetry, plays and elocution. He turned out some good scholars who later on became prominent in the ecclesiastical and commercial world. The lower grades were taken care of by two budding aspirants to the teaching profession, P. J. Moynihan and his cousin Madge Moynihan. These became teachers later on and were assigned to local schools. The lady became Mrs. Cronin and P. J. decided to go to the US where he became very prominent in educational and government positions in the State of Massachusetts. The other teachers were Miss Ellen O'Shea who later married the principal, and an old bachelor named Jack Lynch.

Another figure who was very well known around the locality was a fiddle player named Fred "Gowa" (from the Gaelic word 'Gabha' meaning 'blacksmith') Murphy. He ran a small grocery store east of the village on the main road. From his waist up he was a handsome, normal man but had short, little legs which were partly crippled and he rode around on a donkey when he needed to travel. I heard him play a few times and watched my mother dance for him. He was my father's cousin.

Now this brings me to the other side of my ancestors. My grandfather was about 75 years old as I first remember him. He was grey, partly bald and wore sideburns. My father was heavier built, with a dark complexion and like all the other men of his time, had a full moustache. He was the eldest of six boys and worked on the construction of the Kenmare Railway when he was about 18 years old. When this was finished he worked on the railways around Cork City until he settled down to farming. His education didn't extend beyond the 4th grade but he was largely self educated, was a fine reader and interested mainly in the pursuit of farming.

I had an Uncle Paddy who was a member of the R.I.C. and served in many parts of the country. He was astute, elegant and well groomed. He had jet-black hair and his waxed moustache was very neat looking when compared with the 'soup strainers' of the local farmers. My father wore a moustache too, and in spite of mother's requests, refused to part with it. Of the five uncles on my father's side, three of whom emigrated to the US, I knew the policeman best and he came home every couple of years to visit us. In spite of his eligibility and good appearance, he remained a bachelor until he retired from the force. He was conservative, what you could term a career man and retired with the rank of Head Constable, which was between Sergeant and Inspector. Besides being one of the best shots on the force, he was a weights-and-measures inspector and an amateur detective. He owned a good violin and played it very well. Most of his music he learned from the tramp players who frequented the fairs in the West of Ireland. He often loaned them his fiddle to 'wallop a tone into it' as they played on the streets while he directed traffic nearby. He told me how these tramp players named Smith came to Ballinasloe Fair, which lasted three days and although he would be charitable enough to lend his

The author's parents — Michael J. Murphy and Hannah Moynihan.

violin to give them a start, he was often forced to arrest one or more of their number for drunkenness or disorderly conduct before the fair was over. It was a veritable Mecca for the tinkers of the West of Ireland. Like Puck Fair in Kerry, these fairs were infested with tramps, tinkers, gypsies, ballad singers and plain bums to disgrace the proceedings. William Bulfin wrote a chapter in *Rambles in Erin* describing these characters which is recommended reading.

Many of the old men remembered the famine years of 1845-49. My grandfather told me about a man who lived a mile south of our farm and came for a basket of turnips one day during those terrible years. He only made it half way home and I was shown the place where he collapsed under his load from pure exhaustion and the effects of prolonged hunger. Other tales about the building of the railway were almost as sad. For a few pennies a day, men toiled and sweated, pushing wheelbarrows of earth until they fell exhausted, only to be replaced by another eager workman who waited on the side for such a possibility. A programme of public works was started to aid the starving people and many roads were laid out over new routes, eliminating steep grades and curves but these were never finished. They stand today as they were left over 100 years ago and although sound in engineering principles they serve as neglected reminders of improvements which were long overdue.

On 1 January 1909 the Old Age Pension was introduced. It amounted to 5 shillings a week and was paid to people who had reached 70 years of age. To qualify applicants had to prove their age. Since many records were lost or births never recorded, some people had a hard time proving even their identity. However, a notable event in the country called the 'Big Wind' was used as a yardstick. This was a violent storm which occurred in the winter of 1839. Anybody remembering the 'Big Wind' or born before or during it was considered entitled to the pension, as this would mean they had reached the requisite 70 years of age. There was considerable juggling of elementary mathematics to prove the point. A borderline case had to be decided on the affidavit of an older person. All the old-timers, male and female, who were able to walk, collected the first payment. For many it was the last. Some celebrated the event by having a few drinks and were injured, while others contracted colds and pneumonia. My grandfather was one of the latter. He died a month later. They couldn't stand the 'prosperity'. Some gave up their farms to their sons in order to be eligible and this raised the marriage rate for a while.

One time-honoured tradition which disappeared completely during my youth was 'packing the butter'. Before the advent of the creameries, farmers packed their butter for export into small barrels called 'firkins', which held about 100 lbs. Some middleman at the butter market in Cork graded the product according to quality into first, medium or second. He returned a receipt with a cheque for the proper amount. Farmers' wives in groups of four to six would assemble with their butter in one of the houses to pack a 'firkin' each week during the summer and less frequently as the milking season tapered off in winter. They measured the butter in gallons, quarts and cups and how they remembered what each owed the other is beyond my lame brain. These meetings were not all work and during the afternoon, tea and gossip were exchanged and the affair took on the atmosphere of something between a coffee morning and a bridge club. The whole proceeding was sociable but several coopers (makers of wooden barrels) went out of business when the function came to an end with the establishment of creameries and farmers' cooperatives.

Spraying the potato crop was a chore nobody cared for. This had to be done, however, as the blight which had caused the Famine could be prevented only by spraying the crop with a solution of copper sulphate and washing soda. A neighbouring farmer, while making an apology to the parish priest for a small contribution, mentioned the bad yield of his potato crop. The priest asked him if he sprayed and he answered, "No Father, I left them to God." Obviously annoyed at his neglect to use the only means of conquering the blight, the priest angrily remarked, "You did, and God left them to you."

In those years we had occasional visits from our relatives. It is amazing how far removed families can become relationwise, in the space of fifty years. I remember my grandfather being visited by his brothers-in-law. They all conversed in the Gaelic language. Now and again they broke off into English, and when they did so, I learned that my grandfather had been in England. He had fled there to escape prosecution as a result of some faction fighting which occurred in Killarney. These disturbances, whether political or agrarian, left him with a head injury inflicted by a piece of iron about two inches square and a couple of feet long. I remember as a little lad climbing on his knee and pressing my finger on the indentation in his skull over his right temple, which was very noticeable. It never seemed to give him any trouble and he lived to the age of seventy-seven. Years later his younger brother, who was my granduncle and with him when he was injured, told me all about it. It seems he was unconscious for a while and had a headache for a few days, but was never treated for the injury. Well, they made them tough in those days! Among other jobs he worked at in England (as previously mentioned) was the building of the famous steamship *The Great Eastern*.

The Gaelic Athletic Association had been formed in 1884 in order to stem the anglicisation of Irish athletics. Before this, the ancient games of hurling and hammer-throwing were played, but only in some pasture field. Football was also played but it was a very different kind of game from what we know today. Before the invention of the rubber bladder, a leather ball filled with hay or curled hair was used and the game was called 'Rough and Tumble'. The number of players was not important as long as it was the same on opposing teams. The goals may have been as far as three miles apart and the game was started midway between them. The ball could be kicked, hand passed, punched or carried in any manner by any player, while the participants struggled over the countryside towards their goal. Rivers, roads, trees and fences had to be negotiated and it seemed like a forerunner of the game of rugby. But all that changed when Gaelic football was organised and the game was played under a code of rules in an enclosure. By the turn of the century it was a highly refined type of entertainment and by 1904 the County Kerry team found itself in Dublin playing for the national championship. The team was called the Laune Rangers and they were noted athletes. Kerry had won the hurling final in 1891, but their first football triumph was in 1905.

I saw my first games around 1907 when I had started school. They were played by local teams. At school we played a little football and the names of all the great Kerry players were bywords among the public. Many good, all-round athletes competed at sports meetings and while they were not world-beaters, they had a good effect on the youth at that time. But the schools were poorly situated, having few playing fields, and the children were forced in many cases to play on the roads or in some neighbouring field. This did not promote the best relations between the farmers and the pupils.

The Gaelic League was founded in 1893 to foster the native language. The Irish language was gradually introduced as a subject in the schools. Our new teacher, Mr. Cronin, a native speaker, was also a great fisherman. The village where the school and church were located was only a half a mile from my home. It was composed of two pubs, two general stores, two blacksmith shops, two carpenter shops, one shoemaker shop, a handball court and about a dozen private houses. The storekeepers and craftsmen lived either beside or over their places of business. The railway station was two miles south of the village and the road from there ran north through the village at right angles to the main road. This main road was commonly known as the coach road and was the direct thoroughfare between Mallow and Killarney. Along this road were located at eight to ten mile intervals the stage and mail coach stables where a change of horses was kept in the old days prior to the advent of the railways. Killarney was our market town about eight miles to the west, while about five miles to the east on the same road stood the prosperous village of Rathmore. This place boasted of a police barracks, a courthouse, a creamery, a flour mill, a spinning and weaving mill and a railway station. About 1918, a dance hall and a farmers' co-operative were established and it was gradually becoming the shopping and social centre of east Kerry and part of west Cork. The local hamlet, Barraduff, appeared on the maps under the name of Six-Mile Bridge (but we often referred to it as the Cross) simply because it was six Irish miles from Killarney and a road intersection. Along the side of the main road stood the familiar milestones with the suitable inscriptions under the broad arrow — the official reminder that it was English territory.

The nearest railway station was located about two miles south of Barraduff at a place called Headford. From there a branch line ran about twenty miles to the town of Kenmare — a small seaport. Away to the north, along the Owenacree River, stretched the region known as Sliabh Luachra which translated means 'Mountain of the Rushes'. On account of various conquests and ensuing sub-divisions the whole territory looking northward from the Paps mountains was recorded on the old titles and maps as the Parish of Kilcummin, in the Barony of Macgunihy, almost as far as Scartaglin and Ballydesmond, which was then called Kingwilliamstown. These place names were to figure in most of our youthful activities.

2
School Days and Rural Life (1907-14)

As our house stood alone, I had little contact with children of my own age, and starting school in March of 1907 opened up an entirely new world which seemed very interesting. I liked the teachers and they were very nice to me. One faculty which gave them a lot of pleasure was my ability to read the first book. Little did they know how much work my father had expended on me the previous winter. When I was four years old I got the unfortunate idea of learning the alphabet from the printing on the bags of flour and other merchandise. It was a lot of fun but I called the letters by an entirely different set of names. My system was unique in its own way and very simple. The letters were named after various objects around the house and farm which they seemed to resemble. For instance, O was a hoop, T a pick, H a ladder, Y a fork, and so on. But I reached an impasse when I tried to get these things into words and my little scheme proved to be a bad stumbling block. It took a lot of teaching to break me into the accepted method. I had been well on my way to inventing some new language for fools.

Speaking of language, my father knew only about a dozen words of Gaelic. My grandfather, grandmother and mother were fluent speakers in the native tongue and strange as it may seem, my mother learned most of her Gaelic from an old Irish washerwoman in Cape Cod, Massachusetts. They spoke Gaelic a lot around the house, especially when they didn't want me to know what they were talking about. It helped to keep secrets but it also helped to kill the Gaelic language. Gaelic was not taught in the schools until about 1910 and then only as an option.

I got into trouble one day in first grade when I started tickling another boy. He was very ticklish and he laughed so loud he attracted the teacher's attention. As this was not the first offence, I was chased out of the class into another room and put with the second grade. The new surroundings looked good and I came back there again the next morning. Being able to read well, I caught on to the work fast and everybody forgot about me for a few days. I told my father, — "they put me in the second grade" — but neglected to tell him the reason. I took some money to school the next day and bought the second grade book and I was 'in'. This move proved to be a terrible disadvantage and it dogged me through my entire school years. I was the youngest and smallest boy in the class and as good as the others in everything except fighting and sports.

A new set of altar boys was being trained and I was selected. This gave me something new to think about. Getting around that Latin was a challenge and I served my first Mass with Matt Doherty who later became a priest and a student of distinction at the Irish college in Rome. He has passed away now and is buried in the church grounds where he was once an altar boy. Another incident occurred which caused me a lot of anguish when I was in sixth grade. After some breach of the rules I was being punished. This was administered on the palms of the hands with a rod about two feet long. Having a bruised finger on one hand I refused to hold it out for the 'slaps'. The principal got very angry and grabbed my hand and slapped me anyway. Needless to say it was very sore. When I

The New meets the Old: A new Ford motor car passes a horse and cart in County Kerry in 1907. The Model 'N' Ford (above) built in 1906 was the first Ford to be sold in Ireland. A 15 h.p. 4-cylinder car, it sold for £125 in Ireland and $500 in the USA.

came home that afternoon I casually mentioned it to a man who was working for my father and this opened up the case. There was the usual interrogation and I told the truth though I didn't blame the teacher. My father wrote a letter to the parish priest, who was manager of the school, and a few days later there was a big hearing in the school room during playtime. I was scared and confused but I told the truth again and I was sent outside. The outcome was obvious and didn't help relations between me and the teacher for a few years. I never blamed him but rather blamed myself for saying anything about the punishment in the first place.

As we passed through the village to and from school and church we became acquainted with many funny characters and incidents. There were always a few jokers around public houses and many and varied are the stories that could be told about them. They had a particular humour that is hard to find anywhere except in the films of the famous Irish actor, Barry Fitzgerald (1888-1961). In fact, every village had its 'joker'. An invasion of tinkers and gypsies was the signal to close all gaps and gates as they grazed their horses along the road and they didn't mind if they strayed into your best pasture. When the circus came to our village a double guard was posted. Some children from the circus would attend our school for a week or two and we envied them when they packed up and moved on to the next venue. In those days it was common to see hundreds of cattle being driven along the road from the fairs in the west of Kerry to the grass ranches and livestock farms in the midlands of Ireland. Occasionally some would get lost or stray away and the school was the best place to get word of their whereabouts.

My first automobile ride was negotiated when coming home from school in 1912. The car stopped and one of the men inside asked our names. When I told them mine an invitation was extended as my father was well known to the occupants. You see, one was a member of parliament and it was around election time. He didn't kiss any of us but we decided in our young minds that he was a decent man. As it turned out later, my father was one of his principal backers but we were too young to know anything about politicians then.

There was one source of entertainment that never seemed to lose its edge. It was the local handball court. Though the rate of emigration was high during those years there were many athletic young men left around to give a good exhibition of handball on Sunday afternoons. As kids, we marvelled at their skill and dexterity. Some were members of the police force (R.I.C.), and others were candidates for police jobs in England and the US. Others were college students and a few were home-developed talent. They chased that small black ball around the court for hours for a small side bet or drinks for the participants. The pub was convenient and the local barflies were counted in during some of the victory celebrations.

During a railway strike in 1911 when no trains ran for several weeks, the mail and other important freight items were transported by large lorries. They broke up the roads as these were paved only with broken stone and sand. The steamroller had not yet put in an appearance around there. One such large truck, propelled by steam and with huge solid tyres, pulled up in front of a local pub. The driver and his helpers went inside for refreshment. There were a few local fellows drinking at the bar and a few others half asleep around a table. On the side of the huge body of the truck were painted in large letters the words 'Nat Ross Pantechnicon'. The last word 'Pantechnicon' was a mystery to the local boys and after a few attempts at the pronunciation they dropped the matter, but the pub owner was a little more curious. Aware of the prevailing ignorance, the driver announced that he would buy a drink for the house if anybody could pronounce the word and give its meaning. Up to now, the customers in the pub could not decide whether it was the name of a place or thing. Then the owner of the pub took on the bet. He figured that some one of the customers in the pub or all of them together, between them, would be able to solve the problem. After they failed to do so, they counted heads and everybody had a drink at the expense of the pub owner. He went around and woke up the drowsy ones at the table. One of those awakened asked who paid for the fresh round or whose health he might drink to and was apprised of the situation. He looked out the window and read the word, pronouncing it perfectly (*pan-tek-nik-on*) and giving its correct meaning ('a large truck used for furniture removals'). The proprietor, Eugene Murphy, was furious and chided him for being asleep. "Blast it man, why didn't you wake up earlier?" They had a few more drinks and the truck went on its way. You see, the knowledgable customer was once a school principal by the name of Dan Donoghue who had been dismissed for a weakness known as 'incessant intoxication'.

There was a great selection of old-timers around where I grew up. At one end of our town there lived old Dan Morley, a very old man, bent over at right angles. He must have worked very hard in his youth. His son, Johnny Morley, was a well-known 'Moonlighter' and he told me a story about the transfer of a few guns during those troubled times. I seems that he and Buck Healy were to meet Denny Lynch at Coolbawn, in a furze-covered field to get the guns which Denny was bringing across the hills from Clydagh. Morley and Healy were concealed in the bushes to keep their presence secret. About five minutes before the appointed time, an R.I.C. sergeant and a constable came along to this secluded spot and stopped within hearing distance of the concealed men. The policemen glanced at their watches as the sergeant remarked, "They should be here any minute." For some reason (we found out later it was due to the heavy fog on the hills), Lynch never showed up and the police left when night fell. This will give some idea how the spies and informers operated.

There was 'The Cleaver' who came around our part of the country when they built the railway as did old Dan Hayes from the Bower. 'The Cleaver' had been a dancing master in his youth. A very tall man called Jeremiah Mór, he had been one of those chosen to line the route up along Mangerton Mountain when Queen Victoria took a look at the Punch Bowl on her visit to Killarney in 1900.

Two families of blacksmiths known as the 'Gowas', ran their shops six days a week and ten hours a day. All the boys in both families learned their trade from their fathers. They shod horses, made iron gates and all the mountings for horsecarts, including wheel rims. The carpentry trade was served by Thady Ned Moynihan, Mike Murphy and Thady Sullivan. The latter had a favourite remark; "Tinkers and tailors and makers of brogues, Cannot be compared with the shavers of oak." In the village there were two public houses, one run by Eugene Murphy who was also a blacksmith and made spades and sleáns (spades for cutting peat). The other was owned by Johnny Connor, a bachelor who had returned from America. Old Patsy Carroll served the community well as a veterinary surgeon. Nearly all these old people wore full beards, sideburns or moustaches.

The most common surnames in our area were Moynihan, Murphy, Daly, and O'Sullivan and nearly all the inhabitants were of Gaelic ancestry. All the people of my grandfather's age spoke the native tongue but few of the succeeding generation knew it well enough to converse in it. The political interests of the people were handled by members of the Irish Party who were elected to the British House of Commons, while the lesser items of local government were taken care of by the rural district councillors and the county council. These bodies met monthly in Killarney and Tralee and held some stormy sessions on matters of little importance. Almost all the local people were Catholics and their spiritual needs were administered by Father Tom Sullivan, the priest and his brother, Father John James. We belonged to Rathmore parish while the neighbouring parish included the adjacent village of Barraduff which was our place of worship. The priest there was Father Browne and the curate was Father Kirby. I served as an altar boy for these two priests many times over a period of four years. My associates were Con Lynch, Tom Lyne, David Slattery, Con Cronin, John Murphy and John M.

O'Shea. When we grew too big for the altar outfits some of us joined the choir which was conducted by Mrs. O'Donoghue, a teacher in Barraduff school.

Many people from Kerry worked for the farmers in Limerick and Tipperary during the summer. They were strong and robust and were in great demand. In many cases they had to do this work to earn the passage to the United States. As they returned home on Christmas Eve, they were a happy lot. Leaving the train for a while at each station, while other passengers alighted or got on, they sang or danced steps or square dances to the music of a flute, fiddle or accordion. They never acted like this in March when they went back to work. They were 'all danced out' after the winter. I got acquainted with an uncle of mine on one of these homecomings. I remember well he sported a fancy pipe which had a cover attached with a small chain. Another uncle of mine made a trip from Boston in October 1909, and there were some great parties. The final party before he left for the States was a great occasion. He had emigrated about ten years before and was a policeman in Lynn, Massachusetts. I can still remember him singing *In the Shade of the Old Apple Tree*. He gave me a nice blue suit with brass buttons, a choice item in its day. There were many others who made the trip around that time and some took relatives back to the States with them.

One tragedy which was spoken of very much then was 'The Moving Bog' disaster. This was a spectacular landslide of a large bog which killed eight of the nine members of the Donnelly family. One child, Katie, was visiting the home of her grandmother at the time of the landslide and had a fortunate escape. It occurred on December 28, 1896, about eight miles north of where I lived. The bog was located north-west of the village of Gneevegullia. It was about 1,875 acres in

The sole survivor of the Moving Bog disaster on 28 December 1896 (shown here in her later years) — Katie (Donnelly) O'Donoghue (1882-1964). Katie then aged 14, survived on the night of the disaster as she had gone to visit her grandmother in Mount Cain, Knocknagree, bearing Christmas gifts.

area and was very wet and shaky. Turf had been cut on the south end for some time by the local people. This was also the drainage point for the whole bog. Cutting the turf at this point had the effect of making it solid and dry and slowed down the drainage. In a few years the middle of the marsh was raised higher than the edges and a great many people noticed it but nothing was done about it. On an unusually wet night it broke out about midnight and flowed like lava towards the nearest river. It swept a house off its foundation and carried away several bridges. The debris covered all the level land along the river and ruined some fine farms. Finally, it emptied itself into the Killarney lakes about 15 miles away. It killed all the fish in the river except eels. Five of the bodies of the Donnelly family were found soon after but the remaining three bodies were never found. Many tourists visited the scene of the disaster for years afterwards. The tragedy was the subject of a book and elegy by a local bard. The bard, Joe Dineen, was another 'intellectual' who hung around the local pubs. He had studied for the priesthood in Ireland and the United States but at examination time suffered a mental block, and wound up a 'ne'er-do-well'.

One character who fascinates me to this day was a son of a local carpenter who plied his trade as a journeyman around the country here, there and anywhere. Though highly skilled in the art of woodworking, he was much more admired for his prowess at trout and salmon fishing. It bordered on adoration and was tinged with a little jealousy. His technique was studied and copied as if he had occult powers but few, if any, got the same results. He would fish a few hundred yards of a river and in an hour or so come up with a dozen trout, when others could not even get a nibble. He used to gloat over this and say, "I'm like poison to a river." The trout wound up in some local bar for the biggest admirer or bidder. When the fisherman had drunk the fruits of his success and if he was still thirsty, he sold his rod and tackle and the proceeds kept him going for the next week. And don't think it was hard to sell the rod! Eager fishermen thought it held some mysterious power and its lure would coax any trout to its doom. "Wasn't it John O's rod and cast of flies made by himself?" It surely was, but the new owner never got the same results as John O' did.

One day as I was trout fishing I had an opportunity to observe his technique. I was in the company of one of my school teachers, Jer Cronin, who was an excellent fisherman and always kept good tackle. I owned the usual boy's equipment, a home-made rod and a few flies, with a can of worms as alternative bait. We each had caught a few small trout when we met John O' coming in the opposite direction.

The usual greetings were exchanged and he informed us he was 'not doing so good' with the trout. I listened attentively while the two men discussed the river, the day, the fish and the lures. All the time the 'old pro' was looking at the far side of a nice deep swirl. He had seen a trout rise, he said, and was waiting for a repeat performance. In a few minutes the trout duly obliged. I was instructed to cross the river at a shallow ford and catch one of the flies at the spot where the trout had risen. After some patient swatting I caught one. The two men looked at it closely and 'the expert' proceeded to tie a fly representing the one I had caught. He was not satisfied with the decoy and sent me about two hundred yards back along the river bank to a spot where he had earlier seen a dead rabbit. He instructed me to bring back some of the rabbit's fur and whiskers. He worked some fur onto the body of the fly and took a strand of red wool from one of his socks. He finished off the bait by applying the whiskers as a tail. I was spellbound and had my first lesson in fly-tying. You've guessed it! On the third cast he hooked a good-sized trout. He caught eight trout in fifteen or twenty minutes. This was enough and he quit satisfied, a broad, sly grin on his impish face. He left the fly with my companion and he in turn caught six more trout as we fished over the same water where we had no results an hour earlier. The fish stopped rising and we quit fishing. My teacher had been taught, and he gave me two fine trout.

The first time I ever went to Killarney my mother and I travelled by train. It was a two-mile walk to the station at Headford and an eight-mile train ride. An election result of the previous year had wound up in the courts and the decision was rendered in favour of the plaintiff. There was a large crowd around Killarney courthouse and a big fight broke out. The police quelled the riot and order was restored. I saw a woman using her stocking as an offensive weapon. It sounds flimsy, doesn't it? However, it was reinforced in the toe by a good-sized stone. She was flattening men left and right and I was scared.

The fairs and markets in Killarney were bustling affairs. From early morning large herds of cattle and flocks of sheep were driven along the roads and hundreds of carts containing calves and pigs made some heavy traffic. In the afternoon when most of the animals and produce were sold, the bell man with a very loud voice advertised everything from meals to homes. Beautiful stallions were paraded through the streets, gaily decorated and with dark and fiery eyes. Collie dogs barked loudly driving cattle here and there at their master's bidding. The pubs were crowded and the ballad singers and beggars gave their best performances. If demand and profits were good, the farmers joined in the singing and even loosened up to do a few steps of a jig or a hornpipe. Many American and European tourists in horse-drawn carriages drove through the streets and took some photographs.

The sale of ice cream in Killarney in those days was confined to one pushcart which was operated by a Frenchman during the summer months. Using a mixture of French and English he sold his product (a soft variety between two thin wafers) with ease. It was quite a treat for country children on fair days. He didn't resume his usual occupation after the outbreak of World War I, perhaps he fell victim to that terrible slaughter.

A hardy breed of tramps (itinerants or travellers) frequented the localities of Kerry and Cork. Most of the men were reservists in the British army and were tough fighters with their fists or the ash plant. This latter item was an ash sapling about the size of a walking stick, as tough as whale-bone and recognised as standard equipment for a tinker or cattle driver. An application of this around the head was enough to render any opponent unconscious, even a policeman's short truncheon was no match for it. The tinkers' faces bore many scars of neglected cuts and bruises. They made their living by begging, horse trading and mending pots and pans. They camped sometimes in sand pits and cast flatirons, the bottom surface of which was made smooth by tying them under their carts and dragging them along the road to the next town.

One morning in mid winter, I was going to assist at early Mass and noticed one of their women folk washing a small baby in the icy water of a little stream beside the road. I told my mother when I came home. She went to the place and brought the woman, her husband and another child to our house. She fed them and they stayed the night, sleeping on some straw on the kitchen floor. It was explained to me later that the woman had given birth to the baby during the night in a cart by the side of the road. They had to be tough to survive, or they survived because they were tough. Several of them were killed in France in World War I while serving with the British Army. Many of their ancestors had been dispossessed of their lands or homes during the Famine years and gravitated to this lowly state, though some were a remnant of earlier tribes of beggars.

One practice that had been observed down through the years was the celebration of Mass in the homes of the farmers. It was a vital and practical way of practising their religion and was called 'the stations'. Having never taken the bother to do any research, I am not sure of its origin but it is probably a tradition left over from the days of the Penal Laws when Catholics were persecuted and religion was practised secretly in people's homes whenever feasible. 'The stations' were held twice a year in each townland, and were rotated in order among those capable of hosting them. The houses were cleaned and painted and all the neighbours congregated for Confession, Mass and Communion. Those attending made a modest contribution to the priest and joined him for breakfast. In the evening the young people returned and enjoyed a little music and dance.

No description of Irish country life can afford to omit the beliefs and superstitions of some of the people. It would be impossible to trace the origin of many of these practices, as some no doubt have their source in pre-Christian times. They are a mixture of mythology and legend, steeped in fear and ignorance and leavened by tradition. The product of this brew was deeply ingrained in the people's thinking, but was never accepted by those who did a little thinking of their own. As one practical man commented, "I don't see the sense of sending all these missionaries to Africa and China to convert those people when we have some just as bad here at home." I agree. We had many more important things to occupy our mental processes.

I don't want to spoil all the fun children get from reading little stories about leprechauns and fairies, though the legend of Santa Claus has been somewhat desecrated. There is another far more sinister side to the superstition which is referred to by the Gaelic word 'pishogues'. For instance, if one saw magpies, 'one for sorrow, two for joy, three for a wedding and four to die.' If the rooster did an unusual amount of crowing it was also considered a bad omen. If he happened to crow at night, beware — somebody had not long to live. Deaths often occurred in three's. When one happened, two more followed shortly. During the process of churning butter, if one removed fire from the house, he was 'stealing the butter'. Anyone unfortunate enough to light his pipe and walk out while this work was in progress was considered an enemy and was requested 'not to darken the doorway again.' This was very bad, but there was an antidote. If the person stopped and 'put the size of his head in the churn', that is, to increase the butter production by helping to work the churn, all would be well.

Of course, nobody would dare to level out an old ring fort and not for reasons of historical interest or antiquity. Sickness and accidents were oftentimes explained as being caused by trespassing on the location of an old battlefield or passageway. Diseases like tuberculosis and osteomyelitis were attributed to one being caught in a whirlwind. Strokes were supposed to be caused by fright when the victim had seen someone already dead for many years and who had been sent to summon him to the great beyond. Even these beliefs varied from one county to another.

On three successive years my father tried to build a new cow house. The first year he got a very severe attack of sciatica which kept him in agony for about six months and was cured by a sojourn in a Turkish bath. The following year a large nail penetrated one of his eyes which he almost lost. After another delay of a year he fell off the gable dropping about thirty feet into a narrow drain about two feet deep. I witnessed the accident and wondered why his neck wasn't broken. He was diligently advised by some 'knowing people' to abandon the project as the building was seeming to conflict with some of the desires of a person long departed, who was supposed to retain an interest in the spot.

But there was always the beloved musicians, storytellers and dancing masters who preserved, if only partially, the real folklore and music of the country. An uncle of mine, P.J. Moynihan, won first prize at Killarney Oireachtas in 1912 for playing traditional dance music on his flute. He also inspired the boys and girls in his neighbourhood to learn step dancing and many of them were excellent dancers. He never went anywhere without a tin whistle which he played very well and he also performed on the uilleann pipes. The great fiddle players I remember best were Pádraig O'Keeffe and the blind man, Tom Billy. Also there was the Lucey Brothers, Ned Forde and George Williams. These were the men who made the people dance.

Of the old people who were storytellers, and there were many, the one I remember best was my granduncle, Con Houlihan of Stagmount. He told the stories in Gaelic as well, when he had an audience who understood the language. Being old and stiff when I knew him, he taught the young people to dance while standing at the back of a chair. He was also a great stonemason and a master at the art of making short ropes from the hair of cows' tails, which were used to tie the cattle in their stalls. Twice as a boy I helped him spin these ropes with the 'castóir' (the Gaelic word for 'twister'), as he told me some old stories in English and Gaelic.

I remember one story in particular. A murder trial was being held for a man accused of stabbing another with a hay pike. The defendant spoke no English and the Kerry poet, Owen O'Sullivan, was called in as an interpreter. When he relayed the answers it sounded thus when he pleaded self-defence, 'Him had a pike and him had a pike, and him struck him with the pike. But if him struck him, like him struck him, him would kill him like him killed him.' The case against the accused was later dismissed.

Another story he related also concerned a murder trial. The accused was defended by Daniel O'Connell, the noted lawyer and leader of the Irish Party. The case looked very bad for the prisoner as he was accused of killing some British official. The murder victim's hat figured in the evidence and somehow O'Connell sensed that the witness was paid to give testimony - a not unusual occurrence in those days. The witness had just identified the hat. O'Connell, on cross examination of this witness, held the hat and pretended to be spelling the owner's name from the inside of it. After a few more diverting questions, he asked the witness how he knew it belonged to the victim and the answer was, 'His name was written on the inside of it.' 'Would you swear his name was written on the inside of the hat?' asked O'Connell. 'Yes', replied the witness. This of course was not correct and the case was lost on perjured testimony, leaving the accused to go free.

Births and christenings were considered affairs of little importance as most of the children were born at home without the aid of a doctor. There was very little pre-natal care for the mothers except a lot of hard work on the farm and in the home. They were attended by a midwife or in most cases by a 'handy woman', but in some cases complications arose and a doctor had to be called. These cases were rare but some women paid the price for this neglect by dying at a young age, often leaving young children to be cared for. I remember the third member of our family being born and the succeeding birth of twins. These were followed by three others, all boys. One of the twins died at birth and the last birth was also lost.

The wakes and funerals involved great public participation. Whatever respect the Irish people had for the living, it was not nearly as evident as the respect they seemed to have for the dead. People were mourned and prayed for and remembered far more after death than before it. The wakes were mostly solemn affairs and the general impression of the typical Irish wake is a crude distortion of fact. However, if the deceased was an old person and died of natural causes, the aura of respect was sometimes dispensed with and a few capers were indulged in to liven up the event. Clay pipes and porter were dispensed to the mourners and food to the relatives. At one wake I attended with my father a few of the mourners were pelted with potatoes or 'ciaráins' (small pieces of peat) and the wake broke up in a fit of laughing when the lamp was knocked over with a well-aimed spud (potato).

One other funeral to the local cemetery also provoked a bit of excitement and laughter. An old woman who died in the County Hospital in Killarney had, before she passed away, requested a neighbouring farmer to take charge of her funeral arrangements. She had no living relatives but had been a respected member of the community. On the day of the funeral, this farmer went with a few neighbours to Killarney to claim the body and make the other necessary arrangements. While placing the coffin in the horse-drawn hearse, someone remarked that it was very light, but since the lady was very old and spent, they concluded she 'should not weigh very much anyway'. The pallbearers were hefty farmers and braced with several rounds of drinks. I guess their judgement was a bit on the careless side. Anyhow, they made the trip to the cemetery slowly and in a dignified manner on a balmy evening in September in an atmosphere of leisure and good feeling. When removing the coffin from the hearse, the driver commented on its weight and this caused a temporary pause in the proceedings. Nobody wanted to open the coffin, but the driver being the only one completely sober, lifted the lid. On looking inside they were amazed to find only a fistful of wood shavings. The party returned to Killarney to pick up the right coffin and retraced the journey to the cemetery. There the burial was concluded far into the night in an atmosphere of chagrin and jokes.

On another occasion a namesake of mine in his nineties passed away after a lingering illness. Several times before he actually died, he seemed to pass away only to revive a little later. One night during the wake the corpse was noticed moving slightly as if he was drawing one of his knees up towards his body. He was supposed to be dead for several hours. Some of the timid souls bolted through the doors and windows but one woman proceeded to talk to the dead man. During the one-sided conversation she noticed that a kitten had crawled under the death shroud and given the impression of movement. He had been a very tall man and was one of those selected to line the route to the Punch Bowl on top of Mangerton Mountain when Queen Victoria visited Killarney in 1900. As if to recognise this service his funeral was marked by a military display usually reserved for royalty and out of all proportion to his station in life.

Another event worth recording was related by an uncle of mine. It seems he had a friend who was a great step dancer when they were both young. Later on, this friend got tuberculosis. and died in a hospital in Kanturk many miles away in the neighbouring county Cork. When his death became known my uncle and another friend proceeded by horse and cart to attend the funeral. They knew the route the cortege would follow and intended to drive towards the town and meet it. However they arrived at the town without meeting the funeral and made inquiries at the hospital, where they were informed that there was no funeral as nobody showed up for the remains. My uncle claimed the body and the people at the hospital felt sure it was alright to release the remains to the two men. Both were tired and hungry, so after visiting a nearby pub and getting some refreshments they started towards the cemetery. No doubt they were mellow in their mood and when they passed a roadside dance, the music and dancers stopped out of respect for the dead. Since the man in the coffin had been a great dancer, the driver and his friend decided to do justice to his memory and told the crowd so. They stopped the cart and tied the horse to a bush as he needed rest anyway. Now it would be a shame to inconvenience the dancers so our two men told them to continue and joined them explaining the dead man would have it that way. After an exhibition of step dancing on the platform my uncle's companion had to be persuaded to refrain from dancing on top of the coffin and they left the scene while the crowd gazed in amazement. Well, he loved to dance when alive, why deprive him of it when he was dead?

There was one particular aspect of wakes and funerals which I hated because it scared me so much. This was the crying or 'caoineadh'. This was not done by professional mourners but I doubt if they could do a better job than the people I heard when my grandfather died. I was only seven years old then. The crying was done mostly by women and it terrified me. The wailing followed a set pattern, the notes and sounds of which I can still recall, and it was very mournful. In most cases the participants were dry-eyed but these only joined in when some near relative arrived who usually did some real sobbing. The same procedure was indulged in when my grandmother died suddenly in 1914. She had been very healthy and dropped dead while knitting a stocking and admonishing me and my older sister. Some of those who cried at my grandfather's wake also cried at her wake and I recall hearing one old woman complimenting another on her fine display.

Farming was more a way of life than a business. Most of the small farmers around where I grew up did their farm work by hand. They were healthy, robust men, their biceps being well developed from constant use of the spade, sleán, scythe pick, shovel and pitchfork. They helped one another occasionally by lending horses and grouping together to get the time-consuming work done quickly. A group of men would band together to do the work for one farmer and then another, until the entire group got their work done. This included cutting the turf (peat), mowing hay, making the hayrick and threshing the grain. The latter work was the only one where machinery was used and the band of men was called 'meitheal'. Great, indeed, was the excitement when the threshing machine came to the neighbourhood, and its owner charged the farmers by the day. All hands worked very hard and usually finished each farmer's grain in one day. There was a lot of cooking and extra work on these occasions but the women stood up to it very well and in the evening there was a little music and dance to chase away the cares of the day.

Oats and wheat were the main grain crops and these were stored at harvest time into stacks. They were conical in shape and usually built by some 'knowing man', who took great pride in his art. The stacks were thatched with straw or rushes and erected where it was convenient for the threshing machine. This type of storage was completely water-proof but sometimes mice or rats did a little damage to the heads of the grain which were always in the centre of the stack. Now and then a wise old donkey would figure out where the grain was too and he would chew his way into the centre. When he was discovered (and the only part you could see was his tail) he was usually gorged with oats and it took a bit of beating to dislodge him from his feast.

The straw of the wheat crop was very valuable and was used for thatching the dwelling houses before slate and galvanised iron became popular. This crop was threshed by hand by beating the sheaves against an inverted barrel, or by flail as it would be useless for thatch if done by machine. The flail was made up of a four-foot long wooden handle with a half-inch deep groove cut into one end. Another piece of lighter wood, roughly the same length and called the 'striker', was attached to the grooved end with a strong leather thong. This attachment was secured, but allowed the thong to revolve in the groove while the thrasher swung the striker over his head in a circular movement bringing it down on the sheaves of corn. The sheaves were laid out on the ground in a double row with their heads near each other. A team of four men placed the sheaves in their proper position, two men standing facing another two men, each with a flail. A fifth man turned the sheaves and removed them when the grain was separated. The men with the flails had to be expert in using them properly, and in rhythm with their opposite partner, otherwise it could be a very dangerous operation for the man changing the sheaves. The fore (from the Gaelic word 'fóir') resembled an old-style beehive but was much larger and was made from straw rope about six inches thick and wound into a conical shape and covered with thatch. The wheat, of course, was afterwards ground into flour at a local mill. The flour was heavy and brown and I suppose very nutritious. Oatmeal was also very common and these cereals were an important part of the people's diet in the latter half of the 19th century owing to the intermittent failures of the potato crop. Ireland produced many notable athletes around the turn of the century and some of them are listed in world records and Olympic history from 1904 to 1912. People were not so vitamin conscious then, but a lot can be said for the plain, wholesome diet.

Peat bogs were plentiful where I came from and there was plenty of turf for fuel. But some years there was so much wet weather that the peat was difficult to dry sufficiently to make a cheerful fire. It was cut in May and after being dried in the sun, was heaped up in various quantities and hauled home in horsecarts fitted with creels. Each load weighed between a half ton and a ton, depending on the quality of the peat. It was common to see a rick made from about 50 loads standing near a house around September. This rick was also built skilfully by some 'knowing man' and lasted until next summer's crop. Peat was much prized and purchased by those farmers and town dwellers who had no bogs in their vicinity.

Wood was a scarce commodity in Ireland as the forests had been cut down generations ago and timber had to be imported. Landlords had a three-fold purpose in cutting down the forests — denying shelter to rebels, selling lumber in England and clearing the forests for grazing. The forests were rarely replanted, consequently there was very little wood for burning. There wasn't much coal in the country and the little mined was a hard grade of anthracite which was very difficult to keep alight. But somehow providence had reserved another source of fuel besides peat. This was called 'bog deal' and was the remains of dead trees which were buried under the bogs.

Wood was useful for many purposes and the pine was made into furniture while the oak, which turned black like ebony, was carved into ornaments. The trunks of pine were also split into small sticks about 3/4 inch thick and two feet long. These were used to fasten the thatch on the houses and were called spars, while the smaller pieces were dried and used as tapers for light when candles were scarce. Even candles were homemade from the fat of sheep and cattle as late as 1900. The roots and stumps of the dead trees were excavated and dried, making excellent firewood. These were referred to by an Irish name of 'craughill'. It is worth noting here that while cutting peat small barrels of honey and tallow have been excavated. I once dug up a single moccasin similar to those worn by American Indians. It was covered at a depth of four or five feet and well preserved, but it fell apart when it dried out. We searched the adjacent ground for years afterwards in hopes of finding its mate. What event cast it in these lonely surroundings, no one will ever know. It could have been lost by a traveller crossing the bog a thousand years ago, or it may have floated to this location and sunk in the mire.

The potato crop was very important and much care was lavished on its cultivation. When it failed owing to a fungus blight during the Famine years (1845-49), it was a national calamity. One million people died from starvation and disease while another million emigrated. Indeed, it started a wave of emigration that lasted to this day and changed the whole national outlook. However a French chemist discovered a prevention for the blight and if used properly, the crop will survive but will not be as productive as in the days preceding the blight. Potato stalks have to be sprayed two or three times during the summer and the crop is harvested in October. Many a time after I came home from school I would face the long rows of potatoes shining in the sun and gather them in buckets and baskets. They would be stored in a pit in the field and covered with about a foot of earth which was lined with sod or straw. There were several varieties, of course, some early, some for farm animals and the main crop which was a floury kind and very good to eat. The potato as well as its stalk is very vulnerable to frost.

Turnips and cabbage were able to survive the winters in the ground in Ireland and were harvested as needed, but mangolds were also vulnerable to frost and had to be stored in pits like potatoes. These crops thrived in our locality and along with hay and straw, provided fodder for the cattle and horses during the winter months.

Hay was another crop that required a lot of care and if the weather was wet it was subject to huge losses. When the farmers adopted better seeds and cultivation as well as machinery, the process became less tedious and risky. They also built barns around the turn of the century and this method of storage was better and easier than the hayrick. When a hayrick was built, the job had to be done all in one day, and a fine day at that! This called for a lot of help and if the day rained when half way through, it was a major calamity.

The swing and wheel ploughs, like the mowing machines, took a lot of work off the farmers' backs. A garden planted by hand was a pretty sight indeed, with rows evenly spaced and straight as if laid out with a line, but it was poor compensation for the back-breaking toil necessary to produce it. Some ploughmen with horse or tractor could lay out a garden nearly as straight but a hundred times faster. The old-timers didn't like the modern methods and one incident after another convinced them of their judgement. Here is an example: when my grandfather returned from England around 1860 he brought along some new fertiliser as he had worked where it was manufactured. In his desire to show his neighbours the value of this new concoction he applied it to a crop of turnips. When planting he was careful to pour the fertiliser in the holes and add a few seeds to each hole before covering them. This he felt sure would be an effective way to nourish the young plants, but the only ones that grew were the seeds which had been dropped in the furrows, accidentally. The result, of course, was to condemn all fertilisers and nobody in the locality would use any fertiliser for a good many years afterwards. Poor man, how was he to know the fertiliser would burn the tender shoots of the young plants. Some time after this incident a fertiliser product was marketed in Ireland by a British firm. It resembled guano in colour and texture but was found to be largely composed of brick dust. When this was discovered most farmers were prejudiced against fertiliser for a long time afterwards.

The cattle around our part of the country were a mixed lot of doubtful pedigree. However, as I grew up the introduction of Shorthorns and Jerseys improved the strain somewhat and also led to increased production of dairy products. I remember we once had a cow supposed to be part Ayrshire who gave 30 to 32 quarts of milk per day. She was a very large cow and we sold her during the war in 1916 for a very high price. In the mountainous sections of west Kerry there was a separate breed of cattle called 'Kerrys'. They were black, or black and white, in colour and their milk was of a rich quality but small in quantity. Droves of these animals would be driven along the roads by cattle dealers who bought them at the Kerry fairs and walked them about a hundred miles to the big grass farms in the midlands of Ireland. It was estimated they improved about £1 each in value during the drive, as walking on a level road with plenty of grass on the sides was much easier for them than foraging for food on the steep heather-covered slopes of the Kerry hillsides. Goats and sheep were very plentiful in the farms along the hills and they grazed over the hills unrestricted. It took a lot of work and a good collie dog to keep track of them and each owner had his own special mark on the animals. It was very interesting to watch a man rounding up some sheep with a pair of binoculars and a collie dog. The dog worked entirely from hand signals or whistles from the man maybe a quarter of a mile to a mile away as he watched the movements and marks on the sheep. The dog and man were loyal companions but the dog who did most of the work was usually worn out in five or six years.

The breeds of fowl around our place were nondescript before the Department of Agriculture established breeding stations throughout the country. People could buy the eggs of breeds like Leghorn, Wyandotte, Rhode Island Red hens, Runner ducks and some large White geese, hatch them under any other fowl and raise a good strain of productive birds. Eggs were very dear during the First World War and fowl and feathers carried a high price. A good flock of fowl kept the house in groceries through egg production and exchange was made at the local village stores. Turkeys and geese were raised for the Christmas market.

The author working in the fields with horses.

The pig was considered the 'poor man's bank'. Farmers and even people in the towns bought pigs from breeders at the fairs and markets and raised them to about nine months old when they attained a weight between 300 and 400 pounds. They were slaughtered for home use or sold to jobbers for export. There were some bacon-curing factories in Tralee and Limerick which turned out a very high grade product. Pigs were very easy to feed and keep. They thrived on scraps and offal which would otherwise go to waste. They were finished on cornmeal to give the flesh its best flavour. It was quite a job to kill and dress these animals. Three or four neighbours helped and the butchering was usually done by handy men such as Thady O'Sullivan. The house-cured product was excellent but too fat by today's standards.

The horse, the noblest animal of all, was along with the dog, man's best friend. He did all the heavy hauling, ploughing, harrowing, cultivating, mowing, etc. and was harnessed to a trap or sidecar on Sunday to drive to church or go visiting relatives. Like the dog, he was an animal you could talk to and he seemed to have a distinctive personality. A horse, in spite of his intelligence, must be a very stupid animal. How he got to be dominated and controlled by man a creature about one-tenth his size and weight, I don't know, but anyway he did. Some of them, however, protested strongly by kicking, plunging, rearing and even biting. Nevertheless, man got him to do all the hard work. The breeds popular around our locality were Clydesdales, Shires, Suffolk Punch and a variety known as a common horse which served as an all around animal. Some farmers with large holdings kept stallions which were registered by the Department of Agriculture and these were noble animals. They were exhibited at fairs, markets and shows and the farmers had quite a choice of animals from which to breed. They are, of course, being gradually replaced by farm machinery and tractors. In certain parts of Ireland the entire farm was devoted to just breeding and raising horses, mostly hunters and racehorses.

Going down the line there was the Kerry cob, a breed peculiar to Kerry, from twelve to fourteen hands high. These were very docile animals and economical for a small farmer. And of course there were the ponies which were crossbred to produce the most desirable specimens. They hauled traps and were raced at sports meetings. There were also mules and jennits to do farm work and some of them were tough and vicious. On the lowest step of the beasts of burden was the donkey, a slow, stupid, lazy animal which was used by children and old people to get around to the markets and other short trips. Though he was the target of a lot of abuse he was regarded as a 'blessed animal'. If you look closely at a donkey, you will find a cross of different coloured hair on his back, running from the top of his head to his tail and across his shoulders. Be that as it may, he was a very useful animal around a farm. I was well acquainted with some of them around our neighbourhood and understood their antics, though we didn't own any when I was a child.

It may be of some interest to describe forts and doons (from the Gaelic word 'dún' meaning 'fort'). These are the remains of a type of fortification, a circular bank of earth which, no doubt, was a form of dwelling a long time ago. They are also known as 'raths' or 'lios'. Many placenames in Ireland have a prefix denoting these forts e.g. Rathmore (the big fort), Lismore (the large fort). They are numerous and always located on high, dry ground from which there is generally a good view of the surrounding locality. Some have a diameter of 100 to 200 feet while many are much smaller. They may have single rings but double and triple rings also exist. It would appear that they were made so as to resist enemy attack. In the centre of the enclosed ground there is usually a hole going underground and leading by a stone-covered passage to some secret exit. This may also have served as a drain as the enclosure was bound to be flooded during heavy rainfalls. The hole in the centre also led to underground rooms but few of these have been explored in recent years. I doubt if they contain anything of archaeological value as there was ample opportunity for the invading forces, who were so minded, to loot the entire establishments. However, as late as 1910 two boys found a golden helmet somewhere in the North of Ireland and it is preserved in the national museum. This precious article of antiquity escaped detection for long time due to a superstitious belief which makes these places off-limits. The farmers adroitly avoid any interference with the structures and sinister happenings seem to be going on there all the time. Of course, these places are the dwellings of everything from leprechauns to giants of old and nobody but a hardy soul frequents them, especially during hours of darkness. Fact and fancy runs really wild as the legends and tales concerning these ancient forts are told and retold to succeeding generations. No doubt, their existence is pockmarked by many a struggle of defence or offence and like the round towers which are of much later origin, they stand as silent sentinels of a mysterious and chequered past. People who have entered their dark chambers have been overcome by fright and collapsed, most likely brought about by foul air. This adds to the mysterious aspect of these hidden ruins. I never entered any of them and I refused the opportunity to do so on many occasions, respecting legend and quietly avoiding any such foolhardy expedition. But this timidity is tinged with a large amount of curiosity and if the places were explored, they may yield many clues to the past. Ancient pagan kings were buried in some of them in a standing position, with sword drawn and facing the rising sun. You figure that one out!

One fort in County Kildare was the scene of a ghastly slaughter in the year 1577. The Irish leaders were invited by their English counterparts to a feast and peace meeting at the Rath of Mullaghmast. Travel and communication being what they were in those days, the guests arrived singly or in small parties over an extended period. As each unsuspecting guest arrived, he was attacked and butchered in cold blood by the English hosts. One wary pilgrim to the fort became suspicious and avoided a similar fate by some good sword play. He was the only survivor of the four hundred nobles who were invited to the 'banquet'. This was not an isolated incident, but the most tragic of its kind. Is it any wonder the ghosts of dead warriors are imagined in combat as their dying groans are heard mingling with the wail of banshees in the solemn silence of night? The son and grandson of the English 'host' (Sir Francis Cosby) were slain in a great battle at another fort about 20 years later by a descendant of one of the murdered princes named O'Moore.

In spite of all the adverse conditions, the people prospered slowly, but surely. Not because any famous leader exhorted the population, but because primarily the country was blessed with a mild temperate climate, rich land and a hardy breed of people. The weakling was despised and the less industrious were referred to as a 'cuckoo farmer'; this was because he planted crops when the cuckoo migrated north about the beginning of May, too late to be productive. The growing season is very long in Ireland, much longer than in other lands in the same latitude, due of the influence of the Gulf Stream.

The author and his family. *Rear left to right:* Mary, Margaret (sisters), Jeremiah (author), Patie (brother). *Front left to right:* John (brother), Hannah (mother, with concertina), Michael J. (father). *Lower front:* Michael F. (youngest brother).

The people were well-fed and the children, especially in the country, all had rosy cheeks. Their diet was very plain and unvaried and the Irish have often been labelled as the world's worst cooks. For a people having so much opportunity to grow many varieties of vegetables and fruit, it is amazing how they clung to a few staples. But the staples were nutritious and the only obvious effect of improper diet was the ever present spectacle of decayed teeth. The most common foods were potatoes, cabbage, turnips, bacon, beef, fish and mutton. With plenty of these available, the conclusion can be drawn that the bad state of teeth was due more to a lack of care than nutrition. Very little pastry or dessert was eaten and in the country milk was so plentiful, it was fed to all animals. Eggs were very plentiful, too, but the people in the towns were always a little short on these items. When I was in primary school, ice cream was only something you heard about and apples, oranges, bananas, grapes and dates were sold only in towns. Tea was the national beverage and coffee, concentrated with chicory in a paste form, was added to boiling water but rarely served.

Two notable events occurred while I was a small boy in school. One was the death of King Edward VII in 1910. He was succeeded by his only son, George V. The visit of the former to Ireland, and the difficulties of a war entered into by his successor, did not seem to improve relations either economically or socially between the Ireland and Britain. The other notable event was the sinking of the *Titanic* in the Atlantic in 1912 when it collided with an iceberg. Many Irish and English people were among those lost and the newspapers were very dramatic in their descriptions of the tragedy.

You could spot a Yank a hundred yards away by his clothes and gold-capped teeth. A few of the natives such as professional people dressed fairly well, but the farmers dressed very plainly, almost unsightly. There was only one exception to this. It was the hooded cloak, a distinctly becoming piece of apparel common to the hilly districts of Munster, Connacht and the North. It was usually worn by women of middle age and older and seemed to be more common to districts where the native language survived. The other women wore shawls which looked like blankets trimmed with tassels and were very warm. They were of a light brown or buff colour and carried some designs or stripes. A lighter variety was worn by the younger girls, usually of a greenish colour having stripes and designs also. There were no such things as nylon stockings as all hosiery was hand-knitted by the women at home. Spinning wheels were used in almost every house, but for some reason or other, I never saw flax grown or processed where I came from, though it was a big industry in other parts of Ireland. Some of the men wore 'baneens', a sort of cardigan type jacket, made from heavy white flannel woven at the local mill. This establishment also turned out a coarse tweed which was used for working clothes. The dress clothes were conventional, of course, and fine serges were imported from England for this purpose.

This leads me to the tailors — and they were a distressing lot. The names of many Irish tunes carried references to all the crafts, but one tune I recall was named, 'A Devil Among the Tailors'. Evidently they earned this reputation, as among all those I knew, I can only recall one who didn't 'down' a few pints of stout quite frequently. In fact, I am probably both conservative and charitable in this reference. Not that the members of other crafts didn't drink, but the tailors somehow seemed to deserve the reputation. Before the sewing machine became common, the tailors came to the homes and measured, fitted and finished the suits by hand. Their only tools were needles, tape, scissors and maybe a clothes iron. One member of the outfit, usually the head man, went before the others, measuring and cutting while his employees or assistants followed, doing the fitting and sewing. This procedure necessitated taking over the house for about a week and naturally they got all the women and children into a state of confusion. The regular routine was disrupted and the tables were used as work benches. On these the tailors sat cross-legged, in stocking feet, admired and annoyed by the women and children while they sewed the seams with remarkable speed and dexterity. I watched them often and I could hear the strong thread 'twang' like a fiddle string. Other craftsmen rarely got so well acquainted with the people, as their work was performed in shops or outside the homes. Perhaps this close association became boring, and the tailors sought the refuge of the pub in search of male company.

As long as we are on the subject of crafts and craftsmen, let me tell you a story which was told to me by one who was present when the incident occurred. It seems a place of business was being built. The builders were a noted family of masons, named Moriarty, who had built barracks for British troops as far away as India. They were good at their trade, and as the saying goes, 'had a good warrant to drink a pint of stout.' The owners of the new building were a little superstitious, and on discovering this, the eldest of the masons explained to them that it was customary to put some money, gold or silver, under one of the cornerstones. He didn't tell them that he was a bit sick and broke after a drinking spree and needed a few drinks to bolster his ambition for work. They willingly obliged and placed two half-crowns under the first cornerstone to ensure the success of the business venture. For good measure some holy water was sprinkled around, the sign of the cross was made, and hats in hand, all present observed and approved the ritual. As the mason plumbed the cornerstone to perfection, he tapped it down with his hammer saying, 'Go deo', (Gaelic words meaning 'for ever'). The owners returned to their other house nearby and the work went on — but not for long. With the owners out of sight, the mason tipped over the cornerstone and retrieved the two half-crowns and retired without delay to the local bar where he had a few drinks.

When somebody who was very poor died, a collection was usually made to defray burial expenses. As the coffin was the single biggest cost and all other services were donated, the carpenters got together and made one. They assembled at some carpenter shop in the neighbourhood and 'many hands made light work'. When I was a little lad an incident of this kind occurred in the nearby village. It so happened the deceased was a very big man and somebody decided to make the coffin larger than standard size. Others decided to measure the dead man whose name was Batt. The wake house and the carpenter's shop were a few hundred yards apart and in between a pub was conveniently located. Several trips were made back and forth to measure Batt and measure the wood and others had to verify these measurements. There was no hurry as it was Sunday afternoon and the boys got quite tipsy. The coffin turned out to be a monstrosity and could not be taken inside the wake house. It was proposed to remove the door frame or the window to admit the oversized coffin, but this proposal was rejected by general consent on the morning of the funeral. It was then decided to bring the corpse out of the house and put it in the coffin in the front yard. In the midst of this unbecoming behaviour, the dead man's daughter arrived from England and promptly scattered the jocular mourners. One look at the coffin and she declared, 'My father will not be buried in that thing.' She buried him instead in a fancy casket which she bought in Killarney.

Now they were left with an oversized, odd-looking coffin. What would they do with it? It was returned to the carpenter's shop where it laid in the corner for some time. Nobody would have anything to do with it, until one night the owner of the shop got drunk and had an argument with his wife. He decided to sleep it off in the shop and as it was raining and the roof was leaking, what better place than the coffin for a good rest? He put a bunch of wood shavings under his head and pulled the lid partly over to ward off the raindrops from the leaking roof. In the morning he was awakened by the hammering of his sons and other men working in the place. Suddenly he was seen emerging slowly from the coffin by another carpenter who was probably a bit shaky too. Anyway, this fellow dashed through the door and never came back after seeing the 'apparition'.

Marriage! Ah, this was a state that was achieved by a tedious route. I have read about marriages in many parts of the world, but here it was a ceremony, archaic in its origin, dignified in its performance and permanent in its application. This rare combination may be the reason for the low rate of divorce in Ireland. It has been the subject of many observers from many lands, but I doubt if they ever understood it. A professor of sociology after a lot of research may do justice to the subject. It is beyond the scope of my limited ability to treat the matter properly as a distinct topic. Suffice it to say, I am as well qualified as anybody to describe a typical wedding around the locality where I came from. I speak, or rather write, from experience, as I have been employed to initiate the moves through different ceremonies until the last drunk was straightened out the day after the wedding. The following outline was a typical procedure but whether the couple were plain farmers or social climbers the pattern was much the same. The only difference was the wealth of the parties involved and their hospitality.

Young people kept company in those days just like now, but they were not so sure of themselves. They were forced to emigrate because there was no real means to start a home except one owned a farm or business. If a man intended to give the farm to his son, he looked around for a suitable girl. An 'account of match' was sent by letter or through some third party by one or other of the older people. Those intending to marry may or may not have known each other or have ever met socially. A time and place, usually at a public house or small hotel, was arranged for the rendezvous. The intended bride and groom rarely attended the first meeting, but if there was any prospect of agreement, they were allowed to attend a later session when they were introduced if necessary. Now if they liked each other the tempo grew faster and each side took a sort of cooling off period of about a week to plan strategy. If the affair looked unreasonable, the whole matter was dropped.

The next move was to get the girl's party to see the land and premises of the groom. The size of this party was gauged by the estimated hospitality of the groom's people, but usually consisted of four to six men. For weeks before, the groom's family got everything into ship-shape with painting and improvements and they would not be above borrowing some farm machinery or a few cattle from a neighbour to augment the display. So help me, it was often done. During the tour of inspection the old farmer applied his hospitality to good account, and was careful to emphasise the salient features of his domain while judiciously avoiding things like wet land, sagging roofs and thin cattle. By this time the inspection party was just about able to get on the jaunting car for the return home. During these meetings the nub of the negotiations was the amount of the dowry but there were many side issues which could upset the match. The proceedings had now reached the crucial stage and the fine art of matchmaking was called into play and was used like diplomacy to wring the best advantage from the last delicate items. The match was made — or was it?

One little item remained to be settled. There was always a party given by the bride's parents about a week before the wedding and was similar to the American 'shower'. This was called 'eating the gander'. Remember, so far, all agreements were only verbal. Now nothing was valid until the 'marriage agreement' was drawn up by a solicitor (lawyer) and signed by both parties. The groom could still have a wonderful time at the expense of the bride and still back out at the last hour before 'writing the bindings', as it was termed locally. My own father, God rest him, did so and gave no apology either. A wise girl got the fellow to sign first. But it was better to back out then, than to try two weeks later after a man was roped. The 'gander' was an affair of importance second only to the wedding party, an all-night affair of music and dance.

Now there was only the wedding ceremony, the most important day in a couple's life. It was usually performed before noon, with or without a nuptial Mass. Everybody drove to the bride's house first and only the bride and bridesmaid rode in the wedding coach to the church. Others travelled in jaunting cars or rode on horseback. After the few words were said in the church there was a wild drive to the home of the groom. Bonfires lit by admirers blazed along the way and the groom and best man also rode in the bridal coach which was usually drawn by two horses. If he was generous, the groom gave a bottle of whiskey or money to those who lit the bonfires. The entire expense of the wedding was borne by the groom or his family. Everybody except the very old and very young made merry through the night until daybreak. The dust was kept down by copious applications of stout and hoarse singers were treated with whiskey or porter. At the height of the festivities, friends of the bride and groom, known as strawboys, arrived masked and camouflaged and were given drinks to toast the young couple. Their leaders got the privilege of dancing with the bride. They departed in a short time without revealing their identity if possible. More refined affairs were held in a hotel and the couple went on a honeymoon but these lacked the gaiety of the traditional article.

Many headaches lingered on as an aftermath. One deluded bride asked, 'Who owns all that ploughed land out there?" as she gazed out the front door the morning after the wedding. She was told it was all hers. Alas! She was looking at a heather-covered bog which was covered by a light fall of snow and resembled a ploughed field. A gentle tribute to the fine art of matchmaking! Even physical disabilities were minimised or ignored by the enthusiastic matchmakers and were smoothed over with a little 'drop of the craither' (poteen or homemade whiskey). But this rarely if ever had any effect on the outcome of marriage. They usually lived happily ever afterwards.

This seemingly desirable state of a happy people could have gone on forever but the world was marching on and Ireland had to go with it. Politics and wars have a way of changing the outlook of a people for better or worse. England and Germany were vying for supremacy in those days by building larger and better battleships. This raised the cost of living in the British Isles and prices and wages were rising steadily in Ireland. Farming was getting more interesting and profitable so the farmers were able to buy some badly needed machinery. The appearance of Halley's Comet in 1910 scared the people for a while when its orbit came close to the earth and many believed it would cause the end of the world. But it went as it came, spectacular, yet peaceable.

Kerry, my native county, was competing for the national football championship in 1911. Enthusiasm was rewarded a year later when they won it. Two fine athletes who lived only a few miles away were on the team, Ned Spillane and Paddy Healy. The latter I knew well. He was a rugged man and played in the centre half-back position. Great bonfires blazed on the hillside to greet the returning victors and a good ballad was composed to commemorate the occasion, one verse of which I recall:

And Healy fleet and sure of foot, from beside the Owenacree,
Whose name shall ring in Gaelic fields through ages yet to be,
The games he played at centre half will in future annals gleam,
When men shall write the noble deeds of Kerry's football team.

The Home Rule bill was being steered successfully through the British parliament. The Northern province of Ireland, being Unionist, was opposed to the idea. Its allegiance to England was no secret and on many occasions on the 12th of July, which amounts to something like their national holiday, there were riots and fights between the Unionists and the Nationalists. Several police were sent to Belfast for the occasion and one of them told me how ridiculous the difference of opinion was. He said the whole thing centred on someone, usually half drunk, shouting loudly, 'To hell with the Pope'. Whereupon a passerby Catholic would assault him and the riot was on. Sometimes it took on larger dimensions like burning houses and firing shots at trains or pitched battles on the street. One policeman told me he asked an enthusiastic rioter who the pope was and he received this answer, "Some

Italian who wants to be king of the world." Other rioters did not know either. The Unionist leaders organised a volunteer army to protect their interests when Home Rule would become law. Oh yes, they had to have arms, but England objected, and they procured some anyway when they squawked loud enough. The rest of Ireland, guided by the Irish Party leaders proceeded to train a volunteer force as the official army in November 1913. This force was called the Irish Volunteers (called National Volunteers after 1914), while the northern force was known as the Ulster Volunteer Force. To this day the impasse has not been resolved. What has happened in the meantime is history and will be referred to in later chapters.

3
War, Rebellion and New Horizons (1914-19)

World War I broke out suddenly and had a terrible impact on everything in Ireland. In the first place, all reservists were called up immediately. They were hardly allowed to change their clothes. This stripped the country of a large labour force in all kinds of employment, with a consequent rise in wages. Prices of farm produce jumped sharply. Horses especially, carried a high price tag. A beautiful dapple gray stallion owned by a neighbour of ours was sold a few months before for £40. When the war was only a month old he was bought by a British officer for £80. I remember the animal well and often wondered where he finished his days. Old cattle, if they were fat, were snapped up at the fairs and hogs were much in demand. The farmer was getting his hour of revenge. There was talk of recruiting and someone suggested that all the volunteers be inducted into the British army. The Ulster Volunteers answered with an unqualified 'No'.They were not Unionists now and their leader Sir Edward Carson said so. They were Ulstermen first, Orangemen second, and would fight if necessary to prove it.

The school books were mere propaganda sheets extolling the glory of the Empire, but we were spared the new enlightenment as we were not allowed to go back to school after the summer vacation. We were needed at home to help with the farm work. The National Volunteers who had been training, got suspicious of their leaders when it was suggested that they join the British army. Several decided to go to the US to escape fighting for England. Those all wound up in the US army a few years later when that country entered the war. I went back to school for two days after it opened in the autumn. The teacher of Irish needed a little help from another boy and myself to ensure the class achieved a pass mark. The inspector was impressed and was generous in his praise of our knowledge of the native tongue. It was only surpassed by the generosity of the teacher, Mrs. Cronin, when she gave us a bag of sweets and cakes to divide among our classmates. The class had passed alright and she would be paid for teaching the extra subject.

The Home Rule bill had passed its final reading and only needed the Royal Assent to become law, but the British government decided it should be postponed until after the war. This was a complete rebuff to the Irish leader, John Redmond, and left him with the unbelievable task of telling the Volunteers to fight for England and when the war was won Home Rule would be granted. He did just that but it was the beginning of the end of his political career. At an historic meeting in the Mansion House in Dublin the majority followed Redmond and went off to fight in World War I. Europe was ablaze but fires were being kindled in Ireland also. Newspapers were avidly read. Recruiters were busy. Naval gunfire was heard along the coast. Irish farmers were ordered to grow more of everything. Everybody was busy but not too busy to sing and dance and play. Such was the situation towards the end of 1914.

No period of a man's life can be as exciting and impressionable (for the time being anyway) as his teens, when and if his parents are engaged in some occupation which involves travel and he accompanies them. Life on a farm precludes anything like this and a ten mile radius was usually the scope of our travel. This was also true of many grownups and most of the travel was by horse drawn vehicles, bicycles or horseback. One local observer who was a tailor by trade and noted for his caustic wit, put it this way once when commenting on the death of a nearby farmer, 'The poor man was very honest but his world ended at the horizon.' The same remark was descriptive of many of the small farmers elsewhere in Ireland as well as countless others in all parts of the world. Automobiles were very scarce and only used on the main roads by wealthy tourists or professional people of high rank. Doctors, teachers, clergymen and the like used horses and traps, some of which had rubber tyres. The small, black, little 'donkey' was used by old people and children, and though slow, it was a safe means of transportation. The young men and girls thought nothing of walking or cycling five or ten miles on a Sunday afternoon to attend a crossroads dance or a sports fixture. After enjoying several square dances they walked home in time to milk the cows and do other farm chores.

The scarcity of farm labour was somewhat relieved by the stoppage of emigration in 1915 and many men working in England came back home to avoid conscription. Still there were others who enlisted and were lost in the crowd. They were mostly discontented fellows or others seeking adventure. One local farmer in his desperation was heard to say, "I wonder would those Belgian refugees be inclined to work?" Two of his sons had recently joined the Irish Guards. The notion of conscription in Ireland was unanimously opposed and it was hard to expect otherwise after the shelving of the Home Rule Act. The idea of 'live horse and you'll get grass' did not appeal to the Irish people and it was hard to blame them. England was begging them to save the Empire, which only a few years before was crushing them ruthlessly.

When the Volunteer force was first formed it was intended to be a regular army to take over from the British military forces when Home Rule became effective (possibly Britain had some reservations on this score). They drilled in every village and town and paraded with outmoded rifles on important occasions. Some even wore uniforms. Most of the young men joined up. It was something new and a lot of fun for a while, but before long they found out they were to be mere pawns in the old political game. They were constantly trailed by recruiters for the British army and some of them actually enlisted. One recruiter was a Cork man named Mike O'Leary who had just received the Victoria Cross for gallantry in France. However, there was within the volunteer organisation a remnant of the old Fenian movement and this in time became more influential and gradually took over the leadership. This inside circle was very secret and known as the Irish Republican Brotherhood. Dedicated to the principle that 'England's difficulty was Ireland's opportunity', this sector plotted revolution. The Sinn Féin organisation, which had been formed about ten years earlier and composed of some of Ireland's literary people and artists was closely allied with the labour leaders and both of these bodies were sympathetic to the revolution. A split occurred in the volunteer organisation and in the course of time the revolutionary element became the dominant body.

The leaders of Sinn Féin were quick to sense the prevailing dilemma, and convinced that the young men of Ireland would be sent to France to 'fight for the freedom of small nations' while their own freedom rested on a shelf in some government bureau in London, they decided to do something about it. Public parades and training of the volunteers had been stopped by order of the British government when they organised and planned strategy to resist conscription. England had some long range plans and the Irish were aware of them. Why hadn't the Ulster volunteers been disbanded? Or conscripted? The Sinn Féin leaders decided their hour of decision was at hand. Their plans were not very secret and ostensibly intended to resist the draft. An air of mystery was slowly gripping the country and whispered remarks were quite frequent. But life went on as usual and most of the people were too busy to become aware of the impending catastrophe. This indifference may have been the only thing which preserved them from a terrific bloodbath. They were not prepared for a revolution psychologically, much less from a military viewpoint, and had they engaged in one, they would have been mercilessly slaughtered. England was in no mood to compromise at the moment, and if any proof is needed, you can study the speed with which they executed the leaders of the Easter Rebellion of 1916. She was smarting from the failure of the Dardanelles campaign, a terrific loss of shipping and other reverses at the time, and eager to eliminate anybody and everything with a German or anti-British label.

Easter, 1916, burst on the country like a time bomb. The mystery had been cleared up at last and the newspapers and public were piecing together the parts of the puzzle. Less than a year earlier, on 26 July 1915, there had been a landing of arms at Howth near Dublin and there was talk of a German plot to land an army in Ireland. Anybody in the know did not believe this rumour as long as the British navy was in command of the sea around Ireland, but it served as propaganda to arouse the Irish people against Germany and consequently against Sinn Féin, who were supposed to be German allies. It is a well known fact and a matter of history that a ship named 'The Aud', manned by a German crew disguised as Norwegians, was stopped and searched three times on a voyage to Ireland. When the ship, laden with arms from Germany, arrived at its destination in Tralee Bay, it had to hide near a rocky island to avoid detection. This ship had a rendezvous with Irish rebel leaders Austin Stack and Tadhg Brosnan. Roger Casement, Captain Montieth and others were landed from a German submarine.

A carload of Volunteers from Dublin were on their way to Cahirciveen at this time but this car never reached its destination. Instead, it plunged into sixty feet of water at the end of a pier in Ballykissane, near Killorglin, after taking the wrong road about twenty miles short of its goal. The group had intended stealing a radio transmitter at Cahirciveen. Their plan was to set up the transmitter in O'Donnell's house, Ballyard, Tralee with a trained radio operator named Keating, who would broadcast news of the Rising. All the occupants of the car were drowned except one, but this survivor got away.

I was surprised the car got as far as it did, for it was travelling at high speed with dim lights on a dark night. It almost ran me over a half an hour earlier while I was driving some cattle along the road. The car narrowly missed hitting a cow, but never slowed down — which was very unusual. Of course, I knew nothing about the Rising, and neither did anybody else around there at the time. A neighbour who witnessed the incident remarked, 'That driver must be crazy or else he's a doctor going out on a sick call!'

British intelligence became aware of the extent of the plot when Casement was arrested on Good Friday while waiting to make contact with the local leaders. The whole county of Kerry was covered with British troops before the end of the day and the rising was called off but was scheduled to start on Easter Monday instead. There was no help from the rural districts and the only fighting occurred in Dublin. The Volunteers and Citizen Army fought gallantly for eight days

Patrick O'Connor, Rathmore, killed in action during the Rising in Dublin in 1916 while breaking out from the burning GPO, under O'Rahilly, Ballylongford. He is believed to be the first Kerryman killed in action in the 1916 Rising.

until hopelessly outnumbered by the forces of the empire. Many of the volunteers in Kerry assembled in the hope of being given arms from the ship but when they were disappointed, they returned to their homes and kept the secret. The authorities were none the wiser, but later arrested many people who were known or suspected of being leaders. Vengeance came swift and severe and within a month of the Rising all the leaders were shot except De Valera and Casement. De Valera was saved because he was an American citizen, and Casement being an English knight was given a long trial in London after which he was hanged. So ended the Rising and the British kept all strategic points under guard until the end of World War I.

The only sympathy the majority of people gave the rebellion at this time was a prayer for the dead. Many of the people were patriotic enough, but they had not been prepared for such an event. Some knew the history of Ireland very well and kept it alive in song and story. The neighbourhood had recently been treated to the addition of a library in the local school, and the books were selected by the local curate, Fr. Kirby. He was a mild, saintly man whose charity exceeded his resources when he met up with the travelling fraternity. His choice of literature was admirable and many of the volumes dealt with various phases of modern Irish history, which were not available to the average country boy before this. I often served Mass for this priest and read many of his library books. Another source of my early taste for history came from our next door neighbour, John Murphy. He had been a cattle drover in his younger days before settling on the farm, and his repertoire of songs exceeded those of any ballad singer. These he sang in a grand voice that might have been really famous if it were trained, but that didn't seem to detract any from it once you heard him. He often sang ballads from other parts of the country and explained them to me as I listened attentively.

On one occasion when the local priest visited the school while a history class was in progress, he asked the class who Parnell and Davitt were, but there was no answer. In disgust he deplored the ignorance of the children and added that 'none of them would have a roof over their heads only for those two men.' He left the room, slamming the door violently after him.

The summer of 1916 brought the first airplanes to our part of the country. They were single engine biplanes used by the British Air Force for scouting. An interesting sequel to the Rising was the capture of a German spy whose name, I think, was Lodi. As he was moved from one police escort to another, it was observed that he never ate anything, seeming to get along very well on some pills which he carried and swallowed with a little water — probably vitamin capsules.

Another sequel to the Rising centres around a story about a dog. My father had found a stray dog, a beautiful sky-blue terrier. He brought him home and reported the incident to the local R.I.C. sergeant about a week later. This was a remarkable dog and on one occasion when I took him rabbit hunting, he tore a badger to bits without flinching. Only a dog with plenty of courage and reckless daring would attempt this. A few weeks later the sergeant came to pick up the dog and told the following story to my father:

It seems the dog had been bought in England and was being brought home to Kerry by the lady who owned it. While she was 'airing' the animal at Headford railway station, the dog got away and the lady owner proceeded by train. She reported her loss the following day to the police near her home in North Kerry. Earlier that morning the police from the same station had arrested Roger Casement after he had landed from the German submarine. As they had much more important business than a stray dog on their hands, they neglected to notify the police at Headford for about a week. My father was well paid for recovering and taking care of the animal, a large blue terrier of some Scottish breed, and very valuable. Two years later, the sergeant, a dog fancier himself, told my father that the dog had broken out of his pen and fought with two other dogs of his own breed who killed him. I loved that dog and I called him 'Swank'.

As a military venture, the Rising of 1916 was doomed to failure. No matter how brave the action of the individual volunteers and their leaders, the overall conditions were not favourable. But the hand of the volunteers was forced by developments which unfolded almost daily, immediately preceding the event. In the first place, the plot to secure arms was discovered in the United States through surveillance of the German Embassy, and the information was passed to the British. The mission of Roger Casement in Germany to secure men and arms was not as fruitful as expected. The crew of the *Aud*, with German thoroughness did a first-class job of evasion and seamanship but they arrived at their destination two days early because the plans had been changed after they had put to sea. This delay from Good Friday to Easter Sunday was due to a disagreement among the leaders in Dublin as to the exact time of the Rising. The accident involving the car at the pier near Ballykissane was another adverse development. Besides communicating with the *Aud*, the wireless men were to send out false and confusing signals to the British naval ships in the area. This tactic was calculated to give time to unload the arms unnoticed. Although the pilot was ready on land, he did not expect the ship until Sunday. The failure to signal from shore was due to the change of plans even though a strange ship was seen in the bay. The innocent betrayal of Casement and his subsequent capture after landing from the submarine was another link in the planning chain that broke. The arrest of Austin Stack when he called to Tralee barracks where Casement was being held, finally severed the chain and left the Kerry volunteers leaderless and without plans. Eventually the crew of the *Aud* scuttled and sank it, sending the arms to the bottom of the sea at the entrance to Cork harbour while being escorted there by the British navy. Under all these circumstances, any one of which would be detrimental, the venture was doomed. However, now that the flag of revolution was unfurled and the Proclamation published, there was no turning back.

My honest opinion is that the failure of the Rising at that time was the very reason why later efforts were so successful. Let us suppose the initial events has been successful and Casement and the arms were landed and distributed through the surrounding country. There would have been intensive fighting for a short time but the average man was not trained to fight or support the patriots. After a few generations of English rule since the Act of Union in 1800, the average Irishman was more pro-British than Irish, and at best would have remained neutral while the power of the Empire was concentrated on crushing the rebellion. It may have lasted a few weeks or a month and the resources of the volunteers would have been depleted. The inevitable would follow and the result would be the same as in 1798 or other similar ventures. Subsequent events bear out this conclusion, that it is necessary to have a majority of the people sympathetic to a cause to ensure any success. Even the most dedicated of the volunteers had no combat experience and could not be expected to hold out against the seasoned troops of England.

Whatever effect the Irish rebellion had on the British people, it did not help relations between the two islands. The Irish were considered very disloyal to the 'Mother Country' and the press of both countries joined in the censure. Even the wives of Irishmen serving in the British army hurled all kinds of insults and obscenities at Irish prisoners as they were hustled away to prison camps. The Irish political party leaders made the usual apologies to the government but these were received with disdain. Now the soul searching began and the sympathy of the real Irish came into play. They made up their minds in that slow and obstinate way, peculiar of the Irish character, and almost completely withdrew their support from the Irish nationalist party, placing it instead behind the Sinn Féin movement. The British never liked the Nationalists anyway, though they tolerated them for political strategy. Now the Irish people had no love for the Nationalist party either, so they were left with very few supporters. The police force, always aloof but friendly, were now considered enemies. They helped put down the Rising and arrested the volunteers and other patriotic people. This situation dragged on for a few years. The only activity was the display of tricolour flags which the police always removed. Small bodies of British soldiers camped near vital points like large bridges and large numbers were trained for service in France at the bigger garrison centres such as the Curragh and Kilworth.

The activity of the local athletic groups was curtailed by the formation of the volunteers and the emigration of some of its members. This source of entertainment was sorely missed, especially by the young fellows between twelve and sixteen years old. We decided to do something about it and after much saving and conniving we bought a football in Killarney and started a minor team. The ball got punctured the first day we used it when someone kicked it into a whitethorn bush. But we repaired it and when we felt we were pretty good we challenged a team about two miles away and got soundly beaten. The other team was far more experienced, having had the benefit of training and coaching by the all-Ireland player Paddy Healy and other good athletes. We avoided any invitations to compete for a while and took on another team less dexterous which we beat, but they stoned us afterwards and we were forced to flee. One member of that team, Fr. Jerry Dennehy, who later became Superior General of the Catholic Missions in China, was imprisoned by the Japanese army for several years and is laid to rest in his native land. The following year we had some return matches which were attended and supervised by older people. A spirit of fair play was observed but we couldn't get anywhere with the team from Headford as they knew too many tricks and were highly deceptive. In a few years we lost interest in football and engaged in revolutionary activities.

The taste for music and dance which was hereditary, especially from my mother's side of the family, began to haunt me when I was 15 years old. I heard my mother's brother playing on a flute and it awoke in me the desire to try to play. He was a recent winner at an Oireachtas in Killarney in 1914. There was not very much appreciation of music around where I lived and no chance of taking music lessons in any formal manner. Yet, I bought a tin whistle and tried myself. One day a bachelor neighbour and cousin of my father's, having heard the feeble attempts, asked me for the whistle. He started to play and I was very surprised to learn that he was a fair player, doing so entirely by ear. This didn't dampen my ardour and he taught me several tunes that winter. I found out that he also played for dances in a house where the young people gathered at night. I asked to go along one night and he gave his consent, provided I didn't tell my parents that he made the decision.

This opened up an entirely new phase of life that seemed to go along with the music. The farmers' kitchens were large and permitted some card playing and dancing to be carried on simultaneously. After going to this house a few times and watching the young men and girls enjoying themselves, I wished I was more grown up so I could participate in the fun. My contribution was limited for some months, however, to playing along with my tutor who never danced and preferred to play cards. But one night there were only a few dancers and they needed a fellow to fill out the dancing set. Somebody suggested that I try it, reminding me I would have to learn some day, and the sooner the better. I was flabbergasted but there seemed to be no alternative to complying and I had the wish to try anyway. Set dances in Ireland were done without the benefit of a caller and the dancers were expected to know most of the movements before giving an exhibition of their clumsy attempts in public. They were practised at home or at small house parties and this seemed like the right time and place. The leader of the square dance, or set as it was called, knew all the parts and kept prompting the others if they seemed inexperienced.

The leader of this set was an avid dancer. His name was Malachy Moynihan and his ability to lead was well recognised in the neighbourhood. His decision to perform something long and strange on this occasion terrified me. But he assured me there was no difference between making a mistake in one set or another. He was right and I made enough in that one, 'Set of Erin', to discourage most fellows from trying again. There were many different sets danced in the locality, among them the 'Jenny Lind', 'The Polka Set', 'Victoria', 'Set of Erin', 'The Mazurka' and the 'High Caul Cap' being the most popular. Many of my pals around there learned to dance the same winter. A few others learned to play the tin whistle also, as there was talk about starting a fife and drum band in the village and we wanted to be counted in on it. During a local wedding the following spring only one of the gang, Jerry Daly, had the nerve to dance on that occasion. The music was strange and inspiring but the girls looked 'too strange and too pretty' as one fellow described them. I guess he was a bit too shy.

After hearing a local group of violin players and my uncle giving renditions of Irish dance music, my desire to play that instrument was smothered by the lack of a fiddle and the impossibility of securing one. There was a lot of difference between the cost of a violin and a tin whistle. But the desire to play was so great that one day I cut a flat board in the rough shape of a violin and stretched four strings across a rough bridge. To my surprise it made some sounds and I tuned the strings to E, A, D and G by ear, by straining the strings around wooden pegs. The bow was also made from thread by arching a light piece of wood. If operated in a quiet place and by using your imagination a bit, faint sounds remotely resembling notes of music could be heard. It was feeble but it was encouraging and I decided to read something about the making of violins. In the meantime I took some lessons by note from a man named Mike O'Carroll who played nicely and was also a comfortable farmer and a noted athlete. He had great patience with me, much more so than my pal Jerry Daly who accompanied me one night and vowed he would push me into the river on our way home after hearing me 'scraping'.

About a year after the Rising, quiet prevailed all over the country. Conscription was again mentioned but nothing was done to enforce it. The weather was bad during the summer and on Sundays, when they were sunny, the people tried to save the hay and oats. The young fellows didn't relish this as we preferred to go fishing and looking for birds' nests along Shea's glen or around the Quagmire bridge. I recall one Sunday we gathered at Micky Donoghue's to make a haycock. He had bought some hay 'on the ground', cut and saved it between rain showers and now it was time to haul it home. After a lot of looking at the sky and towards Croghane Mountain and a lot of prayers being said, we started. Several neighbours and friends helped and the haycock was completed on the only fine Sunday that month. If it rained, everything was lost. A few of us climbed Tokenfire mountain the following Sunday and picked some whorts at Doocarrig. We were growing up and looking around for adventure, and something illegal offered the most excitement.

The rivers in our area abounded with trout. Salmon came up these rivers to spawn during the winter months and were much sought after by fishermen and poachers alike. Before the angling season closed in November it was possible to catch an early arrival with a rod and line, but they could only be caught during December and January by the unlawful means of spear or gaff. Although I participated in this practice, I deplore it now as being unlawful and injurious to the fish stocks in the rivers. Two rivers, the Owenacree and the Beheenagh, joined to form the Quagmire close to my home. This junction formed a very large pool known as Orchard Pool and served as the local swimming hole. A little up the Owenacree River there was a cascade in a small gorge of wild beauty. This naturally impeded the movement of the salmon up the river. I heard my grandfather tell, when he was young before there were any conservation laws, that it was possible to catch salmon by hanging a gaff a certain way so that the salmon became impaled when they made an unsuccessful attempt to clear the falls.

About 1900 there was a big explosion around dawn one morning, and when the smoke cleared away the top of the falls about half way across the river was blown away. It was attributed to people living further up the river who had used the equipment of a local quarry to blast away a passage for the migrating fish. This would allow them to go further up the river where they could be caught easily. Anyway, it was a beautiful sight to see those salmon and trout trying to jump up the face of the cascade. Fish between eight and twelve pounds with favourable water conditions sometimes made it and it was common to see a thirty pounder trying vainly to make the grade. Poaching for salmon at night with a torch was a dangerous if not a foolhardy game. Apart from the chance of being caught by a water bailiff or a policeman, there were

Quagmire Bridge — the elevated railway bridge over the Owenacree River. Tokenfire mountain is in the background.

always stone fences and thorn bushes to be dealt with, as well as barbed wire. These things can be treacherous in the dark to say nothing about the cold water, deep pools and ice sometimes hitting your bare shins. However, it was adventure of a sort and occasionally it was possible to sell a salmon for some badly needed pocket money. Where deer were plentiful, poaching was also carried on. But this was very dangerous as the gamekeepers were always armed, — besides, the shots alerted them.

The police became more careless about poaching too as time went on. After all, they were after bigger game and tracking down a wary volunteer offered a bigger challenge. This, of course, gave us a little more latitude to carry out our shady pursuit. I even got brave enough to go fishing alone one night but I was not nearly as confident fifteen minutes later when I saw a salmon so big I was afraid to gaff him. Having heard stories about the 'Bradán Feasa' (Salmon of

Knowledge), I threw the torch into the water and went home to bed. For a while I kept this a secret . . . it wouldn't go down so well with my gang.

In Ireland the next largest wild animal after the deer is the fox. Some of them are pretty foxy, too, in behaviour as well as in colour. Many stories are told of their tricks and they seem to delight young and old. But the landed gentry had their own type of fun when they chased the fox with horses and hounds. These hunts were held during the autumn and winter months, but never around the area where I grew up. The people in the next county of Cork along the Blackwater valley were far more prosperous and inclined that way. Hares and rabbits were very numerous and provided some entertainment for those who liked coursing during the winter and early spring. A good old March hare was nearly as clever as the fox and had several tricks of its own. There were some fine greyhounds in our locality and a breed of terrier known as the Kerry Blue, a docile dog but a very good fighter. I have watched many a hare being chased and many a good dog fight. Many of the hounds bred in our county went on to win big prizes in the coursing classics of Ireland and England.

The other wild animals which were hunted included badger, otter, squirrel and weasel. Game birds were not very plentiful except in preserves, but pheasant, grouse, woodcock and plover were shot in good numbers in certain areas. Salmon, trout and pike were plentiful in the rivers as the water was clean and unpolluted by industrial waste. There are no pike in the Kerry rivers which flow mostly west to the Atlantic ocean, but pike may be found in the rivers of Cork which flow more or less in an easterly direction. Once a cousin of mine caught a nice pike when he suddenly jerked it out of the water as the fish got a hold of his finger and tried to make a meal of it.

Now that everything was quiet, politically and militarily, all of

The 'City'— an ancient pilgrimage site at the base of the Paps mountain.

us young fellows and girls enjoyed ourselves as best we could. We were at an age, in our mid-teens, when we had little or no responsibility. This is the age when most of the youth of Ireland are neglected. Instead of being formally educated and receiving some technical training, we were left to just grow up, but we enjoyed it. There were crossroad dances or 'patterns' in each community during the summer, weather permitting. At the base of the Paps mountain lies one of the oldest pilgrimage sites in Ireland. Known locally as the 'City' — this ancient spot was the location for religious ceremonies even in pre-Christian times. On May 1 each year, people assembled here at this site with their cattle for a summer pilgrimage to the mountain pastures. The Druids performed blessings for the health and fertility of the people and animals. These May Day pilgrimages to the 'City' have taken place each year down through the centuries — through Paganism, Druidism and Christianity.

The 'City' pilgrimage site — note the crosses deeply engraved on stones by thousands of pilgrims to this site down through the centuries.

Whit Sunday was a similar observance day at Ballyvourney and so was the last Sunday in July at Cullen. Attendance at these events demanded some pocket money so we pilfered and sold some farm produce to come by it. Sports and football matches were held in the neighbouring villages and an 'aeríocht' (open-air concert) was a popular affair. I earned my pocket money by planting onions and a new variety of early potato which could not be imported due to the war. These I sold to local merchants. I also made baskets and sold them to the farmers. All these little bits of activity and social life kept us going from one Sunday to another and it was the only respite. Life on a farm may slow down at times but it rarely stops, and the eight-hour day was not popular as yet.

My early education having been curtailed, my father prescribed a course of home study which he insisted I pursue. It consisted of a resumé of English grammar and vocabulary and the text was an old spelling book belonging to my uncle. He examined me once a week and after incurring his wrath a few times I soon found out it was much safer to study than neglect it. My uncle Paddy treated me to a fine arithmetic book and introduced me to equations and trigonometry. This also I had to keep a secret in fear of being taunted by my comrades. So there was a little play and a little learning. Gaelic was spoken very little since my grandmother had died in 1914, and my interest in this dropped off.

In spite of the apparent failure of the Rising and the apologies offered for its occurrence, it had the reverse effect on the Irish people. The organisation remained intact and secret. Although many of the second line leaders were in prison, others held meetings whenever possible. The Gaelic League continued to hold an annual 'aeríocht' or open-air concert in every town and village of importance. These events were rather quiet and consisted mainly of music, singing and dancing. The tricolour flag of the Republic, proclaimed on Easter week, was displayed on the stage and after being objected to by the local police was usually removed by them. This did not make the police any more popular than they were at the time of the Rising, when they were armed and helpful in arresting the rebels. Each succeeding event seemed to create more animosity and, after a few riots occurred, a company of soldiers or a cycle patrol attended public gatherings. Some leaders even addressed the audience and were listened to attentively by a police sergeant or military officer for signs of sedition. When this was noted, the speaker was ordered to stop or be arrested. The crowd usually moved about sullenly or dispersed quietly, even the timid ones refusing to be pushed around.

In the spring of 1918 Lord Derby, who was in charge of the conscription scheme, made a further bid to force the draft of Irishmen. By now the whole population, incensed by the tragedy of Easter Week, had enough backbone to resist the compulsory service. If one enlisted it was his own private affair, but everybody, even the clergy, opposed conscription. The slogan was, 'If you have to fight for the freedom of small nations, fight for the freedom of Ireland first.' It was a logical principle and men, women and children marched in protest parades. They expected nothing from Britain and the authorities made no show of force. The British were cautious and didn't want to alienate their new ally, the US. Many Americans were of Irish birth or descent and the alliance was a delicate one. Britain was also trying to negotiate a loan from the US and it was no time to strain relations. The Irish won their point and were very pleased with their performance. Sinn Féin collected money and organised clubs in every village. It also floated a bond in 1919 to carry on their government in hiding. This was all very secret and the outward show of parades against conscription covered up all the activities. The RIC (Royal Irish Constabulary) were becoming more unpopular and the government, as a result, were lacking intelligence of the real scope of the movement.

Nearly all youths, eighteen years and older, joined the volunteers. The older people ran the Sinn Féin clubs and all joined together to run a sports meeting or 'aeríocht'. It was a loose combination but the hard core was composed of a few dedicated men who rarely made themselves conspicuous. They belonged to an inside circle which only themselves were acquainted with. This took very delicate manoeuvering, which the average volunteer did not understand. Many moves were made which were beyond his comprehension, but he had taken an oath of secrecy and lived up to it.

The Murphy family outside the old thatched farmhouse in Kilquane.
Rear from left: Mary (holding fiddle), Patrick, Margaret, Jeremiah (author)
Front from left: Michael (brother), Mrs Hannah Murphy (mother, with concertina), Michael J (father), John J (brother).
Holding the horse: Elizabeth Collins from Newbury Port, Massachusetts, USA (nurse and member of A.O.H.)

The farmhouse was built by Con Houlihan (mason) brother to author's grandmother originally from Stagmount. The stone and mortar walls were two feet thick with no windows at the rear which faced Barraduff. During one incident bullets came through the thatch and some fell to the floor, still hot. Some bullets embedded in the rafters.

In July, 1918 most of the young men in Ireland became very restless. Drilling and organising were carried out by night and farm work had to be done by day. Many of our parents didn't know where we spent our spare time and couldn't understand why we were so tired all the time. This led to some bad feelings between father and son so I decided to run away to some other part of the country. I got everything ready secretly on a Saturday night and at first streak of dawn, I sneaked out of the house and took off on a good bicycle which had been given to me by my uncle, the policeman. I headed east towards Cork and met no one, but an aunt of mine who lived about three miles away was rising early and just caught a glimpse of me as I rode past her house. I could really push a bike in those days and I made about 15 miles before most people were up. Besides, it was cool in the morning and I wanted to get into strange country before anyone recognised me. As the morning wore on, the sun got very hot and I took the first rest after about 20 miles. While eating breakfast in a small restaurant in Newmarket, I asked directions from another cyclist. He seemed friendly and from our conversation I learned he was going in my direction and looking for work. At least we had something in common. We proceeded at a much slower pace and he pointed out the grave of Sarah Curran (Robert Emmet's sweetheart) as well as the scene of the tragic murder of Bridget Gayer. He was a native of this locality. We rode through Kanturk and on to Buttevant. We visited some friends of his there and attended Mass at 12 noon. I had put a respectable distance between me and my home. His friends knew someone who would hire me and after thanking them, I rode two miles to the north of Buttevant. As I had little money I decided on two things. First I would have to start work as soon as possible, and second, I must change my name. I was not a criminal but I hated the idea of being caught.

A Mr. Hutch opened the door when I presented myself and with little ceremony he hired me and gave me dinner. He was a tall, good looking man in his late thirties and very unlike any farmer I had ever seen before. After dinner he asked me if I knew anything about pigs and having answered in the affirmative, he took me to a well-kept piggery and showed me a sow which was preparing to have young bonhams. She looked me over. After all, I was to be her companion and midwife for the afternoon. There was a lot of straw in the place and a large wooden box about two feet high lay in one corner of the room. My new boss brought me a chair and I started the long vigil. After all, it was my job, and I was thoroughly familiar with all its intricacies. The afternoon rained and I was tired, but I kept from falling asleep by snipping and tying up each navel string. When Mr. Hutch relieved me for supper, there were twelve little bonhams in the box all doing well. He looked over a few and congratulated me on the operation.

While at supper I learned more about my surroundings. Mr. Hutch was a veterinary surgeon. He was married and had three children. He had a large two storey house and his mother-in-law also lived there. He employed one servant girl, a groom for the horses, two farm labourers and two other permanent workmen who lived in their own houses on the farm and whose wives helped out when times were busy. He owned about 400 acres of land, 2 brood mares, 4 draft horses, a large strawberry cob and a black pacer stallion with a white forehead. He also kept 40 milking cows, several dry cattle and many pigs. All the stock were of good blood lines and the farmyard and buildings were well kept and orderly. After supper I went back to my job and Mr. Hutch suggested we leave the young ones out of the box to their mother. I told him the straw was too long and asked if he was going to put a stick along the wall to keep the sow from crushing the little ones. He told me to fix it up the way I thought best. I took care of these items and when he came to see me later he remarked, 'I see you know your pigs'. We let the young ones run around and afterwards he asked me a few more 'getting acquainted' questions. He told me he had a car and would like to teach me to drive. It was time to retire for the night.

The famous Model 'T' Ford made its debut in Ireland in 1908.

I engaged in all the farm work and enjoyed it very much. The groom, whose name was Tom Dooner, took the milk to the creamery in the morning and I took it in the evening. He was about 19 years old and we became friends easily. All the others were men in their 40's and we had little in common. The weather was rainy at one time and we had to hustle to move the hay away from the rising flood. One day, Tom and I were resting after lunch on a fence near the gate. Tom suggested I get on the horse's back and as I did so, I scared the animal, who reared up and took off around the farm. He tried to throw me but I held on for dear life. I finally threw myself off into a clump of briars and he tried to kick me as I fell. It was a terrifying ride and I had no idea he was so wild. I learned afterwards that he was almost impossible to break into harness. While putting the cows in the stall one morning, I slipped and fell on my back on a sharp edge of concrete. A collie dog drove about twenty cows over me but none of them stepped on me. I was crippled for about three days and I got an idea to apply for another job that I saw in the 'wanted' ads.

Since I was going to leave Buttevant anyway, I reasoned that if I wrote a letter home, and even if someone came looking for me, I should have already left there and, leaving no further information, it would be impossible to find me. Knowing that my parents were concerned about my disappearance I wrote to my mother and gave no address. However, my father noticed the Buttevant postmark. He borrowed a relatively new bicycle from Jeremiah Cronin, the local school teacher. Bringing the bicycle with him, he took the next train to Buttevant. He arrived in Buttevant and knowing the routine, he inquired at the local creamery. The manager was cooperative and told my father where to look for me. When he arrived at Mr. Hutch's farm I was already packed and he walked right up to me as I cleaned my shoes. He handed me a letter from my mother which pleaded with me to come home. I had no other alternative and we rode home by way of Mallow and Rathmore. My father had the idea that I might bolt on the way home and as he was almost 50 years of age and I was just 16 years, he knew that he might not catch up with me again. He reasoned that if I was riding Mr. Cronin's bicycle I would not try to bolt and get away again. That was sound logic as he knew that I had special respect for Mr. Cronin. However I had an accident on the journey home and I ran off the road and wrecked the new bicycle against the fence.

I settled down to work on the farm and tried another scheme to make some money. Fuel had been expensive because coal was hard to get during the war and by cutting some turf, even late in the season, I hoped to make some money. I sold the idea to some pals of mine but the 'weather man' refused to cooperate and the turf didn't dry before the war ended in November 1918. Prices dropped and I sold the turf the following year at no profit.

The end of the war brought a lot of rejoicing but the farmer missed the high prices and demand for farm produce dropped off gradually. The parades against conscription were no longer necessary and many of the young men, with the danger of war removed, got careless and there was a strange loss of excitement, a sort of vacuum. Ireland's bid to be included in the peace negotiations having failed, and Ulster causing as much disturbance as possible, put the rest of the country on a sort of neutral status. The old question of Home Rule was re-introduced and rebuffed to the delight of the Ulster leaders. In December of 1918, a general election was held. Prior to this, most of the Irish revolutionary leaders were released in a general amnesty. These were greeted by the people with wild demonstrations and many made speeches of gratitude. A few of the leaders had been elected in by-elections since 1917. Now, Sinn Féin had the support of the electorate to such an extent they were confident enough to contest nearly every seat held by members of parliament from Ireland. Even some of the Nationalist Party leaders saw the 'writing on the wall' and rather than go down in ignominious defeat, withdrew from the contest. There was a very good reason for all this course of action.

When that scheming old statesman, prime minister Lloyd George, was thinking of enforcing conscription on Ireland in April of 1918 he conveniently 'discovered' a new German plot to land more arms and troops in Ireland. This was only an excuse to round up the Sinn Féin leaders. The 'plot' was afterwards proved to be a hoax but it supplied the necessary reason to re-arrest many of those who had previously been released. Anyone lucky enough to evade arrest went on the run. The police (RIC) and military carried out many raids and searches, continuously harassing the peaceful population. This was particularly true in the cities and towns where the police knew every volunteer. So the wanted men moved to the country areas and carried on the work of organising from there. This proved to be a boon, as up to then these areas had been more or less neglected. The allegiance of the stalwart country people was well known and proven many times before.

Among those arrested in May 1918 was Eamon De Valera. In February of the following year he escaped from Lincoln Jail with the aid of Michael Collins. It made us feel proud in later years to learn that among those who planned and organised his escape were a few Kerrymen, one of them born less than a half a mile from my home. 'Dev' as he was known, made his way to the United States where he made some speeches and organised the sympathisers. Large sums of money and some arms were collected there. Of course, he was among his own people as he was a native of New York. Unfortunately, two ships containing arms were captured in New York and impounded by the US government. They contained the new and much prized Thompson sub-machine guns which would have been a boon to the IRA. To the US it was a duty, to the IRA it was a sacrilege.

Public bodies all over the country and in England had censured the government for its handling of Irish affairs. Coroners' inquests had returned verdicts of murder against the government where prisoners had been killed or mistreated. In the case of Thomas Ashe, who had died as a result of forcible feeding in Mountjoy prison, American congressmen had forwarded resolutions condemning the British policy and supporting the Irish resistance. Local bodies, such as county councils and urban councils — even the clergy, never an element to support the patriots — voiced their disapproval of the high-handed methods used by the government to smother Irish aspirations. Important individuals, who heretofore had remained silent and neutral were loud and clear in their sympathy for the harassed population. Sinn Féin was the only organisation that seemed to have a definite policy and in a short time, thousands of clubs under this banner were formed in Ireland and the USA, as well as Britain, Canada and Australia. It was time to stand up and be counted and to separate the 'boys from the men'. And the men were separate, at least at night, and in lonely places. They drilled and organised in secret and when there was an opportunity to parade in public, their leaders were arrested and handed stiff prison sentences. Other men came forward to fill the vacancies. Emigration had ceased since 1915 so there was no shortage of manpower.

Where the Nationalists had put candidates forward, every consideration was afforded them by the authorities. In Waterford city where the Sinn Féin candidate was discriminated against, it was necessary to draft some young men from other areas to protect his campaign. Several men from Kerry took part in this movement. When the noise and excitement had cleared away, Sinn Féin had won a landslide victory. Out of 105 seats, 73 had been won by Sinn Féin and of those elected, 43 were in prison and 26 at large (De Valera won 3 seats and Griffith won 2 seats). They were at liberty to take seats in the House of Commons, but having campaigned as abstentionists, they would not sit. This was a new twist to the lion's tail. (Actually, the Irish Party members had walked out of the House in a body when the conscription bill was debated in April.). The newly elected members proceeded to carry out their mandate; refusing to recognise British authority in Ireland and announcing that they intended to form their own parliament. It was sedition at its worst. But England was not in a risky war situation now. She could afford to bide her time and toy with the issues. She had some long-range plans and could test them at her leisure. Why hurry? Had she not toyed with Home Rule for fifty years? The Irish Party had been voted into oblivion and a new set of leaders had come to the fore. These were not as experienced in parliamentary procedure as their predecessors, but they didn't need to be. Their approach to the Irish question was different and they intended to solve it.

Since there was no emigration during the war years, the number of young adults had increased considerably. These became enthusiastic enough to form athletic clubs and bands and engaged in many worthwhile projects. Football and hurling teams played more games and every village and town held some kind of a programme of entertainment, generally a 'Feis' or a sports day. Our district organised a very successful aeríocht sponsored by the Sinn Féin club. A tug-of-war was formed under the leadership of Jiles Cooper, who had been a member of the Manchester Police team in England. The new team was composed of Jimmy Daly, Mike Doherty, Dan Murphy, Patsy Hayes, Mick O'Carroll, Mick Dennehy and Malachy Moynihan, all big, muscular men. We cheered them on to many a victory. At the sports meetings the young college men dominated the events but some local men gave them stiff competition, especially in the weight throwing. One event in particular created a lot of interest. It was the pony race which was usually held at the end of the programme. Two entries by local owners, Jeremiah O'Leary and John Singleton, staged a regular duel over a number of years.

Dancing platforms were built at many crossroads and the general atmosphere was of social gaiety, in spite of constant harassment by the police.

The great influenza epidemic at the end of the war was disastrous. It weakened the lungs, making a person subject to pneumonia, which was fatal in many cases to people who had any respiratory disease. It began in Europe and was spread all over the world by the discharge of troops to all countries. Ireland, of course, had its share of visitors, returning soldiers and some Americans seeking their relatives or the place of their forebears. Very few people escaped the 'flu' and the medical profession seemed powerless against it. During the spring of 1919 it was particularly virulent in Ireland and people were advised to avoid crowded functions. Eucalyptus was sprinkled on handkerchiefs and inhaled, in hopes of combating the disease. However, an occasional house dance seemed innocent enough but it took only one house party to prove the wisdom of avoiding crowds.

All my pals attended that dance, but a few days later we got very sick. Some had already died and the rest of us were fearfully awaiting our turn. The saddest example was the death of a young man and his wife leaving four orphaned children. At the party he had sung 'The Battleship of Sinn Féin'. One of my brothers complained of pains in his legs which was regarded as a general symptom. After several days my father was able to get a much overworked doctor to see him. He diagnosed the illness as osteomyelitis, a disease of the bones. The doctor was forced to open my brother's leg with a penknife, in order to relieve pressure. After two other similar visits and two more openings he was taken to Cork where he underwent major surgery. My father and mother accompanied him and remained there for a few days, during which they contracted another bout of the 'flu. They hurried home and all the family got very sick for about a week. It was impossible to get any work done but our neighbours took care of the farm stock and chores but they would not enter the house.

Some of the returning soldiers joined the volunteer ranks. Even visiting Americans gave military advice and enjoyed meeting their Irish cousins. They were very different from British soldiers. Besides being more friendly and better behaved — which was expected — they had plenty of money. One of these visitors was a cousin of ours from North Dakota, named Houlihan. He didn't drink or smoke and entertained his relatives with a few days on the town while telling them stories about the 'Wild West'. His father had emigrated from Ireland about 1870, married a Swedish girl and settled in North Dakota about one hundred miles from the nearest town, where he owned a large wheat farm. This US soldier had a fine physique, was a good boxer and wrestler and was minus one of his ears which had been bitten off by a horse. This was quite easy to understand after listening to some of his stories. He started school when he was about twelve years old. The school was in a settlement that sprung up around the station when the railway was built about forty miles from his home. The journey took two days each way. He attended school two days and rested on Sunday. He went there to school for four years but only in summer. He landed in France the day the Armistice was signed. Others of my acquaintance were not so lucky. A cousin of my mother, named John Foley, who had been a policeman in Ireland, England and Australia respectively, was killed in action in France in 1916. Another returning soldier was a young tinker named Denis Harrington who was a nice step dancer and served with the Munster Fusiliers.

Many memories of the Great War lingered on. When the liner Lusitania was sunk by a German submarine off the south coast of Ireland, life-saving crews, Coastguard and Naval craft brought some more activity than usual to that area. A relative of ours was a policeman in Skibbereen and he spent some time searching the shoreline for some of the victims of the tragedy. Though the sea was about twenty miles from our home at the nearest point, we frequently heard the sound of naval gunfire along the coast. The fishermen sometimes profited from the wreckage along the Atlantic seaboard. Much valuable material such as timber and foodstuffs were washed ashore. A side of beef or a ham was not spoiled by a little more application of salt water, or a container of flour protected by its outside surface (turned into dough by contact with seawater) was only spoiled in part. Of course all the material was not so useful. An occasional mine also floated onto the beaches. At one time the British soldiers carried their rifles along when going on leave. When they ran short of money they sold them to eager buyers from the Sinn Féin volunteers. Of course they suffered the consequences and the practice diminished. The army platoons which had been guarding bridges, etc. packed up their gear and went elsewhere. I conversed with one officer who was stationed at the Quagmire bridge near Headford and he seemed to have no quarrel with Ireland. Of course he was typical English middle class and might have been only trying to gain my confidence to get information.

During the years between 1916 and 1919, when the police were eagerly rounding up the volunteers it was found convenient to search for and confiscate all arms. This profound logic was based on the idea that a people without arms could not defend themselves. There was only one thing wrong. It was not only too late, it was also in the wording of the Defence of the Realm Act (D.O.R.A.). Long before, the volunteers had made some raids of their own and collected any useful arms. Many patriotic people willingly gave their weapons to them. The pro-British aristocracy made a big show of turning in some useless or needless arms while secretly keeping possession of some good rifles and small arms. Some of these people served as intelligence agents for the British as, at some time or other, they had been connected with government service.

As the authorities were putting on more pressure each day and noting anyone patriotic enough to make himself conspicuous, so too the volunteer organisation was taking notes of those who were carrying out the arrests and searches. Several local people in every community came forward, with courage, to plead the cause of the newly established republic. The speeches were no gems of oratory, but the message was getting across. It was frank enough to appeal to the man in the street and painful enough to hurt the feelings of those supporting the crown. The duly elected representatives had formed a government, even if it was in hiding. A bond had been floated to carry on its work to which most people subscribed. Large sums of money were collected in many parts of the world where Irish people or their sympathisers lived. The volunteer organisation had changed its name to the Irish Republican Army. Police were appointed from members of the IRA. A system of courts and a code of laws were organised. All of these developments were carried out by people assigned to work while evading arrest. Those arrested refused to recognise the authority of the courts. Some of the prisoners spoke only in Gaelic which the old judges didn't understand. So both sides continued to goad each other in every way short of war.

One event, held in the nearby village of Barraduff was the occasion of a lively exchange. A fife and drum band from the Anablatha district was approaching the village before the start of an aeríocht. The police and a military officer met the leading file on a small bridge and stopped them with the order, 'Stop the music!' The band obliged and after being admonished by the police sergeant they asked to be allowed to proceed. They were refused and told something about unlawful assembly. Several of us boys were standing about fifty feet away and saw every move. The bandmaster gave the signal to march and the officer barked an order to the alert soldiers. In less time than it takes to tell it, the band was dispersed with broken fifes, drums gored by bayonets and several cuts and bruises. It was our first experience of an unnecessary show of might. The rest of the programme was carried out in an orderly manner. The leader of the band was 'small' Jack Fleming and he was confronted by Sgt. Jack Hastings of Headford. Young men and girls started dancing in the handball court and this was also objected to. The musicians countered by pointing out that the only ones creating trouble were the police. However, they stopped playing when it became evident the police meant business and the military began to clear the village.

Then the real trouble began. Two or three soldiers headed for a house where the committee was entertaining the visiting band among others. Somebody alerted the diners and there was a mad rush through the back door, but the structure couldn't stand the strain. It was torn from the walls and carried out into the back garden. Out on the road one intrepid youth, Denis O'Sullivan, waited on one knee for two pursuing soldiers with fixed bayonets. He had a stone in each hand and when the leading soldier came into range he nailed him on the head with a well aimed throw. The soldier crumpled but his companion took up the chase. The next stone missed its target and the odds were too great to ignore flight. The soldier didn't follow. By now there were very few people in the village and everyone was heading for home.

Of course, there was an aftermath! Five policemen (RIC) were returning to their station in Rathmore after putting on a display of force all day. They came on a few fellows pitching pennies on the road. Dismounting from their bicycles, they proceeded to punch the unwary pitcher around, while at the same time delivering a sermon about abusing the image of the king on the coins. But some of our boys had a reception prepared for the police half a mile further on. At a turn in the road, they greeted the unsuspecting police with a fusillade of stones from behind the fence. The police were supposed to be without arms, - a very dangerous situation. Although they were all knocked off their bicycles and stunned, one of them scrambled to a low part of the fence and fired some shots after the retiring attackers. The leader of the IRA was the only one armed and it was lucky he had used this precaution. He boldly stood his ground and fired the only rounds in his outmoded revolver. When the police realised they were being attacked by armed men they made good their escape on their bikes. This was the first brush in our locality against the forces of the crown, — weak, but spirited. Later in the year the R.I.C. abandoned the barracks at Headford and the local IRA burned it to the ground. Another dragon slain!

My desire to become a scientific farmer was motivated by a little reading and by some of my father's reforms — his avowed intention was to improve his lot. Though he succeeded in accomplishing some of his objectives, his effort could be best described as 'scratching the surface'. I am inclined to think he entertained some good ideas but was a little cowardly about putting them into practice, for fear of being criticised by his neighbours. If the idea failed, he could be the target of much scorn. As proof of this timidity he borrowed a neighbour's donkey and cart one day to haul some cotton and linseed cake which he had purchased in Cork. This stuff was used for cattle feed and its effect on milk production was highly recommended by Department of Agriculture leaflets. He read many of these leaflets and was well aware of the messages they conveyed. Yet he feared the reactionaries enough to want to prevent their becoming aware of his experiments, by using another man's cart to deliver the goods, which were fictitiously consigned to a local merchant. I became aware of this plot a long time afterwards.

So in the winter of 1919-20 I decided to attend an agricultural school which was located in the Temperance Hall in Rathmore. My fellow students were Manus Moynihan, Dan Courtney, Malachy Moynihan, Jer Ryan, Michael Reen, Michael O'Sullivan and a Courtney lad from west of Killarney. We were all eager to learn one of man's oldest skills with a new approach. I failed to get any of my pals interested, so when the session ended, I got no encouragement to pursue my studies any further. But I learned a lot, or at least enough to whet my curiosity and the little knowledge acquired there served me well later on.

I also attended dances in that same Temperance Hall on Sunday afternoons and became acquainted with many fellows and girls. The music was supplied by the renowned player, Tom Billy. Though completely blind from smallpox and crippled by polio, he never failed to delight his audiences. His only means of livelihood was his fiddle and his transportation was a donkey on which he rode around from one place to another. He played at weddings, house parties, fairs, markets and gave music lessons. I knew two of his pupils very well, Bill Sullivan and Denis 'The Weaver' Murphy. It is a great loss that his music was never recorded. He was witty, too. While changing a broken string on the fiddle, he might say to somebody standing near, 'Come out of my light'. Or he may ask, 'Who is that nice blonde girl I saw you dancing with?' The person often answered unconsciously never realising he was completely blind. The last time I saw Tom Billy he was astride the donkey, facing backwards, going towards Knocknagree from Rathmore. A large herd of cattle was being driven along the road from the fair to the railway station. There he was, in the middle of about one hundred half crazy cattle, trying to drive the donkey against the thundering herd. He was 'half gassed' and was urging the donkey on by hitting him on the backside with his violin case. What a picture!

The Sliabh Luachra area of east Kerry, a few miles north of where I come from, is the source of some of the finest traditional Irish music in all of Ireland. This area around Ballydesmond, Gneevegullia, Knocknagree and Scartaglin produced many a fine musician, particularly fiddle players — among them, Tom Billy Murphy, Pádraig O'Keeffe and Denis "The Weaver" Murphy.

The history of the Sliabh Luachra area probably has a lot to do with its prolific output of renowned music and famous musicians. Hundreds of years ago only the southern half of this area, along the southern hills, was inhabited. The remainder was just bog, rushes, marsh and woodlands — a home suitable only for refugees trying to evade the authorities. After the plantations of Laois and Offaly (1558) and Munster (1585) and the Battle of Kinsale (1601) many dispossessed and poverty-stricken people moved into this area. O'Connor, a popular surname in Offaly at the time of the plantation, is a common name in Sliabh Luachra today.

The remoteness of the area and the barren soil proved attractive to the dispossessed people as the authorities were less likely to bother them in this new inhospitable environment. People in the area suffered great hardship and deprivation. They felt isolated from the outside world. In such circumstances the communal and social skills of music, poetry and dance often thrive.

Sliabh Luachra has its own dancing set comprising of six figures which finishes with a slide and a hornpipe and it lasts about thirty minutes.

Tom Billy Murphy (1879-1944) from near Ballydesmond, was one of a family of seventeen. Blind and partially disabled from a young age as a result of illness, he could not work the family farm and had to learn music to make a living. His repertoire included 136 reels as well as many jigs, slides and hornpipes.

Tom Billy Murphy (1879-1944) — a rare photograph of the gifted blind fiddler, with two ladies from Sliabh Luachra.

Pádraig O'Keeffe (1888-1963) from Glanthane, near Ballydesmond, was a national teacher but he found the discipline of the job too much and resigned to concentrate on playing the fiddle. He could read and write music and had his own unique style. He never married and called his fiddle 'the

Pádraig O'Keeffe (1888-1963) — one of the greatest traditional Irish fiddle players of all, playing in Lyons Pub, Scartaglin with one of his best known pupils, — Johnny O'Leary.

missus', often saying 'she's no trouble at all. One stroke of the bow across her belly and she purrs.' He spent much of his time playing informally in local pubs in the area.

Denis "The Weaver" Murphy (1910-74) from Lisheen, near Gneevegullia, was a distinguished pupil of Pádraig O'Keeffe. A fine fiddler noted for his dynamic and rhythmic style, he collected hundreds of tunes, some of which bear his name today, such as *Denis Murphy's Slide*.

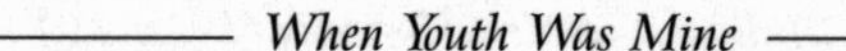

4

Rebellion Spreads: Armed Resistance & Guerrilla Warfare (1919-21)

The next few years were among the most momentous in recent Irish history and produced examples of courage, betrayal, murder, pillage, ambush and tyranny not experienced since the rebellion of 1798. It started gradually in 1919 after the results of the general election in December of the preceding year. Sinn Féin members of parliament, now backed by a mandate from the people, challenged the 'establishment' in all departments, taking over the work of government. England now recognising the fact that its hold was indeed slipping, issued many orders and directives, most of which were ignored or disobeyed.

The courts of law were deserted by civil litigants, in favour of Sinn Féin courts which had been established by the rebel Republican government. The majority of defendants in the regular courts were political prisoners charged under the Defence of the Realm Act (D.O.R.A.), and its provisions had plenty of scope to arrest and convict, for even slight offences. The general populace was calm but the government in hiding and the elusive patriots throughout the country initiated the moves which had to be countered by the British forces. The police (RIC) were forced to make many arrests and since the task was very distasteful, they resigned by the dozen. Only those who were nearing retirement, or those strongly pro-British, stuck it out and these became very unpopular. Few candidates had joined the force since 1916 and as a result of being undermanned and despised, it was reduced to impotence. When its members became overzealous in trying to carry out their orders, they were ambushed and killed. Sinn Féin issued a manifesto calling on them to resign as a body.

Some resignations came about and one in particular made the headlines. As he was a native of our locality, Tom O'Leary by name, we were very interested. He wrote an open letter to his superiors, submitting his resignation formally, giving the reasons for his actions and remarking, 'I cannot serve two masters, so I prefer to serve the duly elected government of my country.' When he returned to his native Kerry from Mayo, where he had been stationed, he was closely watched and evaded arrest by keeping out of sight.

The greatest drawback to the active members of the IRA who were on the run was the lack of arms to defend themselves. There was a time when our local company had only one Lee Enfield rifle as its most formidable weapon. This was passed around at drill meetings and all members were taught to handle it, assembling and disassembling it with alacrity and reverence. Most registered arms had been collected by the RIC after the 1916 Rising, but a few outmoded, unlicenced rifles and shotguns were collected by the IRA, sometimes forcibly and always by masked and armed parties. It was very important to keep the identity of the real leaders secret.

One way to come by arms, which proved successful in other countries, was to take them away from those who possessed some, namely, police and soldiers. This involved ambushing small parties of police or soldiers or attacking their barracks. Stealing or buying rifles and ammunition from British soldiers also proved fruitful. A great many small country barracks deemed incapable of defence were evacuated by the RIC and these buildings were burned down by local boys under cover of darkness. Such incidents caused another wave of arrests but the real leaders evaded this by remaining incognito in their usual employment, under the eyes of the authorities. Long before this, the Irish people were convinced that the British were playing a game of 'cat and mouse' (which they were), trying to force the rebels into open confrontation. Another Easter Rising would be 'right up their alley', as they could release their forces from any obligation of government, Home Rule or otherwise. Besides, no attempt had been made to resolve the situation in Ulster and the IRA in that part of the country had to fight the Irish Unionists as well as the British. Reinforcement for the RIC was deemed necessary by the government, so they accepted recruits from England or anywhere. When these new men were mixed up with regular members, much dissatisfaction and quarrelling occurred. The new recruits were a profane and obscene lot or rowdy opportunists who could never measure up to the high standards of such a force in the first place. There were quarrels for other reasons. In Listowel and Milltown some visiting officers gave a pep talk to the members stationed in these towns. The speech was so effective that several men resigned. Throwing their guns and badges on the table in front of their superiors, and telling them how they felt about the new police orders, was an act of mutiny. One of the officers, a Colonel Smyth, laid his revolver on the table while speaking, as if to threaten the men. Strong language was exchanged and a scuffle ensued, but the police resigned anyway. This news was heartwarming to the rebels, but there was always the British army to be contended with as the last line of defence.

England had to stay her hand for a while. She was negotiating for another loan in the US and did not wish to start shooting down innocent people as Colonel Smyth had suggested. There was no formal declaration of war by either side and all disturbances were supposed to be handled by police action. Besides, the rebels were getting too elusive to corner. Many post offices and trains were held up at gunpoint by the rebels in order to try to get information on the strength of the forces in occupation, the names of their officers, condition of police morale and, if possible, on suspected spies. The latter had become very busy, and as the police were not the shrewd, dependable operators they had been in the past, spying became a very dangerous but lucrative game. Meanwhile, the IRA did some spying too, and Colonel Smyth was cornered in Cork city and shot dead. They had come to realise the best defence is vigorous offence. Many spies were caught and convicted by rebel military courts. Some of those convicted were found tarred and feathered and tied to some church gate for all to see. This humiliating experience was not recommended by the clergy either, as they deplored all acts of violence committed by both sides. It was standard treatment for female culprits to discourage them from fraternising with police officers or soldiers. But the male spy, if convicted of a serious offence resulting in the capture or conviction of any member of the rebel forces was usually shot and his body labelled, 'Spies and Informers Beware.'

As a result of constant activity on the part of the government and its overwhelming power and international influence, the Sinn Féin organisation found it increasingly difficult to keep the people informed of their aims and objectives. *An Phoblacht*, its official publication, had been discontinued for a while, as the British forces had smashed the printing facilities and arrested some of the workers. However, they resumed publication, at grave risk, from underground plants on a limited scale. Its editors strove to counter the propaganda of the English and Irish press and tried to encourage the people to be patient in adversity. The British posted many proclamations outlining penalties for various actions in public places. These were read by day and torn down at night. Often they were replaced by signs such as 'To Hell With The King' or 'Up the Republic'. Numerous tricolour flags of the newly proclaimed republic were displayed on tall trees, or other lofty and almost inaccessible spots and more than once the police woke up in the morning to find one waving in the breeze from the top of the building they were occupying. It took a lot of nerve to pull off such stunts and it was of little material advantage but it had a bad psychological effect and irritated the authorities no end. The RIC cut down the flags whenever possible, but some were made so inaccessible by those who put them in place that more than a few servants of the crown were injured in the process of trying to remove them. One can easily imagine their chagrin.

The British government could ill afford to let this situation continue right on their own doorstep. Curfew regulations were put in effect in many towns and districts. Conditions in the cities, especially Dublin and Cork, were even worse than those already mentioned and the city boys were leading the police and soldiers on a merry chase. They harassed the military at every street corner and faded into the next building or through cellars to the next street. It was an entirely different strategy from that employed in the country. The city lads seldom carried rifles or shotguns, a revolver or a hand grenade being much more effective weapons at close range. After a few lorries were bombed, the British covered their vehicles with strong wire mesh but very soon the city rebels put a cluster of hooks on the grenades and dropped them from the rooftops. They became attached to the wire mesh before exploding and the result was terrifying. Casualties rose and there was an outburst of indignation from both sides of the

Irish sea. From the U.S.A., Canada, Australia, — anywhere there was a considerable number of Irish or Irish descendants — came all sorts of protests and suggestions to settle the Irish question. At coroners' inquests held in Ireland, the British forces were condemned and verdicts of wilful murder were returned against them. The British government could see no reason to heed these warnings, with ten times the population and ten thousand times the resources of Ireland. These developments put more pressure on those in charge and finally the British government declared martial law in Ireland, with all sorts of authority to seize, search and execute, or suspend any activity at will.

There was no pretence about it now! What the Irish leaders had predicted all along had come to pass. They countered with similar declarations, calling themselves the Irish Republican Army, with a mandate from the election of 1918, and based on the Declaration of the Republic in 1916. The British bulldog intended to chew up what he had bitten and the Irish terrier was just as determined to prevent him. The Irish cause suffered a severe setback when its delegation was refused recognition at the peace negotiations in France after the Great War ended, so they decided to go it alone and go all the way. It was war to the hilt and the stakes were the same as in the time of Cromwell or Wolfe Tone. The British reinforced many points and evacuated many troops who had become accustomed to life in Ireland. After all, they had no quarrel with the Irish, being regular garrison troops with little interest in Irish affairs and were merely serving in their country's armed forces. They could not be blamed for any of the acts which had been committed so far. A new breed of soldier was introduced to the country in March 1920. It was called the 'Black and Tans', and was composed of ex-commissioned officers who had seen service in France. These cadets were

Beaufort Bridge, Killarney. A Crossley Tender troop carrier with Black and Tans in the 1920's. Scene from the film *The Dawn* 1935. The director was Thomas G. Cooper from Killarney, who owned the taxi firm where the author worked 1924-25. Mr Cooper is the gentleman wearing a hat (partially hidden between two men) on the right-hand side of the bridge.

led by ambitious officers who vowed to put down the disturbances at all cost and in many cases volunteered for that particular service. They were backed up by martial law and the impotent RIC was pushed aside. A large force of intelligence agents was spread over the country and others with particular skills were used in special areas of resistance. The new force was to have a free hand, operating independently of any other authority except the War Office in

London. This may give an idea of the seriousness of the situation.

When 1920 rolled in, there were so many IRA men on the run that they were forced to band together and move about frequently to avoid capture. They were fairly well armed, but short of resources and ammunition and took no foolish chances, because there was no mistake about their fate if caught. The local IRA men, who were not under suspicion, guarded them and their arms. The British intelligence arm became aware of their existence, as the disappearance of certain individuals from public circulation was disturbing to say the least. There was only one way to find out — look for them. All atrocities were attributed to these active service units or 'flying columns', and the work of guarding them became much more difficult. Local men did sentry duty at night and if a patrol or movement of troops was noticed it was made known by the blowing of horns. Some of these horns did a similar service many years before, during the evictions of the 1880's and one belonging to my grandfather served as a model for others which were made for our company. The 'heat' was on now and every man, woman and child old enough, was on the alert for twenty four hours a day.

An order was issued to post the names of all occupants at the back of the doors of all residences. This piece of strategy hurt, and many men who had been getting along under some disguise before, were now hard pressed. Some made secret dugouts and one fellow who had resigned from the RIC and was active in the IRA was captured in one. He was taken to Kenmare police station and tortured all day to reveal information. In a moment of desperation he seized a hand grenade and pulled the pin. He blew himself and his inquisitors to bits but gave no information. This incident was in the best tradition of patriotism; 'Kill or be killed, but don't give any information!' Many others died bravely under similar circumstances. It was time that intelligence should bring results.

The Lord Mayor of Cork, Thomas McCurtain, was murdered in his home by Crown forces in 1920. Some time later a party of four men and a chauffeur left Cork and drove out about thirty miles west of the city into a hilly district. They were disguised as pedlars and fishermen. The driver picked them up in the evening at different points. This trick was repeated once too often, as the local IRA had interpreted their designs and fishing skills. One evening, when they were assembled as usual to head for home, they were surrounded and captured. Their identity and purpose having been established, they were immediately shot and buried without a trace. All were British intelligence officers.

By the autumn of 1920 the flying columns of the IRA had been brought to some degree of efficient fighting units. No longer were they a bunch of frightened men trying to evade arrest. They had all seen some action during the course of barracks attacks. An important meeting of the IRA leaders from various parts of the country was scheduled for Dublin about this time, to assess the situation and coordinate the effort. The presence of a new group of British intelligence men was reported to those leaders who were responsible for the safe conduct of the meeting. This presented a dangerous situation. It may be they were ready to spring a trap. Instead of playing it safe, our men decided to go on the offensive. Michael Collins was in charge and he was a resourceful, daring leader. All the other men had a price on their heads, having nothing to lose except their lives, which were not worth a penny if captured anyway. One Sunday morning, a squad of hand-picked IRA men, unnoticed and unrecognised, entered the hotels and rooming houses where the 'gentlemen' were staying. The IRA men had information about room numbers and the occupants. They knocked on the proper doors and shot the agents down on sight. Some of the latter on becoming alarmed, ran out into the hallways amid a hail of fire. Fourteen men, most of them British agents, were shot and killed. During this operation one IRA man was killed and another was wounded. The British evened the score, however, in the afternoon. Three prisoners who had been picked up earlier were murdered in Dublin Castle, and the military turned guns on the spectators in Croke Park as a football match was in progress. As a result one player and eleven spectators died and over sixty people were wounded or injured.

Before this, the RIC and Auxiliaries having failed to put down the 'disturbances', were inclined to shoot any IRA men they captured. Having been driven into the large towns and cities, the British forces lacked information, while the rebels roamed the countryside. Since the rebels kept out of sight they could not be arrested. The police then wreaked vengeance on their property and their next of kin. Many innocent people were killed in this way during the course of reprisals. The 'noble British Lion' was wounded now and he was very dangerous.

One day a small party of Auxiliaries in a lorry stopped at the neighbouring village of Gneevegullia. They made a quick search of a few homes for no apparent reason, but this was not unusual. They noticed a picture of the volunteers of 1914 in one house, and the man of the house among them. He was questioned about his IRA connections and though he was not implicated since 1914, he was arrested. His house was burned to the ground and he was taken away. When the lorry reached Tralee his legs were tied to the tailgate and his head dragged

The Creamery, Rathmore, burned in 'reprisals' by the Black and Tans.

along the road. 'He had been shot while trying to escape' or so his captors claimed. Incidents like this gave the IRA an idea what was in store for them if captured and steeled them to some barbarity of their own. The object of these sorties was to force the rebels into open revolt and to terrify the population. But the people refused to be stampeded or give the armed forces an opportunity to annihilate them.

Commandant Tom Barry, of the West Cork Brigade, gave the Auxiliary force its first taste of real action at Kilmichael. A few lorry loads of this unit made a habit of driving around between towns in south-west Cork. It was hostile country to them and this was just what they wanted. They were organising some action or hoping to surprise an unwary group of rebels, or 'Shinners' as they preferred to call the IRA. Barry prepared an ambush position and waited for a few days. The enemy showed up late one evening when least expected. They almost overtook a sidecar bringing some additional IRA men to the scene, who were fortunately detoured onto a side road by an alert sentry. This incident almost wrecked the whole plan. Barry was an experienced soldier, but most of his men were never before under fire, so he divided them into four sections, with an experienced man acting as each section leader. When the lorries slowed down at a bend on the road, the rebels opened fire and the result is a classic example of guerrilla warfare. The rebels lost a couple of men when the Auxiliaries pretended to surrender but resumed fire on those who came from behind the fence to accept it. Barry gave the order to 'wipe them out' after this piece of treachery, so his men did just that. They collected the arms and burned the lorries. The IRA commandant drilled his men amid the carnage to prevent them from getting the horror jitters. A good antidote, I would presume.

Many tricks were used to lure the IRA out into the open such as the following one. A party of military came into the village of Ballyvourney in west Cork. They let it be known that one of their armoured cars was broken down and would have to be left behind. Having locked the doors and announced they were coming back the following day to tow it away, they presumably went back to their headquarters in Macroom. All the time they had been watched by some IRA scouts who reported the matter to their company captain. He decided to look the juggernaut over and estimated it could be destroyed. Suddenly the shutters were raised and blistering fire from the vehicle cut down the captain and one of his lieutenants, while others escaped. A few intrepid British soldiers had remained inside the armoured car and had heard the conversation. They had got their man, too.

The shortage of arms still prevailed, but the supply was increasing all the time. Since the enemy travelled mostly by lorries, the land mine was developed as a means of blowing them up if they tried to run the gauntlet through ambush positions. When mines were suspected, the British soldiers, well trained in all tactics, put out flanks of infantry to encircle the ambush position. This made ambush difficult and the strategic ground was well known to both sides. As a means of saving rifle ammunition, shotguns with buckshot were frequently used at close range. It was mostly homemade as were the land mines. Instruction classes were held to disseminate these crafts and it was a very dangerous occupation. Many accidents occurred when working with crude equipment. It is miraculous how many escaped through an element of luck. However, a reserve of material was built up. A new type of hand grenade was designed and manufactured somewhere in the cities and this was as effective as a British Mills grenade, but not as dependable. An accident occurred in this department to an instructor I knew. While thus engaged, something went wrong and realising the grenade would explode, he shouted to his pupils, 'Lie flat'. He then threw himself on top of it and was killed, but he died bravely, giving his life to save those of his comrades.

The IRA had some intelligence agents in strategic locations. One of them overheard a conversation between two officers having a few drinks, that proved to be a good tip. A British troop exchange was to be carried out, so it was decided to ambush the outgoing unit from Killarney, at a place called 'The Bower'. It is located on the Kerry side of the Cork border on the main Killarney-Mallow road about three miles west of Rathmore. The site was well chosen and the road was mined. The shotgun section was posted close to the road, in case the mines failed to explode or missed the trucks. A Hotchkiss machine gun was set to enfilade the road and several riflemen were located at many points to snipe the enemy if he occupied certain points for cover. Seán Moylan of the North Cork column was in charge of the operation and was supported by groups of men from the local Cork and Kerry battalions. After three days of waiting, information was received that the number of troops being moved was much larger than originally estimated. It was also learned they were aware of the prepared ambush. This may or may not be true, as it could have been a trick used by the British to frighten away any opposition, thus granting the troops free passage. Nevertheless, Moylan, a shrewd commander, decided to pull up stakes and pitch another tent. He and his staff reasoned, as there was no other likely ambush position between Killarney and Mallow, except 'The Bower', the enemy would not expect any trouble and could be attacked at some other location. It was sound strategy and it worked.

I was an eye witness to the movement of the convoy as it went through 'The Bower', as I was driving a horse-cart through the area about 11 a.m. Living less than two miles away, I was aware of the planned ambush and the withdrawal of the column during the previous night. I could not estimate the number of British troops, but there were many trucks and most of the men were on foot. The flanks were well protected by advance parties who made a wide sweep on both sides of the ambush position and every man was at the ready. Even some high officer who was well attended in the middle of the convoy carried a small carbine at the trail. A lieutenant stopped me and ordered some of his men to search me and the cart. They questioned me about my business and after a thorough search told me to 'carry on'. Boy, they were efficient!

About twelve miles further east they were attacked by Moylan's column. Major General Cummins and a dozen other troops were killed. Fate played many tricks during this ambush. First, a couple of lorries going in the opposite direction passed through the ambush position a few hours earlier, untouched, when the mines failed to explode. Second, a prisoner being carried as a hostage escaped during the confusion. Was he lucky! He ran through a hail of fire towards the Cork part of the column where no one recognised him. The military took cover on the wrong side of the road, thinking the attack was being directed from the high ground. Third, the IRA machine gun went out of action early, becoming jammed. Fourth, the enemy armoured car which had collided with the lorry in front of it finally got into position and kept up a sustained fire until the whole party got reorganised and made good their escape. The annihilation at Kilmichael some weeks previously was too fresh in their minds to fight it out. And finally, our column had to retire from an empty victory as they were located between three enemy strong points and could easily have been surrounded. If the mines had been effective, the result might have been quite different. The little 'IF's' played a very important part sometimes.

Many other attacks were planned which had to be abandoned or failed because of some last minute changes in circumstances. When you consider the conditions that prevailed all over the country — searches, ambushes, patrols and reprisals — it was no wonder everybody was in a constant state of jitters. Roads were cut, bridges blown up and trees felled across roads to impede the movement of troops by truck. If these vehicles could be used freely it would be easy to surround IRA columns and capture them. Our signal sections were doing a good job and regular routes and riders were appointed. I saw service in both branches and had a close shave one afternoon. While taking a dispatch by cycle, I held the piece of paper in my hand, rolled around a small stone and tied with a string. I heard the sound of approaching lorries and dropped my packet in the long grass by the side of the road, noted the location and continued cycling. Four military lorries went by in the opposite direction but the last one slowed down. The occupants looked me over with suspicion but didn't stop or search me. After shouting some profanity they went on their way. I returned to where the packet was lying and delivered it without any more trouble. On another occasion I had a dispatch to be delivered in person to a certain officer. When he was finally located, he and his colleagues were in an ambush position and I was not allowed to leave immediately. I realised the importance of the situation and left when allowed, after a lecture on secrecy.

The principal aim in attacking patrols and barracks was the procurement of arms. Since it was impossible to import any, the main source was the enemy. No IRA leader was so silly as to think the British occupation forces could be defeated, but they did believe, by making the process of government too costly, the enemy could be forced to make some decent agreement. Public opinion was already weighing heavily on the side of the Irish, so the struggle went on and neither side could afford to relax its grip. Some posts were attacked on account of their location being valuable to the enemy and others because their capture seemed feasible or they housed a large quantity of arms. The more isolated the post, the greater the store of arms, for in case of attack they were expected to hold out until help came from surrounding posts. Speedy help was not always possible as the relief force was sometimes ambushed and repulsed. No troops relished the idea of relieving another post during darkness, as it was nothing short of suicide. So the pattern was set. A barracks was usually attacked during the night and if not captured by daylight, the siege was lifted. Reinforcements arrived the next morning and engaged in reprisals, which consisted of burning down several homes and shooting up the town. Sometimes innocent people were arrested and beaten mercilessly, while being compelled to ride around on the lorries as hostages in order to insure the safety of their captors. The 'noble lion' was hiding under the mouse's arm!

Rathmore railway station (as it looks today) with the same signal box (on the left) and foot bridge. The double-gabled building on the extreme right was Rathmore barracks.

One particular post that defied capture was the Rathmore police barracks. It was built of brick and stone — a precaution taken many years before — and stood inside a wall near the street, on one side of a small, bare field. The railway ran east and west in front of the barracks, about one hundred yards away. The street crossed this railway line close by the entrance to the station. The barracks was a stout two-storey building, with an attic in which there was a machine gun nest, and all the windows were fitted with steel shutters and sandbagged. There were many rolls of barbed wire around the lawn. The main entrance was a strong porch of stone and brick, approached by a winding passage through the barbed wire entanglements. It was manned by a relatively small force of men, as fortresses go, but the exact number was never public knowledge. They were a tough lot and among them were a few the IRA wanted very much to eliminate. For this same reason, they were extremely cautious. Several ambushes were planned, but when the police ventured out, it was always in some unexpected direction or they didn't travel far enough from the barracks. Many hours had been spent studying their movements to no avail.

Finally a plan of attack was agreed upon. A number of men from the Glenflesk company of our battalion, were to mingle with a crowd of people departing from a religious service one Sunday evening. It was a desperate gamble. As they walked past the barracks, they were to rush the front and back doors and shoot on sight. This was called off only at the last minute and another plan was tried and carried out. A few chosen men were to open the attack by placing a large home-made bomb onto the upper floor, by resting it on a hod with one hinged side and raising it to the window with extension handles. The bomb had a powder fuse and exploded with a roar. Almost immediately a muzzle-loaded cannon, set on a gondola type railway car was pushed west out from the station and stopped at an exact spot on the tracks in front of the barracks' entrance. The bomb had been charged earlier, bound to the car and the angle of elevation as well as the exact spot on the tracks was carefully calculated in advance. When the cannon blast had blown down the entrance, the main assault was to be directed under cover of rifle and buckshot fire. Alas! The gun failed to fire and the assault never materialised. The attack simmered down to desultory fire while the gondola had to be pushed away and unloaded of its 'not so deadly' cargo. The assault failed badly, but the bomb killed and wounded some of the defenders. A few days later, the same gun still charged, was fired at the gable wall of a disused stone building and demolished it. 'The best laid plans of mice and men gang aft

The bullet holes are still visible to this day in the walls of the building that was Rathmore barracks.

agley' (on that occasion at least). But many other successful attacks were carried out in other parts of the country and the amount of arms was always increasing.

I made at least one personal bid to increase the number of rifles in our company. A large force of military were moving west towards Killarney, a few days before Christmas, 1920. They were behind schedule and it was already dark. While a few of us local lads were standing in the village of Barraduff, suddenly a lone armoured car with dim lights came from Killarney to meet the others. Some members of our company were at the Headford P.O. raiding the mail. We went towards home and found the armoured car had sunk in a soft spot on the road. Two of my companions lived near the place and decided to give it a wide berth. I remained at a safe distance for a few hours and learned from another passerby that the first lorry of the approaching convoy had collided with the sunken armoured car and turned over on its side. It was obvious the troops were drunk, as they were very noisy. Anyhow, they were stuck in this place all night and swarmed into the two houses nearby.

The following day I found some excuse to pass by and examine the mess. The road was blocked and the place was alive with soldiers. Some were engaged in raising the armoured car while others were trying to right the capsized truck. Sentries were posted east and west of the scene on the road and a machine gun with a tripod was set up on the railway tracks nearby, overlooking the road and the surrounding fields. My aunt lived in one of the houses close by and I went there. She owned a small grocery store and carried on a dressmaking business. Scores of rifles were lying on the floor and piled against every piece of furniture. The day was raining and the arms had been put there to keep them clean and dry. At a moment when there was no soldier in the house, I picked up one of the rifles and examined it. It was fully loaded and in fine condition. I replaced it and got some ideas.

My father owned the land at the back of my aunt's house and I knew every inch of it. The Beheenagh river flowed along the field at the base of a deep glen bordering the river in both directions. At this point the river, road and railway ran parallel. I told my cousin, Pat O'Donoghue, it would be easy to steal some of the rifles, as many of the soldiers were drunk. He considered it and agreed, so we rehearsed some of the movements. He was to put about six rifles out the back window of the bedroom at night and I was to approach from the glen and throw them into the river about a hundred yards away. It seemed a sound plan so I told my captain about it. We reasoned out all the details and on his advice we let the matter drop temporarily. He decided to talk to his lieutenants about the plan, but we never carried it out. If we did and were caught, I would never write about it. The following day, after another night of drunkenness and noisy confusion, one soldier shot himself accidentally. By the evening the whole contingent had cleared out of the area.

The troops had decapitated and eaten some of my aunt's chickens, leaving their heads sticking out between the stones in an adjacent wall.

Another young cousin of mine found a Mills hand grenade and with some other youngsters were rolling it along the road, when his older brother spotted it and added it to his collection. It was found to be primed for use.

Both sides stepped up activity in the spring of 1921. In fact it had abated little during the winter, but certain tactics were impossible because of weather conditions or enemy pressure. The farmers were pleased with any respite, but the number of men on the run and billeted in their homes was constantly increasing. This put a terrible strain on their food reserves and the supply, often very low, had to be acquired by the local quartermaster and his aides. But they bore the inconvenience with great patience and were the unsung heroes of the struggle. If suspect, they shared the same fate as a captured IRA man. When the food supply was exhausted, the flying column had to move to another location. All agreed that the current year would be one of much activity and suffering. Each day's newspaper carried an account of ambushes and reprisals, or the capture of some IRA men. In some cases these were tried by a military court, which the defendants refused to recognise, but if they were caught with arms or ammunition during an attack, they were usually shot immediately. The press reports on these activities were exaggerated and as both sides never admitted their setbacks, it was hard to know the exact number of casualties. However, by comparing the reports of known activities with the actual facts, the struggle seemed to be in our favour.

The railways were still operating but were not essential to the enemy. Long before now, he had moved all his heavy equipment into place by road and rail, so food for the occupation forces was his only necessity. However, the farmers needed the railways for supplies and marketing of produce and the general public had no other means of travel except horse and cart. Bicycles were fairly plentiful but it was hard to keep them in good repair. We had to borrow them frequently to run dispatches. Later on we commandeered some bicycles from postmen. As these were government property and painted red, we had to keep them out of sight or paint them black. The few civilians who owned automobiles were closely watched by both sides, 'in case they gave aid or comfort to the enemy' and if the owner came under suspicion, the auto was taken away or burned. Some autos were taken to do a special quick job and returned a while later to their owners. The same policy applied to those who owned large homes or small hotels. Many fine buildings were burned down to prevent them from being used as barracks. In fact, all the large hotels and public buildings had been occupied by British troops by the autumn of 1920.

These buildings were safe from attack on account of their size and, being equipped with radio, telegraph and telephone, were never isolated. However, the wires were often cut or tapped and we spent many hours listening to communications in code which was useless. The 'bush' telephone on our side was not so efficient, so the railways were allowed to operate, for reasons already stated, as well as a means of communication. They were the only means of quick travel which could be used by our top officers and couriers in disguise. Even the enemy used the railways when moving important officers or prisoners. By mingling with the passengers they felt secure and sometimes a British officer rode in the same compartment with an IRA officer in disguise. They even swapped ideas or commented on the political, economic or disturbed state of the country. It was a dangerous game, but the stakes were high and the odds were in favour of the IRA man, while his British counterpart had little to fear.

Nevertheless, there were some attacks on trains and small parties of soldiers were captured and disarmed after sharp exchanges. The engines were manned by soldiers as well as the regular crew. On many occasions, a sniper would take a pot shot at a soldier sitting on top of a pile of coal on the tender. The engineers and firemen often walked off and refused to operate under such conditions and some of them were arrested and shot at. Two of these, a fireman named Jack Hayes and a cousin of mine, were fired at in Tipperary when they walked off a train in such circumstances. When moving prisoners, the British usually took over a separate compartment of the train for privacy and this very tactic often led to the prisoners' release. Their liberators had to act swiftly, in one offensive stroke, and shoot their way out. One very daring raid was carried out at Knocklong when Seán Hogan was released by his comrades while being transferred to Cork under heavy guard. It was no place for a faint-hearted man!

By the beginning of 1921 many IRA men, especially those 'on the run', were well trained in the use of conventional arms and possessed many good ones. The flying columns consisted of twenty or thirty men, each having a standard British Lee Enfield rifle. Some men carried revolvers or pistols. There were a few machine guns and an occasional haversack full of grenades. It was adequate for a short fight, but the lack of ammunition and automatic weapons put a long engagement out of the question. Each brigade area had its own flying column. There were two brigades in County Kerry. As already mentioned, the special services were operating smoothly. *Cumann na mBan* (Women's Association) had received instructions in first aid, dispatch riding and other duties necessary to the support of the IRA. Some obtained valuable information and others risked their lives in the cities, by carrying arms to the scene of a fast operation and returning them afterwards to places of hiding. In the country, the girls were always cooking for the 'boys' or knitting socks to soothe their aching feet. They were also very valuable in warning of the approach of the enemy, and many a woman gave up her bed to a harassed rebel, while she slept on a chair. Many a man in public office in Ireland years later, owed his existence to some gentle countrywoman who cared for him in his hour of need.

A course of instruction was initiated for officers and conducted on a battalion level in various locations. The venues were a highly guarded secret and only half of the officers attended a session. In case of betrayal or accidental contact with the enemy, the whole force could be surrounded and wiped out in one fell swoop. The loss of arms would be irreparable too. One such camp came to grief in East Cork when an IRA contingent was wiped out after a bloody engagement.

The long days and short nights were now approaching, the bane of all guerrilla fighters. Security measures were tightened as there were indications of large scale activity in the near future. Several road bridges which were not considered a security risk before were now ordered to be destroyed. Even railway bridges came under this order and rust gathered on the rails. The stoppage of rail traffic interfered with markets and the farmers felt the economic pinch. So did everybody else, but this was a 'knock 'em down, and drag 'em out' fight, which was going to be contested to the bitter end — no matter how bitter. We were given many talks on loyalty, that 'now was no time to weaken' and reminded that 'it was more important to live for our country than to die for it.' And live we did, not well, but dangerously. As long as a fellow had not made himself conspicuous in the early days he was fairly safe but the wanted men had to stay together. There was some safety in numbers.

As if the innocent people hadn't enough trouble, the British came up with something new in reprisals. Where an ambush had taken place, the local creamery or farmers' cooperative store was put to flames. This was in addition to the usual half dozen or so houses which were burned down after an attack. Indiscriminate burning of towns and cities under the guise of 'official reprisals' was the popular 'outdoor sport' of the British authorities in Ireland in the latter half of 1920 and up to June of 1921. Several suspected leaders were also assassinated, as well as the mayor of Cork, a few priests and some innocent people.

Our battalion was composed of six companies, one among the hills, three bordering on the mountains and two out on the open country. The main road between Cork and Kerry ran right through the middle of the area. The three villages of Rathmore, Barraduff and Gneevegullia were located in the shape of a rough triangle over the level part of this terrain. It formed an irregular outline about ten miles by twelve and was composed of small farms, workshops and stores. It was good fighting country and the loyalty of the people was never in doubt. When harassed, we could always retreat to the hills or beyond and very few other places enjoyed its strategic advantages. The Paps mountain was anchored in the middle of the range and commanded a broad vista to the north, as far as the eye could see. The main road ran more or less parallel to the mountain range, about three miles away. These hills were often the target of British planes and telescopes.

The battalion officers' camp was held in March. At its conclusion, all hands dispersed to their homes on a Saturday afternoon. When I arrived home about midnight everybody was asleep and the door was bolted. I decided to go to Jim Daly's house about a quarter of a mile away. We had parted only an hour before. While we were having a cup of tea, the barking dog alerted us. We had a rifle and a shotgun, but not much ammunition. As we hurried to go outside, a man wearing a uniform, with a rifle and a steel helmet, peered through the window. My heart sank as I thought we were surrounded, but my companion was as cool as ice. My nervousness eased when his sister shouted, 'It's alright!' She had been in conversation with the men outside and had recognised them as some of the flying column. It could just as well have been a British patrol. Boy, was I scared!

The presence of these men, some of whom I recognised, meant only one thing — no sleep that night. One of them, Denis Sullivan, the captain of Barraduff company who was on the run, told my captain they were an advance party and the main body would be along shortly, travelling by side-car. He suggested someone meet them at Bealnadeega Cross and direct them to their destination. I was the only one available at such short notice, so he handed me a Webley revolver and sent me on the errand. As I approached the cross, I was startled by a donkey as I was a bit jittery from the earlier experience. The cars had already passed the cross and were off the main road. When I returned, six or eight farmhouses had been opened up to the column and cooking was in full swing. Sentries were posted by the local station and after a little music and a few songs in one house the boys 'hit the hay'. Paddy Lynch from Kenmare played the accordion, Mossy Galvin, from Farmer's Bridge, was the singer. Others in the group whom I met for the first time were Mossy Carmody, Peter Browne, Tom (Scarteen) O'Connor and Den Batt Cronin. I hit the hay, too, in a neighbouring haybarn.

After Mass on Sunday, which the flying column did not attend, Dan Allman and Tom McEllistrim, who was in charge, met with Jimmy Daly and other local officers. They decided their location was an unsafe one. A spy had been captured the day before so it was better to move nearer to the hills. Being close to the main road, with a network of byroads behind them, made the place too vulnerable. They were right, but they hadn't counted on our sentry system. However, after a little music and dance at Tim O'Sullivan's, the column moved to Gortdarrig at the foot of the Paps mountain. Paddy Lynch and Jim Bailey played the music and a good exhibition of step dancing was given by two girls named Burns, one of whom was home on a holiday from Australia. It was a merry hour, there being little thought of the sad state of the country. However before the next day was over, another contribution would be made to the tragedy.

Intelligence had reported a section of enemy troops would travel by train from Killarney to Kenmare, on Monday, March 21st. Their objective was primarily to deliver rations to the garrison at Kenmare. It was about twenty-eight miles by rail and this was considered a much safer route than the shorter distance by road through the Moll's Gap. A cattle fair was being held in Kenmare on the same day and it was usual to make a show of force at such gatherings to reinforce the local garrison. Crowded conditions like fairs had become favourite places to pick off a specially obnoxious policeman or to disarm a few soldiers. The route of the troops was through Headford Junction, where it was necessary to change trains for the branch line to Kenmare. They were due at Headford at 2.55 pm on the return trip. Two other trains were due there at 3.00 pm, going in the opposite direction on the main line. The plan was to ambush the troops when they had crossed the tracks to wait for the Killarney train. The platform ran along an embankment which rose about twenty feet high, affording good cover and a good view of the whole station. There was only five minutes to complete the job and leave the scene, before the two other trains — probably with a large numbers of troops on board — would come into the station. Their arrival could be slowed by setting the distant signal against them.

With these plans hurriedly agreed on, the column marched speedily towards Headford. I had just received a dispatch for Allman (the O.C. of the flying column) and in delivering it, met the column in Doocarrig, about two miles from their objective. He gave me another dispatch to be delivered at Rathmore immediately. He also told me to look after a suspected spy, whom they had left at their encampment, to make sure he was properly guarded. I checked on the spy and learned from his guards the location and nature of the intended attack. Riding hard on the hilly road, through safe country, I delivered the dispatch and returned by the shorter route on the main road. When I was about two miles from Headford the firing started.

A view of Headford Railway station — the scene of the attack (as it looks today).

It was rapid fire for about two minutes and then tapered off for another minute. I saw two of my pals, Tim Daly and Jack Murphy, running towards the station about a quarter of a mile away, so I ran in the same direction along the railway track. Very soon the train from Rathmore passed me by. I had hoped the other two fellows had orders to derail it. The sound of gunfire was still coming from the station. In a few seconds the incoming train would be there and the job was obviously not completed.

Actually, the attack had failed. While the men were being assigned to their positions, the train from Kenmare entered the station a few minutes ahead of schedule. There was no time for Allman and his comrades to get to their positions, so they ducked into the toilets to keep out of sight. When two soldiers entered the toilets the IRA men were forced to shoot them for their own protection. Since a shot was the signal to open fire, the men already in position on the embankment fired at the soldiers who were moving about the platform, unloading their equipment among the passengers. There was terrible confusion and only the close range and good marksmanship prevented many innocent people from being killed. Some of the troops — skilled in their art — used the prone passengers and their dead companions for cover. Eleven soldiers were killed in a futile attempt to get back into one carriage. This seemed very strange, but, it was learned later, there was a machine gun in the car — an item which had not been anticipated. A few soldiers had ducked under the train and Allman, Jim Coffey and Johnny O'Connor tried to rout them. While thus engaged Allman was mortally wounded. His comrades tried to help him but saw it was no use. Jim Bailey was shot through the head above the embankment. Our men had set the distant signal red, but the train, loaded with troops, continued on its way slowly, when they heard the firing. The casualties were: twenty-four British soldiers killed, two IRA men killed, two civilians killed and five wounded.

As in many other cases the little 'ifs' played a big part. Our men retreated in different directions and assembled later near the Tokenfire mountain. They were tense and grave and it was a few hours before all the details were pieced together. 'If' the Kenmare train had only arrived on schedule, preparations could have been completed. 'If' the Rathmore train had been stopped further away. 'If' the troops had crossed the tracks before being fired on, they would have no cover. 'If' all the IRA men were in a firing position. 'If' the train could be moved away from the platform it would expose the men under it. After all, the IRA men were not professional soldiers and the time was limited. Both sides fought well, but there was no time to finish the job before reinforcements arrived on other trains.

Fortunately, there were no reprisals. The IRA dead were taken to Killarney and given to their relatives. Dan Allman was a big loss as his cool daring was hard to replace and Jim Bailey, the fun-loving fiddle player of the night before, was sorely missed. The passengers who were able were used to help the wounded and lay out the dead. Among the passengers was one of our local men, Dan Hayes, who filled us in on the gory details. It was a bad setback, but not disastrous. There were to be other opportunities to even up the score. Tommy McEllistrim took charge of the column.

One may wonder at this point, what the social life was like. In short, there wasn't any. With martial law in force, the British army busy patrolling here and there, the Auxiliaries burning and looting, the RIC checking residences against the list of names on the backs of the doors, there was little time for gaiety. Bereavement for a fallen comrade was another reason for a grim and austere atmosphere. All the young men were too tired to feel like dancing. At night they cut roads and felled trees, or made mines or ran dispatches, or did sentry duty. When a patrol was noticed leaving their barracks, our sentries blew a horn and kept out of sight. The next sentry heard the blast and did the same thing. In that way the whole countryside was alert in a few minutes. It was that simple. Sound travelled faster than a Crossley Tender. But you had to be at home when a search was made or be suspected of unlawful activities.

All of the litigation that usually goes on between people seemed to abate considerably, since they had something worse to worry about. However, there were some cases, large and small, that had to be resolved. This was done by judges appointed by the Sinn Féin organisation. Sometimes the proceedings were conducted by people having some knowledge of the law, but most of the small cases were settled by arbitration, by people whose only criteria were the Ten

Commandments and common sense. No lengthy arguments or legal technicalities were indulged in and the litigants seemed satisfied with the settlement of their differences, just as well as if some English judge with a wig and an impressive show of jurisprudence had done the job. Certain members of the IRA were appointed as police and they took care of seeing that a few fundamental regulations were observed by the public. And the public responded very well to the discipline. One may wonder, also, how spies were treated. As far as any who were picked up in our locality, the answer is — they were treated well. If proven guilty after a fair trial, religious consolation was granted, if requested, followed by an humane execution.

There was an order to arrest a prowler around our locality, who seemed to make a speciality of bothering women, during the summer of 1920. He gave his name as Tom Malone, admitted he was once a British soldier, while being vague about his present occupation. This was enough to keep him under surveillance on suspicion of being a spy. He claimed to be shoemaker by trade and this was evident by the work he turned out when we supplied him with some tools and a few pairs of shoes. His repair jobs were very neat and of very high quality workmanship. Once he took off across the fields about daybreak while I was guarding him, and I never trusted him afterwards. He was moved around only at night, blindfolded, and would be obliged to walk about a mile across country to change his location only a short distance. But this little trick didn't fool him and he was always able to orient himself by certain landmarks.

This shrewdness led us to believe he was much smarter than he pretended to be. On a few occasions he displayed his education rather beautifully by going into a monologue of the finest English we ever heard. He was well schooled in the classics and his recital of poetry was a treat to his audience. In spite of providing entertainment for us he was moved away to another area. There were conflicting reports afterwards that he escaped and that he was shot as a spy, but we never found out for sure. Anyhow, he was well educated, but his wiles may have been all part of his act.

Several spies were apprehended during the spring and early summer of 1921. Some of these pulled the old pretence of being deserters. How they expected to get away with such a slim veneer baffles me yet. The authorities were desperate for information, or these fellows must have been overly anxious to serve in that capacity. Either way it was suicide. Two of these strangers were seen riding on bicycles along the main road to Killarney. They were overtaken by Denny Reen and others from the Rathmore company and taken along for further investigation. They readily admitted being deserters. No charges could be held against them, but they were held and moved about from one company to another for some weeks afterwards. By this time they had become acquainted with a lot of places and people. The IRA reasoned that this might be their intended strategy. A little later they helped convict another spy and this only served to thicken the plot. They were young, carefree, agreeable and intelligent - typical middle-class English. We will find out how they fared a little later on.

This sudden rash of spies around this particular locality was interpreted to mean only one thing. The British were going to make a big drive around here in the summer and they wanted as much advance information as possible. Otherwise, why should so many 'deserters' show up in this part of the country? In May, several large patrols came into the neighbouring villages and stayed around all day rather aimlessly and rather passively. Nobody on our side could figure out their intentions, but the British had a long range plan as usual. They were planning a big roundup but it was not apparent yet.

The scene of the Bog Road ambush near Rathmore.

One spy, who was a tramp, got caught and convicted. After being executed, his body was placed on the side of the Bog Road near Rathmore. It was appropriately labelled. A passerby who saw it, spread the word in the village and the police decided to investigate. Nine men went out and found the body about a quarter of a mile from the village. They walked in pairs or alone, moving cautiously and well armed with rifles and revolvers. As the men approached the corpse, they formed in a circle around it. When the eight men had gathered thus, they suddenly became aware it could be a trap. And it was! Before they could take cover they were fired on and in a few minutes, only one of the eight was still firing. He made the mistake of changing his position after a few close calls and was also killed. This fellow was named Sergeant Woodcock. When this was discovered later, one of the attackers is said to have remarked, 'He's not the first woodcock I bagged.' The ninth man escaped and got back to the barracks. Some of these men had been very lucky a few times before but their luck finally ran out. Reprisals were

Manus Moynihan, I.R.A., O.C. at the Bog Road ambush.

inflicted on the neighbouring farmers for this attack, known as the Bog Road ambush. Four homes in the vicinity were burned down but no people were shot.

Tim (Foxy Tim) Moynihan, Old Road, Rathmore, standing outside the ruins of his home burned by Black and Tans as a reprisal for the Bog Road Ambush, Rathmore in 1921.

On another occasion a few local fellows were arrested for some breach of the peace and we got the job of escorting them to a remote area. When we arrived there was an unusual commotion. One of the flying column had just shot himself accidentally. This happened while he was climbing on a sidecar. His gun discharged accidentally and hit him in the head. There was nothing to do but bury him. That afternoon a few of us dug his grave in an unoccupied corner of Kilquane cemetery. He was Patrick McCarthy of Killarney and his remains were later transferred to a cemetery in his home town during the Truce. Information of a large-scale roundup came through. Our two young English 'gentlemen deserters' who had been arrested about a month before were now shot as spies. They were buried in a lonely bog, but their remains were given to their relatives some years later by the Free State authorities. A rather tragic end to a mission that must have appealed to them when they took it on. Well, someone has to get information but it is too bad when one gets caught at it.

As secluded areas were suspect and constantly searched, it was sometimes found safer to carry on our activities nearer to the beaten track. One night we took over a blacksmith's shop, on the side of the main road, about half a mile east of Barraduff village. After posting sentries on both approaches, we worked through the night and about dawn had made two large mines. Our orders were to send them to a place about ten miles away, as soon as possible. We used a local farmer, Phil O'Connell, and a fifteen year old boy, Pat O'Donoghue, to transport them in a horse and trap that morning. We reasoned, as it was Sunday, they would not attract any attention among others going to Mass. A mine was placed under each seat and the dangerous cargo was delivered punctually and without incident. Had they been caught, our gratitude would have been piled on dead heroes. As for the rest of us, we struggled to keep awake at eleven o'clock Mass.

A few days after the above mentioned incident, Tim Daly, Ned Hickey and I were experimenting with a type of weapon, recommended by headquarters, known as a punt gun. It consisted of a section of pipe, closed at one end, charged with black powder and pieces of scrap iron. This was intended to be used at a bend in a road and being buried in the fence, would be fired electrically or by a short fuse, at an approaching truckload of military. We had fired one shot at the front of a lime kiln and being satisfied with its range and spread, we loaded another charge to check its penetration. While making up the fuse a twenty-five pound bag of blasting powder, which was lying nearby, exploded with a dull but frightening blast. We were enveloped in flames and my comrades were badly burned on the faces, hands and chests. Their clothes were blown off and they ran blindly, throwing themselves into water in a nearby ditch. For some reason I escaped miraculously and the gun, a few feet away, did not fire. These two men had an awful time recovering, which was made more difficult and dangerous by the presence of enemy patrols. However, they recovered completely. About the same time, several men of the Rathmore company were engaged in making explosives. When somebody fouled up the procedure, there was a flash fire in Reen's house at the Old Chapel. Fortunately, nobody got hurt and a larger container of explosives did not ignite. If this had happened, the house and its occupants would have been blown to bits. These are only a few examples of what was happening all over the country at this time.

One Saturday about the middle of June, large bodies of regular British troops moved into every village and town in East Kerry and North and West Cork. Strong garrisons had already occupied the larger centres such as Bantry, Macroom, Millstreet, Kanturk and Killarney. We got the word that the long expected roundup was about to begin and all hands were alerted. Regular British troops patrolled all roads between the villages and it was very risky to move around. On Sunday, they were reinforced by many more with a lot of heavy equipment. A few of us had taken to the hills on Saturday night and slept in the open on top of the Tokenfire mountain. The weather had been unusually warm for some time previously. We left the mountain about 10 a.m. on Sunday and moved down towards the village of Barraduff where we lived. As yet we were not acquainted with the extent of the occupation. The previous weekend a large patrol had forced the people who attended Mass to repair the bridge east of the village. We had watched this performance at a safe distance and expected a similar one, but dared not to go to Mass. Our scouts brought information that the military were posted in every house in the village and had tents and field kitchens. We strained with our weak binoculars and could see a large telescope on a stand in a field, aimed at the hill. There were all sorts of military equipment in the village. This was 'IT'!

Word was passed around to keep out of the way and not to take any chances of getting caught. It was quite easy for most of us to go about our daily routines, but the wanted men, those that had done the real fighting and planning, — where were they going to hide? By this time their identity had been established. No doubt they were known to the RIC, as some pictures of the early parades were available. Nobody seemed to know where the column was located. Neither did anybody know what form the sweep might take. Would every man of military age be taken away or would they search every house? Questions like these could not be answered, so everybody worried a little more than usual. Young and old had become so search conscious that the slightest clue was not overlooked. A few of us younger fellows decided to go home and stay there, but the older fellows were almost conspicuous by their absence. We spent the afternoon studying the movements of the British troops. The only information we picked up was that 'they were all strangers to our part of the country', and they had been watching some men on top of the Tokenfire mountain in the morning. They had probably been watching us alright, but they seemed strangely relaxed — and why not? They were resting.

Before dawn, they moved by the thousands towards the hills on every available route. When the sun rose, rifle, machine gun and artillery fire were heard coming from that direction. On examining the route over which they travelled, it was apparent the advance troops had worn sneakers. Large trucks shuttled between the villages and other vehicles moved men and equipment towards the hills. As the morning wore on the gunfire died down and by noon it had stopped completely. Waves of infantry, in extended formation, had climbed over every accessible part of the hills, gone over the top and over other hills beyond. They strafed the inaccessible parts with rifle and machine gun fire and shelled the cliffs. By late afternoon all the troops had moved away and the IRA men started to come out of their holes and hiding places to compare notes. Some had worked all day on their farms and paid slight attention to the troop movements, minding their own business. Others had got by with some disguise. The Kerry column managed to get outside the ring, but Tom Barry's West Cork men were almost cornered.

When reports came in from different points it was evident a roundup of immense scope had been carried out. The bases from which the troops were moved were located over an area roughly in the form of a circle about forty miles in diameter. Reports said about 14,000 men were assigned to the operation but it seemed more like 40,000 to us. It was evidently well planned and highly coordinated, with all means of communication and air observation participating.

The weather was as near perfect as possible for such an operation. There was only one thing wrong. It didn't net one

IRA leader. Only a score of men of no rank, who were unknown, was the total capture of the 'Big Round-up'. These unlucky fellows could be charged with nothing more than running or taking cover from gunfire, a crime for which they could hardly be blamed. In addition, several people were tending sheep on the hills and a few others who got scared and ran ahead of the troops, were killed and wounded. The press reports glowed about all the Sinn Féiners who had been killed and captured. It was a good exercise for a highly trained army but it got very poor results.

As far as the IRA in Cork and Kerry was concerned, the big roundup had little or no effect and could be written off as a failure. It proved a few pertinent points. First, the British had a poor or inadequate intelligence system as a result of our vigilance, and second, the strategy employed had not produced the planned results. Evidently, the plan was expected to work this way: by camping on the low country and being very active for a few days, the British had hoped to drive the rebels into or near the hills and by surrounding them in an ever decreasing circle whose centre would be around Ballyvourney, capture or annihilate them in one powerful stroke. A master plan indeed, but it did not work that way.

Now the authorities were at a loss to know what to do and so were the IRA. So everybody waited. There were rumours of a truce, and it would be welcomed. Both sides had reached an impasse but not their limit. In spite of all the oppression by the British, the IRA had become immensely stronger and the people had cultivated a will to resist, which was the ingredient with the greatest effect. People who had grown up in the 1880's and 1890's and were scared by a few RIC men had rendered that force impotent and caused the complete breakdown of all government agencies. They had replaced them with a brand of their own and watched the British army make fools of themselves. It made the Irish feel important for the first time since Davitt and Parnell pulled them out of the mud and hopelessness of peasant farming.

A few more patrols moved around our locality during the end of June. Their objective was not apparent, but they could not afford to lose face. With their immense power they could crush any rebel force four times their number, but we didn't fight that way. This was very frustrating for them. We had the advantage of selecting the time and place, if we chose to fight, as well as the element of surprise. We were also fighting for a cause, to preserve our race and our freedom. At best the British were fighting a war of attrition with public opinion, even in their own country, highly critical of their every act. What could the government hope to accomplish anyway? Give a demonstration of savagery? Or teach the world, at the expense of the Irish, a lesson in colonial subjugation? Even if they wiped out the IRA it would be an empty victory. The country and its people would still have to be given some concessions in order to exist. With pressure from abroad and criticism at home, the government gave up the fight and a truce was arranged. To the eternal credit of our leaders, they had waged a successful campaign with very inferior equipment against a modern, powerful army. They had refused to be goaded into any foolhardy action and had taken every step, psychological as well as physical, to counter the enemy on every move. But above all, they had shown the people how to resist injustice and the people had preserved and guarded them, sometimes with their lives.

Numerous incidents, tragic and humorous, could be related here. The tragic ones are amply recorded by those best able to describe them and are a matter of history. A few samples of the humour should be sufficient, but it would be necessary to

Droum Bridge — a road bridge over the Owenacree River, close to Headford Railway Station.

know those concerned to appreciate them fully. As this is impossible, the reader must rely on my inadequate description. One concerned the manufacture of black powder, which was widely used for mines and other devices. One day while a few of our company were secretly engaged in this procedure at a very quiet location, a local man happened to stumble on our project. He was acquainted with all of us, but could not understand our behaviour. After a few questions concerning it, his information on the subject was still quite limited. He looked around at some containers and bottles which had labels such as 'Highly Explosive' and 'Deadly Poison'. These had been put there for just the purpose of inquisitive visitors. He shied away from them and concentrated his enquiry on a large cauldron which was being used to make charcoal. He recognised only one familiar element, the wood, when his queries were cut short by the passing of a military scout plane. He dove for cover pulling his coat over his head, and left when all was clear. A short time later he confided to a local farmer that he couldn't understand how we were going to beat the British government with 'burnt chips'. His knowledge of chemistry was somewhat less than our ignorance of it.

One night, after working particularly hard to demolish Droum bridge (over the Owenacree river, near Headford), an effort which was only partly successful, our company retired just before daybreak. I retired to a small local cemetery at Kilquane and slept soundly for a short while near my ancestors' graves. When I was awakened by the song of a bird I became aware of a subdued cough. Without moving, I listened attentively. It may have come from a person walking outside the wall, I reasoned, but it also could be from a member of a patrol. On hearing the same sound again, I estimated it came from inside the wall. Raising myself on one elbow, I noticed a human head rising slowly from the ground, as I peered through the long grass. I was startled but not scared, so I lay there to await developments. The third cough, which I recognised as that of Jim Daly, my company captain, brought me much needed relief. If I had seen the head and not heard the cough, my conclusions might have been quite different. He too had sought the cemetery for a quiet sleep. At least our 'sleeping neighbours' wouldn't keep us awake.

Just before the Truce took effect, movements were under way to saturate certain unruly areas with new troops. IRA headquarters had plans going to get a large shipment of rifles from Italy and several Thompson sub-machine guns from the US. In the midst of these preparations the Truce was called and took effect on July 11th, 1921. Immediately after it was arranged a general reorganisation was carried out. Before this, the county of Kerry had been divided into two brigades areas. Now it was divided into three brigade areas. This was much more realistic geographically and saved time and travel. The various battalion areas were also re-defined and elections were held within the battalions. As a result our battalion (5th Kerry No. 2 Brigade) wound up with an almost entirely new set of officers and one company (B Co. Barraduff) changed its captain. Unfortunately, these elections, though valid under organisation rules, did not produce the good feeling expected of them. Therein lay some of the seeds of animosity and opposition which were taken advantage of during the Civil War later on. But the new organisation worked smoothly and the work went on at an ever-increasing pace. Remember, this was only a truce so far and hostilities could break out at any time. We were still sadly deficient in firepower and ammunition and in no way equipped to withstand a sustained attack. Past performances in dealing with Britain demanded a certain amount of scepticism, so the fighting men took a rest and let the politicians work on the problem for a while.

5

Divisions Grow: Old Comrades Fall Out (1921-22)

The Truce brought about much needed rest for many harassed IRA men and a little relaxation was indulged in. Some who had not been home for a year were able to see their families again, for they had not been operating in their native territory. They were either too well-known, or the districts might have been largely pro-British, or the terrain was very unsuitable for guerrilla warfare. But the majority of the men were able to be at home most of the time and didn't suffer from the worries of the wanted men in the flying columns. Even the British seemed to enjoy the newly found freedom and rode around on their vehicles with little or no arms and less caution. The troops acted friendly but their officers were aloof and sullen. Our leaders cautioned us about undue optimism and warned that hostilities could break out again very easily.

As the weather was beautiful, the remainder of the summer gave plenty of opportunities for such things as swimming and fishing. It was the finest summer in many a year and I learned to paddle a few strokes in the river south of Barraduff bridge. Later on, when I became more confident I tried Orchard Pool, but I was never at ease where the water was deep. The cross-road dances and 'aeríochts' which had been banned for almost two years as unlawful assembly, were reorganised and people returned to the same carefree customs as before. They planned bigger and better events, travelling further to attend them. People were acquainted with a wider circle of friends and seemed to enjoy the diversity. Sports and football matches were quite frequent, with the familiar pony races for good measure. A story made the rounds about two English officers walking along the wall of some park in Dublin. On hearing some commotion beyond the wall one decided to have a look and saw a group of young men playing hurling. The other inquired, "What's up, mate?" He got the dry retort, "Just 'ockey played by savages."

Behind all this veneer of peace, the IRA leaders were cautious and pessimistic and used the respite to plan strategy in the event of a recurrence of hostilities. A large-scale programme of training was planned and carried out. The battalion and company officers of East Kerry were located at a place west of Gneevegullia in 'F' Company area. The high point of the proceedings was a full parade and sham battle of the 5th Battalion which was held on a warm Saturday in September. It consisted of over 600 men. They were instructed to show up with any and all arms. Some even came from our company with dummy guns which had been made for training purposes. The turnout was inspected by some brigade officers. After a little close order drill in the morning, the whole outfit consumed a large quantity of food in the open, prepared by *Cumann na mBan*. These girls had also received some instruction in the use of arms, first aid and other useful services. The afternoon was a hot one and the whole battalion was manoeuvered by each Company Captain in turn. When the turn of our Company under Captain Jimmy Daly came, the battalion was on high ground in the centre of a large field. His efforts were being watched and evaluated by other members of the Battalion staff and brigade officers. He gave an order, 'Battalion, on the right, form!' The officers of

'B' Company marching ahead of us misinterpreted the order and gave the order, 'Right about, turn!' Now this occurred in a low, wet corner of the field, where some surface drains had been left open from many years before. The long grass and rough ground was bad enough, but when the other company came charging back against us, there was complete chaos. Much swearing and laughing was indulged in amidst general embarrassment. It was the subject of a lot of funny conversation for a few days. The sham battle gave us an awful workout and there was little laughing as we returned home that night.

The battalion staff moved their headquarters around from one company area to another. They were usually billeted in some farmer's house and carried on business by day only, returning to their homes at night. Secrecy was not such an important factor anymore and the nearest enemy post was about eight miles distant. Our battalion even used a typewriter for ordinary communications. Nobody paid any attention to the less frequent patrols as the British troops leisurely swept along in their Crossley Tenders and they seemed less interested in the farm carts as they toiled over broken bridges and pockmarked roads. The age-old practice of 'rambling' after a day's work was in vogue again and it was common to see a few fellows around the cross-roads at night. This was the standard way to come by the local gossip. The newspapers were read aloud in some houses where a few people congregated to play a game of cards. These were the only means of keeping up with the news in those days.

Headquarters decided that too much of this tranquil existence might not be the best thing for the IRA. Peace negotiations were being carried on in the meantime and the leaders of both sides seemed very far from agreement. So, another bout of training, this time with the special services, was carried out at the battalion level. This included munitions, signalling, engineering and first aid. Our instructors were men who had remained very much in the background before, but as the programme started to unfold, it became obvious who the people were that directed the struggle all along. I found myself located in an unused house near Rathmore with about a dozen others from the other companies where we had reported for instruction. The classes for engineering and munitions were conducted by Dave Crowley. Some other fellow taught the signalling course and I happened to pick up enough of this to get a place on the team. It was quite obvious how useful this addition might turn out to be sometime.

We were billeted locally but one night we decided to meet some girls in the village and showed up late for muster in the morning. My pal and I got ten rounds of the field 'on the double' as a penalty, under the watchful eye of Denny Reen, the Battalion Quartermaster. We lost a little sweat but it was worth it. We learned how to make a few different explosives and towards the end of the week we made a small mine. This was buried in the road, and when it exploded, it blew a hole about ten feet in diameter and threw up a bogdeal stump in the process. A device made from flashlamp batteries and a Ford coil was put together to set off the mine. Soon after coming home we imparted our new-found skills to others in the company.

In October, the 3rd (Kenmare), 4th (Killarney) and 5th (Rathmore) Battalions were ordered to report for a parade and inspection at Glenflesk near the church. Each of these units had held camps at battalion and company levels. The brigade and some divisional officers wanted to make an appraisal of the results. About a thousand men were being

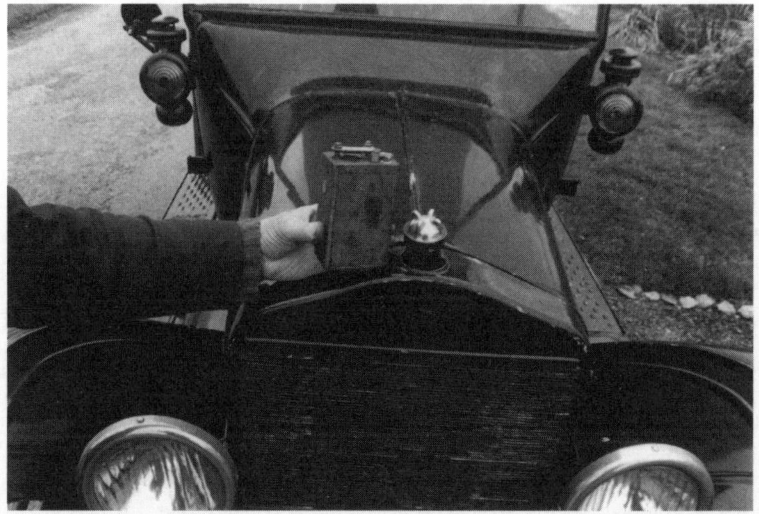

Trembler Coil: Every Model 'T' Ford had 4 trembler coils mounted on the floor to provide increased energy for the ignition spark. These coils could also be used to provide the energy to detonate explosives.

manoeuvered about the field when a group of five or six British army lorries came along and parked on the side of the road beside us. They may have been going about their business and stopped out of curiosity, or they may have heard about the proceedings and decided to 'review' us, too. We never stopped our movements or paid any attention to them. Some men alighted from the lorries and lined the fences. They displayed no arms except the officers who carried side arms and binoculars, but of course their rifles and machine guns were in the trucks. After watching for about twenty minutes they drove away. There on that field, especially among the officers, were some of the men they had been looking for during the past year and all they got was a good look. We were all armed with rifles and shotguns, and one section, which was specially trained for town fighting, was equipped with revolvers and grenades.

No matter how important these assemblies were, they invariably had their lighter moments and this was no exception. There was always some little incident which caused a snicker among the bunch of us fellows who had grown up together. On this occasion we were not acquainted with all of the officers who were present. While the engineering section was being examined orally, the fellow next to me drew my attention to a member of the revolver and bomb squad who had lost his pistol during a crawling exercise. This fellow was going through his drill with no gun and just pointing his finger at the target. I burst out in a subdued laugh and Brigade Comdt. 'Free' Murphy asked me, "What is so funny?" Before I could answer he popped another question. "What type of detonator is used with a six-volt battery to explode a mine with leads of 250 yards?" After a few stammers I answered correctly and he passed on. 'Free' Murphy was a schoolteacher and a big imposing 6 feet 3 inch tall Kerry footballer. I also remember J.J. Rice, Tommy Mac and Con O'Leary among the officers.

Smaller instruction camps were held during the late autumn where many men learned how to make mines, hand grenades, explosives and other devices. At more select camps, men were making trench mortars and shells, learning how to run railways, and even building armoured cars as well as planning daring strategy to be used in case of renewal of the fighting. I got involved in an accident while testing home-made cartridges. The shotgun exploded and my left wrist was punctured with broken steel. This became the subject of some lectures on safety — a much neglected subject in the past. I remember the date, December 8th, very well. This injury gave me plenty of opportunity to take time off for a while from work of any sort but it did not deter my attendance at dances and other amusements. One morning when returning from a

A view of the Owenacree River flowing through a ravine between Barraduff (on the left, out of picture) and Kilquane (the background on the extreme right).

dance at Knockanes, Pat Daly and I walked along the Quagmire river. An otter splashed into the water ahead of us, so we surmised that a salmon was close by. A little poaching came into our minds quite naturally as there were no police or gamekeepers to bother us. We saw some gravel disturbed in the bed of the river - a sure sign. After a little preparation during the day, we arrived at the spot after nightfall and saw two nice salmon. I held a gaff, though my left hand was in a shoulder sling, but I didn't intend to go in the water. My pal gaffed one fish but he was afraid to hand it to me and exchange gaffs. As the other fish was moving away, I waded in and made a swipe at it with my lamp, and I got it. While walking backwards, waist-deep in a slight current, I slipped on a wet sloping rock. With one hand still in the sling I went under, only to be rescued by my pal. We got two salmon, one eighteen pounds, the other twenty pounds. A few minutes later another party came along to try the same spot. As there was no law enforcement our movements were unhurried, so we chatted for a while. It was very nice to watch the salmon jumping at the cascading waterfall that winter. A few were taken but not as many as could be, considering the lawless state of the country.

Late in November, before I hurt my hand and nearly blew my head off, an incident occurred in our neighbourhood, which was a good lesson in prudence, as well as a bit of luck. As we were constantly increasing our arsenal we kept our eyes peeled for ways to acquire anything that might be useful. We needed some Ford coils to make the detonators already mentioned. The means of procuring these was not important, but we certainly wouldn't shoot anybody to get them. One Sunday, late in the afternoon, I was walking from my home to the main road, just rambling. It was almost dark but I heard a man running along the road being chased by our neighbour, Mike Murphy. On enquiring I learned the stranger had been tampering with a Ford car which had been left in the neighbour's yard by some British officers, when it supposedly ran out of petrol. Pat Daly and I looked over the car and with a few sly winks we knew what we wanted to do. It seems the officers had asked two young men, who happened to be passing by, for help to push the car off the road into the yard. My neighbour knew these two young men and having secured the car in the yard, they went on their way. The officers continued on foot to the village of Barraduff, about a quarter of a mile away, to await help. There was no phone in the village, but by prior arrangement a search party would come to meet them from Killarney, if they did not arrive at their destination on time.

Help came all right, but instead of taking the car away, the officers took over the farmer's house and spread hay on the floor. They raised the window and placed the table in the centre of the kitchen. Putting their revolvers on the table, they ordered the farmer to bed and in complete darkness five resolute looking men took up the vigil. They had noticed the coils disturbed in the car and guessed that it was IRA men who wanted the coils. In the meantime, Pat and I decided to steal the coils around midnight when everybody should be asleep. We had no hint of the trap being set. We walked past the house about 11.30 pm and saw the car. All was quiet and the people inside apparently were gone to sleep. We got a shotgun, a revolver and two masks and proceeded to the car. When about 200 yards from the house, a man came along and he recognised us. He was slightly inebriated. He offered to help us, but he had no idea what we were up to. Besides we couldn't trust him, so we decided to call the whole thing off at the last minute. We were lucky we did. The five officers waited all night for the raiders to return. At a range of fifteen feet they could have riddled anybody tampering with the car. It may have been another stunt like the armoured car incident in Ballyvourney, but we didn't think about that at the time. Incidentally, the fellows who had helped to push the car were two other members of our company, Tim Daly and Mike Houlihan. They had the same idea as we had but they were scared away earlier when the farmer surprised them. They had even contemplated a second raid, but had seen too much activity around the house to feel it would be a success. Well, we were all very lucky that time!

During the autumn there had been a few good sports and race meetings which were well attended. The people, glad to have freedom of movement, enjoyed themselves as they danced any time an opportunity came along. At one of these gatherings, I met a fellow named Bill Sullivan from near Gneevegullia. He was a very good fiddle player, being a pupil of the blind player, Tom Billy. When we held a sports meeting in our area, I asked him to play for the dancing. Having secured permission from Eugene O'Keeffe, the principal, public dancing was held at Meentoges school. I had the honour of playing for a few dances with him and his easy style fascinated me. The committee were very enthusiastic when they heard a sample of his music. He told me about a fellow he had met at the Killarney races, who had invited him to his home in Muckross to do some playing.

It would be well at this point to make a few observations regarding the respective positions of the British and the Irish, to evaluate the political climate, and to give some explanation of the situation which shaped the course and direction of subsequent events. Nobody will dispute the fact that Ireland (though geographically referred to as one of the British Isles) is a separate entity. Its people, despite all the invasions, conquests, plantations and emigration, are mainly Celtic. It is a country of farming, having very little manufacturing since the time of the penal laws. It was always, even under British rule, treated as a separate unit regardless of population or religion, and politically recognised as such, by its representation in the British parliament since the Act of Union in 1801. Then it would seem logical that any negotiations between the two countries should be on this basis. However, since the Home Rule bill had been passed in 1914, British leaders had made many subtle moves to divide the Irish. They were uneasy and jealous of Irish progress and wished to have Ireland as a place to hunt, fish and relax, as well as a source of cheap labour and army recruits. It also provided a nearby source of food and in case of war, they wanted to ensure it was kept free of any alliance with other European countries.

Four meetings between De Valera and Lloyd George in July, failed to produce any definite results, but they didn't provoke discord to the point of resuming hostilities either. But the British leaders didn't lack for prompters. Some of these wanted to send about 100,000 additional troops to Ireland. To break the deadlock, it was decided that a delegation from each country would meet for negotiations in London to seek agreement. (The negotiations were to last from 11th October to 6th December.) Both sides were hopeful. It would be well to point out, that even though a radical section within the Dáil (Irish Parliament) wanted to settle for nothing less than complete independence, a more practical element were in the majority and were for acceptance. Herein lies the tragedy. How could such resolute, responsible men as comprised the Irish delegation, who six months before defied the might of the British forces and rendered all agencies of the government unworkable, become so soft and amiable in their attitude? Many answers have been offered, chiefly: the people were tiring of the struggle, the unsettled conditions were ruining them economically, the agreement seemed workable and capable of revision — or the alternative was a resumption of hostilities. Bunched together, they presented an awful problem I suppose, but individually these difficulties were nothing the Irish people had not endured before.

Be that as it may, the agreement presented nothing more than a poor bargain to an uncompromising patriot. In reality, the exclusion of the North was disastrous, if not fatal, and the retaining of the three seaports in the South was unpardonable. A separate referendum was to be held in the North and a commission was to be appointed by the British to establish a boundary. Certain other details were calculated to restrict trade expansion and hamper the development of the new government. All these impediments represented a poor bargain and not in the best interests of the Irish people. An amount of pressure was exerted on the members of the Dáil from the press, business, religious circles and public opinion, which swayed the decision of lukewarm members. When the Articles of Agreement came up for ratification in the Dáil, it passed by a slim majority of seven votes. Considerable excitement prevailed as the outcome was very much in doubt. Even one of the delegates who had signed it repudiated it. It is not my intention to dig up any graves at this late date, or reopen any wounds. Let history be the judge. The 'Treaty' as the agreement was called from this time on, was signed on 6th December 1921 and approved by the Dáil and the House of Commons on 7th January 1922.

After some tricky technical manoeuvering a government was formed. The Sinn Féin government, while still in being, yielded to the new Provisional government, which was formed to carry out the Treaty. The members who supported De Valera walked out as a body. The Headquarters Staff (largely controlled by Michael Collins and Richard Mulcahy) which had been the main driving force behind the whole movement, were now trying desperately to remain neutral. It is very difficult to understand that there were four different governments and four different armies all operating within the island of Ireland at this stage. The South was trying to run its area under a provisional government, while taking over from the British and appeasing the IRA. The Sinn Féin organisation was forming a new opposition party and taking over some of the British posts as the latter moved out. The British were trying to wind up their affairs and sit back to watch the Irish tear each other to pieces over the spoils. An observer said, "Each seemed dedicated to his own task. Ye gods and little fishes!"

Rear from left: Jeremiah Murphy (author), Kilquane; Dan Hayes, The Bower, Rathmore; Tim Daly, Kilquane, Headford.
Front from left: John McSweeney, The Bower, Rathmore; Pat T. O'Sullivan, Kilquane, Headford. (guns — Lee Enfield rifles)

While this three-cornered chess game was being slowly conducted, the people waited patiently. Britain made the moves, Belfast made the counter moves and Dublin were the pawns in the game. Now that the threat of war was no longer hanging over our heads, the remainder of the winter was very enjoyable. It was 'on with the dance.' We became acquainted with a great many girls and just about danced our legs off. But beneath this carefree attitude a slow, steady change was taking place. About ten of us fellows who had grown up together, met often. We talked politics seriously and the conversation was often very interesting. Having all passed our 20th birthdays, it was no longer kids' stuff. We suddenly realised we were men, or at least we thought we were. We were too young to do any fighting during the preceding two years, yet we were acquainted with the techniques and tried to imitate the older men in the IRA. Except for a few, we all worked on our fathers' farms and the spring was close at hand. The British garrison was moving out of Killarney and two of our gang were called to that post. They were Tim Daly and Pat T. O'Sullivan. A few men were called from each company to occupy each post as it was evacuated by the British. Killarney was the Brigade H.Q. and smaller posts were located at Rathmore, Kenmare, Farranfore and Blackwater Coastguard Station. Some fellows were disappointed at not being called, so they went to Dublin and joined the newly formed Free State Army. In fact, the general public was beginning to line up behind their favourite leaders. Trouble erupted in Limerick city when competing forces took over from the British. One post was taken by the IRA while another was occupied by Free State forces. Similar events occurred in many parts of Leinster, but Munster and Connacht favoured De Valera and the Republican cause.

A few months passed by and my hand had healed in the meantime. I met Bill Sullivan again. He had to do some work for a farmer near his home and when that was finished we planned to go to Muckross together. In order to get his work completed sooner I worked with him for a few days. We went to Kingwilliamstown (now Ballydesmond) to see friends of his named Tarrant. These people were great bike riders and one of the girls operated a home knitting machine. There was a dance held in the hall that night and we played music for some of the sets. We walked back to his home in time for Mass on Sunday morning and after a sleep and something to eat we went to my house that afternoon. He gave an exhibition on the fiddle which compensated somewhat for my father's disapproval of my absence from home for the past few days. We struck out for Muckross that night, but on the way we became aware of a dance in Kelly's at the Iron Mills. It was not very difficult to be diverted, so we danced and played there until dawn. Arriving at Muckross about noon next day, we introduced ourselves, had lunch and fell asleep. Our host, Patie Lynch, was at work but his parents and sister joined in some pleasant conversation. He finally arrived about nightfall.

The next day we occupied a bungalow on his place and played the fiddles while getting acquainted. The day after, we accompanied Patie all over Torc mountain as he was gamekeeper for Sir Arthur Vincent. The scenery, the view and the herds of deer made the setting idyllic. Next day it rained, so we played all day and our host told Bill about a project being contemplated by Mrs. Vincent. The good lady wished to teach music and dance to the children around the estate. A noble gesture indeed, and Patie thought Bill was the right man for the music part of it. It was necessary to be introduced through the steward, one Angus McLeod, as fine a Scot as ever roamed the Highlands. Patie had an appointment arranged at the steward's home. After I had played a few tunes for Angus, he asked if the other boy played, too. Bill shyly obliged with a few simple tunes, but he was not putting his best foot forward and already Angus had become aware of his style. He coaxed a few more tunes out of Bill, who by this time was warmed up and he cut loose with some of his favourites, which left Angus spellbound. The Scot excused himself and left the room. In about five minutes he returned, fully dressed in kilts with his bagpipes blaring away. He had been touched by Bill's music and gone into a sentimental frenzy while he played the music of his native highlands. There was no doubt that the job would be Bill's, but a few weeks later, tempted by the offers of a recruiter, he left home and joined the Free State army. But we met again under different circumstances, as you will learn in a later chapter.

While the majority of us young fellows were enjoying ourselves, the leaders and politicians were planning strategy. The IRA police were displaced by an official body to be known as the Civic Guards. Several of the old RIC joined this new force and helped to get it on its feet in the early stages. Of course these were fellows who had been sympathetic to the Irish cause or at least neutral. Recruiting for the Free State army went on apace. Many IRA men joined it. This trend also reduced the ranks of the unemployed. It was hard to blame them, at least they had a job and plenty to eat. De Valera formed an opposition party, repudiated the Treaty and the IRA took over the Four Courts in Dublin as headquarters. Arthur Griffith and Michael Collins, who had signed the treaty, held the opinion that it was the best agreement at the time and provided a stepping stone for revision later on. Britain had ratified the agreement and at once began to shower praise on its supporters. This was the tipoff.

The Dáil had approved the Treaty by a small majority and some of those in favour had done so with many reservations. The die was cast. Britain had some good statesmen, as subsequent events proved. The IRA now tried to help their more unfortunate comrades in the North by sending men and arms to stave off the Orange mobs. The evacuation of the British was going on gradually and they turned over a lot of equipment to the Free State army. They did not evacuate the North (nor have they to this day).

Killarney was our Brigade H.Q. (Kerry No.2). John Joe Rice was the brigade O.C. and the quarters was in the new Railway Hotel. The British had been quartered also in the more luxurious Great Southern Hotel but this was returned to the railway for redecorating, and heaven knows it needed it. The walls reeked of a coating of blasphemy and obscenity. The 5th

Battalion staff were located in Rathmore. Denis 'D' Reen was the O.C., Francis O'Donoghue the Battalion Adjutant and Denny Reen the Battalion Quartermaster. This was a typical setup in most of the country in the spring of 1922. The larger posts were evacuated last, being handed over to the new Irish Free State government, which proceeded to staff them with the new recruits. Places such as Beggars Bush, The Curragh and Dublin Castle were all in the hands of the Free State army.

By March, 1922, the leaders were deeply divided and De Valera launched a move to take the question to the people, while making it plain he didn't want two armies. He spoke at big meetings in Killarney on March 18th and in Tralee on March 19th. By some gift of vision, he had perceived the tragedy of disunity and pleaded before large audiences for patience, unity and loyalty to Sinn Féin. The items that irritated him, as well as many other leaders, were Partition, the Oath of Allegiance, and to a lesser extent, the Governor General and the retention of three seaports as British bases. In truth he had a strong argument because the utterances of those who voted in favour of the Treaty were strongly against those articles. His tour of Kerry was followed up with a big recruiting drive by the Free State army. Some IRA men defected, enticed by commissions and other jobs. It was amusing, if it were not so tragic, to see two posts in one town, manned by competing armies wearing the same uniform and trying to be neutral. When the election was held, it was a farce, as the Constitution was published that same day and few had time to digest it. Of course, it had already been swallowed, so now they could live with the belly ache. A few minor clashes between the opposing forces did occur, but the climax was reached when the Free State government got orders from the British to oust the IRA and take over their barracks.

De Valera, by participating with Collins in the agreement known as the 'Pact', hoped to preserve unity and give the people a chance to acquaint themselves with the 'fine print' in the Treaty. In comparison with the preceding months, events moved rather swiftly during the month of May, 1922. Collins was in favour of the Pact and declared so publicly while Griffith and O'Higgins were not enthusiastic about it. On Collins' return from a meeting in London all pay was stopped to the men holding the IRA posts. A relief fund, known as the 'Green Cross', had come into being the year before to aid those who had been wounded or whose homes had been burned. I had been awarded thirty pounds but never received it. I believe my political sympathy had something to do with it, as those who interviewed me were well known Free State organisers. The IRA was ordered to disband and relinquish their posts or join the Free State army. This they refused to do.

Public opinion was now on the side of the government and an uneasy peace prevailed. Both sides started to reinforce their positions, politically and militarily. Some IRA barracks were handed over by treachery. A contingent of 120 Free State soldiers on a recruiting drive in North Kerry were captured by Brigade Commander 'Free' Murphy and his men. They were disarmed and talked into turning back. In Cork a large shipload of arms was being returned to England by the evacuating troops. While under light guard, the arms were seized by the IRA of that city and distributed to the inland barracks. In our own area, many men were called up to reinforce the garrisons, as there were fears of an attack by Free State sympathisers. Meanwhile in Dublin the British were turning over large quantities of arms to the Free State army, as their leaders started to renounce the Pact. In the midst of these developments, the British suspended their

From left: Jeremiah Murphy (author), Dan Hayes (The Bower, Rathmore-standing) Pat T. O'Sullivan (Kilquane). Picture taken by Tadgh Sullivan, photographer for *The Dawn* movie.

evacuation. Wholesale rioting, burning and shooting were taking place in Belfast and other Northern towns. Between January and June 1922, 171 Catholics and 93 Protestants were killed in disturbances and a great many Catholics were fired from their employment, just because they were Nationalists. Sir Henry Wilson, long a foe of the Irish, was shot dead in London. The British were furious and demanded revenge. They ordered the Free State to repudiate the Pact, implement the Treaty and get rid of the IRA. The bonds that had held Irishmen together were straining now and ready to snap. And snap they did!

After a twenty-four hour ultimatum had expired, the Free State army attacked the Four Courts which housed the IRA headquarters, and the Civil War began. It is very difficult to understand what drives a country into civil war. The cause never seems to justify the result. Yet many nations, such as England, France, United States, Italy and Germany had their own civil wars and they were very bitter struggles. It seems to be part of the growing pains of a nation. I could understand a civil war between the North and the South in Ireland, but then it would not be a civil war for long. It would be aborted into a struggle between Ireland and England. The IRA men in Ulster had been receiving help from both sides in the South and now that help was cut off, leaving them at the mercy of the British troops and the Ulster Specials. The latter force was a sort of home guard organised to bolster the Orange mobs and fight against the IRA. Many men retreated South and joined one side or the other as their loyalties prompted, and some were bitterly disappointed later.

I had visited my pals at the post in Killarney on a few occasions and we conversed about the prospects of army life. They were not particularly enthusiastic, but said it was easier than farming. We engaged in a bit of hurling one afternoon, the O.C. was a good hurler a few years back. A number of IRA police were stationed in the old RIC barracks on College Street under the supervision of John Kevins, an ex-RIC man, from Beaufort. It was a quiet place except on Fair days. The shooting was far away yet, or at least so it seemed. Those of us who were not needed had reverted to a steady existence of farm life. However, many of us kept in touch, but since it was a volunteer army there was no strict discipline. I often thought afterwards, we should have studied military tactics at this point instead of resting on our laurels, but nobody expected it would be necessary.

6
A Winter of Conflict (1922-23)

In those days there were no radios to flash the news, so the first inkling we got of something unusual was the trains not running on time. You could almost have set your watch on their regularity. But one day they were running away off time. It was June 28th, 1922. I noticed a lorry load of armed men passing by in the afternoon and asked a neighbour if he had heard anything new, but he had no news. Later in the day my cousin, Mike Reen, came to see me and told us what he knew. The news was bad. 'Fighting has broken out between the Free State Forces and Republicans in Dublin,' he said. He asked me to report to Rathmore barracks as soon as possible. I had been gathering hay all day and I left with him.

The first night in the barracks was a wild affair. The place was divided into two separate, yet integrated, departments, police on one side and military on the other. The police were all big men and I knew them all, except one. He was Jim Buckley from near Killorglin. The military men were all on the small side so we took an awful teasing from the bigger boys. I was assigned a bed in the corner where the bomb was pushed in the window two years before. The boys were careful to tell me that nobody had slept there since. After I was sound asleep my bed fell apart, aided by a string pulled by the police from across the hall. Awakened by the crash, some fellows from the other department came to investigate. As I bent over in the darkness to fix the bed, someone gave me a slap of a leather belt across the bare thighs. I ran around the room being chased by the others and all my room-mates woke up. They protested, but were also pulled out of bed and worked over by the police. Francis O'Donoghue got a few swipes of a piece of insulated wire cable as he tried to get away from them. I escaped in the darkness and got the idea of hiding in the lockup, but I chose the machine gun nest in the attic instead. After searching around a while, Manus Moynihan guessed where I was and I heard him saying so. He failed to find me as I had crawled between the sandbags and the roof and he was too big to get through the hole. I didn't get much sleep, but it was all by way of initiation, I learned later.

We posted guards at night and tightened the defence somewhat. We also got land mines to place on the approaches, but never used them. Once before, in May, when it was expected to be attacked by Free Staters, the post was reinforced by a few of us who were called in for a few days. Johnny O'Connor and Mossy Galvin brought a Lewis gun also for that occasion.

After stubborn resistance, the Four Courts was taken by the Free State army. Four top officers were taken prisoner. One more was killed in the fighting in the city and another was captured and executed. The Free State troops were using the equipment that was turned over to them by the departing British and were using shrapnel shells initially. However, they fanned out from Dublin and Kildare towards the south and west. As they advanced, their numbers grew, but Collins was biding his time as most of his troops were green. To check his advance, large numbers of Republicans from the posts in Munster were hurried towards Kilkenny, forming a line diagonally from North Tipperary to North Waterford. When these opposing forces met, a series of skirmishes were fought, while the Republicans fell back slowly until they formed a line, running from Limerick City on their left, through North Cork into Waterford on their right. They captured the Free State post in Limerick and started to hold their ground for a few weeks. In the meantime, more men and material were moving up towards the line.

The British government made a nice move to support the Free State forces at this time. Having no colonial war on their hands, they found it convenient to disband the Irish regiments in their service, except the Irish Guards. Most of these seasoned troops threw their lot in with the Free State. They had only to change their uniforms, everything else was the same. This reinforcement of several regiments of first class troops gave them an edge in the fighting, which had not been going too well for them up to that point. The majority of the Republicans were experienced fighters, but sheer force of numbers and superior equipment gave the government troops a decided advantage. Their sympathisers throughout the country supplied information and the former IRA men among them were familiar with the personnel and layout of all our strongholds. The east and centre of the country fell rather quickly as the Republicans were spread very thinly. The West was doing fairly well but could not support an unbroken line like the South. Every train and truck was loaded with men and supplies to support this line, but even then there were pockets of Free State agents behind the line.

Jerry Riordan, O.C. Kerry No.3 Brigade, returning from the line to his own area was running low on fuel. He gave us a fine James motorcycle in return for four gallons of the precious fluid. We enjoyed riding this novelty and it was funny to see Manus astride it, smoking his pipe, with D. Reen in the sidecar and I on the pillion in case it got any ideas of stopping. One fine morning after Paddy Murphy and I had the guard duty all night, we took off on a trip and soon the engine stopped from dirty fuel. It took us a long time to get it started, and we got a dressing down when we returned to the barracks. An hour later, my pal and several others left for the line.

We acquired an old Ford car from the Brigade H.Q. After a few lessons from a local chauffeur, Charles Dineen, I managed to drive it. It had many dents on the body and fenders, and was without a top. We christened it 'The Indestructible' and it was almost that. We took it on many trips to commandeer food and supplies, such as bread and cigarettes. Once on a hunt for horses we were almost struck by the car bonnet when Manus drove it too fast over one of those bumps on a narrow bridge. On another occasion I was sent to pick up some of our men who had been on leave and were to return to the line on a troop train. We were speeding along around Bealnadeega when a large cow, belonging to Michael O'Connor, dashed out in front of us. The cow was killed, of course, but the car was not damaged. There was no time for explanations as we could hear the train approaching. The road was very rough and we had to drive fast. Francis O'Donoghue was complimenting me on my 'skill' when, suddenly, about a quarter of a mile from Rathmore, the car took a sharp turn to the right, jumped the sidepath and struck a wall. I made a quick effort to right it but it made a sharp turn to the left and mounted an earth fence about two feet high. It stopped in this position when the dislocated radius rod got buried in the fence. This unusual position might seem funny, but on the other side of the fence there was a thirty-foot drop to the railway tracks. Leaving me with my problem, the others hailed a passing horse and cart and made the train connection. I repaired the damage the day after with parts from another wreck which had been left abandoned at the Killarney barracks. I drove Den Reen and Con Moynihan on the motorcycle to collect cigarettes on another occasion and escaped a swipe of a tongs from a local shopkeeper as she protested at our commandeering of her property. But these actions were necessary for survival.

Lest our actions be misunderstood, let me hasten to explain that the seizure of private property was covered by an order from H.Q. as long as we issued a receipt for the goods. Of course, the resistance to commandeering was an indication of things to come, and it was more evident when the fighting grew in favour of the Free State. At one time there were no questions asked, as all merchandise could be taken and paid for. We had to call up more men as the garrison was constantly being depleted by calls for men from the front line. One day I found myself the senior officer in the barracks. This was not a pleasant feeling, as I lacked the experience of running an establishment of its kind. I missed the other men of senior rank who took care of this obligation with ease. Receiving dispatches and orders from my superiors on which I was forced to act, or make decisions, was not very pleasant at times. I was also more than a little worried that the post might be attacked, if our enemies knew the strength or weakness of the garrison. Consequently, I kept a man on the alert and put some security measures in practice. From dispatches and the press, we were aware of the sagging front line.

This situation might have continued for a long time but the British were involved as usual. With most of the coastal areas in the South stripped of IRA men, it was only natural that the strategy changed. The advantage we enjoyed at the front line was soon offset by an equal disadvantage from the sea. Our officers became aware of this when some strange vessels were seen hovering along the coast of Cork and Kerry. A unique incident occurred towards the end of July, which bears relating here. While bolstering up the forces along the coast, a large cannon drawn by four horses was moved from

Killarney to the Coastguard station at Blackwater in the Kenmare Battalion area. The station was a stout building of stone, built by the British, commanding a broad and picturesque view of Kenmare bay. One morning after the arrival of the 'artillery', a large British cruiser steamed slowly into the bay and anchored about a quarter of a mile offshore. A boat was launched and when it was about half way to the shore our men at the station opened fire with rifles and a machine gun. A cannon ball was fired but it missed the British cruiser completely. The action signal sounded on the cruiser and sailors idly watching before this, rushed to battle stations, while those in the boat got around on the other side of their ship and scrambled on board. The next cannon shot went through the rigging and the cruiser replied with a shell which hit the gable of the Coastguard station. This blast stunned most of the occupants but nobody was injured and they all left the building. A rapid fire was kept up on the cruiser as it steamed away. It fired several shells, one of which went through the front entrance, through the building, and buried itself in the hill at the rear, before exploding. Parts of the shells recovered later indicated that six-inch shells had been used. It was amusing to hear Mossy Galvin and Mike Quill talk about 'the day they attacked the British Navy.' Years later Mike Quill went on to become an influential trade union leader in New York during the 1950's and 1960's.

With the coastal threat large numbers of Republican troops were recalled from the Limerick-Waterford line. These were sent to various points along the coasts of Cork and Kerry. Free State troops were landed at Fenit and Kenmare, but these points were far apart and it took some fighting before their position was consolidated. Johnny O'Connor and Tim Daly, with their Lewis gun, were among the defenders, but they got cut off in a flour mill in Tralee. They were forced to abandon the Lewis gun to prevent its capture but they recovered it later. The landing at Kenmare was made under the command of Comdt. Tom O'Connor (Scarteen) who had been a well-known member of the Kerry No.2 Flying Column. It was his native locality so he knew how to avoid resistance. It was evident now that we could not stem the tide of Free State troops, so it was just a matter of how long we could hold the remaining territory. We were ringed around when the landings were made along the coast. It was expected that they would move inland as soon as a supply line was established, so our command decided to make their advance as difficult as possible. We received orders at Rathmore to remove all arms and supplies to places of safety, and be prepared to leave the place at short notice.

There wasn't much material to be moved. It consisted of old guns, ammunition, mines, several bicycles and bedding. These all seemed useful — and they were at a later date — so after all the other items were hidden in the hills, we carefully packed the mines in hay into the rear seat of the 'Indestructible'. We had driven only a short distance when the hay caught fire because there was a hole in the floor, over the exhaust pipe. As the mines were filled with black powder they were very dangerous, so we decided to leave the car to its inevitable fate. But the flames died down and we came back. After beating out the rest of the fire we repacked the cargo and eventually hid it in a dugout. There were five mines, each of which were capable of destroying a large bridge — and some later did. Our luck held, and the old car was still the 'Indestructible'. Next day I went to Killarney. The garrison had moved out towards Tralee, burned the police barracks, and left only a few men at the hotel. On returning, I was handed a dispatch which read as follows; "To: O.C. 5th Battalion H.Q. Destroy all available bridges. Evacuate the barracks and destroy same at your discretion. From: O.C.

Kerry No.2 Brigade." I knew then it was the beginning of the end.

It was obvious that we couldn't hold the barracks and do the job on the bridges also, so we called in some more men. After securing a hand-car from the railway station nearby, we set out for the west towards Killarney along the railway tracks. Our tools and supplies rode on the car and we pushed it west of Headford station. There were no bridges of importance further on, and we had no knowledge of the advance of the enemy. No trains had run since Tralee was occupied about a week before. We burned a few bridges, wrecked the signal equipment at the station, and removed some rails at a bend. The idea was to make everything as difficult as possible to replace. We built a large fire of railway sleepers and piled a lot of rails on top to be bent by the heat. My colleagues wanted to burn the Quagmire bridge, but I reasoned it could not be destroyed, as it did not contain enough wood. While throwing some rails off this rather high structure into the river, a few of us almost got our skulls smashed by a teetering rail. At Barraduff bridge we knocked out another span. Here we scrounged some grub and returned to the post late in the afternoon. We were thoroughly exhausted as we had worked all through the night with no rest and little food. Reports of the enemy advance were conflicting, but we knew that Cork City was occupied and the enemy was moving inland. We also expected a three-prong drive on Killarney — from Kenmare, the north, and along the main road from Tralee. The Rathmore barracks was set on fire and, as the flames broke through the roof, the 'Indestructible' was given the torch also and left to its doom. The barracks building had stood as a symbol of British domination long enough anyway. As we left, we got word of a convoy of cars and trucks approaching from the east.

The village of Rathmore was suddenly filled with armed men, hungry, tired and dejected. They were our men, and soon we recognised those from our battalion among the crowd. It was a very inhospitable form of welcome - a burning barracks, no food, no place to rest, and a lot of wild reports of the enemy approaching from every direction. After a few greetings and comparing notes, we were ordered to mount the trucks, so somebody knew what he was doing. It gave us a feeling of strength and security to be together again. We drove west to the Forge cross and, after a meeting of those in charge, we proceeded through Gneevegullia to Scartaglin. Our men had returned from the collapsed line and we, too, had not slept for forty eight hours. After a good night's rest, we marched to Killarney the following day. Here we were all equipped with clothes, shoes, arms and ammunition. During this diversion, I spotted my old pal Jerry Daly. He had returned from Limerick with the retreating troops, some of whom he knew well. There was a general regrouping here, and men were able to get back into their own local units. That afternoon it rained, and several trucks, loaded with men and guns, travelled through Glenflesk and the Loo Valley to Kilgarvan. Around Minish, we got a flat tyre on our truck and, as we repaired it, along came Fr. Allman and he gave us general absolution. He was a brother of Dan Allman who was killed at Headford, the year before.

The driver of our truck was a fellow named Tim Shea from the Kenmare Battalion. I had helped him repair the flat tyre and when he discovered that I knew the road and was able to drive, he asked me to sit up front. The road was narrow and winding and his lights were poor, but he did a good job. We got another flat tyre at Morley's Bridge and repaired it, but the column moved on and left us behind. Billeting in the village of Kilgarvan, we slept all next day and I spent the next night as sentry at Artully bridge. This place was half way between the opposing forces but neither side sought to make contact. Both sides were on the defensive until they knew a little about the other. We were low in ammunition, as well as organisation, and could not undertake an attack, but we would be obliged to sustain one. Our section was close to the railway bridge and Fred Healy was amongst us. He had recently been disbanded from the British army with his brother Pats, and both were veterans of World War I. These two men and Patie Reen of Rathmore had joined us only a few days before. About midnight, Fred removed his glass eye, a casualty of the war in France, and told us we could take a nap and 'I'll keep an eye out.'

The following Sunday we decided to go to Mass in Kilgarvan. The church was so crowded with armed men that the regular congregation could not enter. Here we heard another sour note against our presence and our motives. The parish priest told us to leave the church and he loudly denounced us. Dan Hayes, one of our group, argued violently with the priest, who was a Free State sympathiser no doubt. This greeting was entirely new to us, but it became familiar as the weeks passed.

The next day we reconnoitred as far as the Cross Roads near Kenmare and found the Free Staters had been there the day before. Another night was spent around Artully and the next day a fellow from the Kenmare Battalion blew up the railway bridge. He used guncotton and seemed to know what he was doing. A locomotive was capsized there also and was leaning against the embankment. In the meantime, Killarney had been occupied but it was assumed Kilgarvan would not be for some time. Our battalion was withdrawn and sent back to our own area without any action. We had not long to wait. While we were away, Rathmore was occupied by strong forces, and we heard another convoy was to travel there. After a good night's rest, it was decided to attack this convoy.

Our old system of signalling had broken down or been taken over by Free State sympathisers, consequently, our information was very unreliable. The convoy reached Barraduff about 3pm and then split up. Those who were marching continued on the main road, while about a dozen trucks with men drove south towards Headford and across the bridge at Droum. Jerry the Cock (he owned fighting cocks), and I tried to blow up this bridge the day before but we were only partially successful, as we were short of explosives. We cut a trench on the Droum road near Cooper's house and took positions on the side of the hill, two hundred to six hundred yards away. Our party consisted of about seventy riflemen.

The first vehicle to come along had a cargo of soft drinks and bottled stout, which we diverted to a safe hiding place. Soon afterwards, a large touring car, followed by an armoured car and ten trucks, came along. The touring car was plainly marked with a red cross. While the occupants of this car filled in the trench, two of our men accidentally walked into them. Our Vice Comdt. Jerry Kennedy and Tim Daly had been making last minute preparations and came around a bend on the road and were fired on while the rest of us stayed out of sight. Our men wounded one of the car's occupants, Jim McGuinness, and disarmed the others. The Free State troops had been riding in the Red Cross car, fully armed with rifles and revolvers. Nice fellows! While trying to drag the extra arms along to our position, the enemy armoured car opened fire on Kennedy and Daly, who were lucky to escape. Then both sides opened up in full, but it was impossible to capture anything, as the armoured car moved up, covering those filling in the trench. So we held our fire. They also dropped a few shells amongst us from an 18-Pounder gun but nobody was hit. This was the only time this gun was used in east Kerry. They were forced to abandon two trucks, which we burned. Once again, their superior numbers and armament had held us at bay. But a few of our men did capture the stout and drank enough to sleep through the entire engagement!

The occupation was complete by now, as every town and large village had a garrison of troops pledged to enforce the laws of a government which was implementing a treaty — that was proving to be unpopular among many of the people — against the wishes of an opposing army, which had been the mainspring in wringing that same treaty from the British. What a paradox! We were back where we were two years before, but there were only half of us now, with less resources, and our enemies knowing every move we could make. It was a dubious outlook at best, and there seemed to be no immediate solution. There were talks of a truce, but nobody was sure what the leaders were doing, or what the overall strategy might be. If we had quit fighting then we would all wind up in a prison camp, so we were forced to fight on for no less a reason than self preservation. If the leaders could have arranged a truce, some compromise could have been worked out. Of course there was a large matter of principle involved and a certain amount of false pride. This was the point where a scar became a festering wound, and has ever since plagued the nation. Much property was destroyed and many good men lost their lives in the subsequent struggle. To make matters worse, these losses were tragic at the birth of the new nation, at a time when it needed all the resources of leadership it could muster. Britain, and especially the press, gloated that the Irish were not able to govern themselves, while they had created the very conditions that made the division inevitable.

On our side at least, we thought that by making the occupation by the Free State troops as miserable as possible, they might come to some sort of agreement, as the British did. But conditions were very different now. The British had had a big army for sure, with a compliant police force and a few spies, but the Free State had an army, half the people, the British government and public opinion on their side.

We decided to go underground as before. There was no use waiting around to be captured. Another movement of troops was to be expected. Their plans were very simple. Since most of them came from Leinster and their overland movement southward might be challenged, they chose a route by which we could not contest them, namely, by sea. Then they would finish the occupation of Kerry and Cork from the seaports over a shorter land route. This was why they had come from the west. We took up a position at The Bower, on the main road between Barraduff and Rathmore and waited three days without making contact. We needed a victory to boost our morale and our supplies, but we got a rebuff instead from people who had been our greatest supporters a short time before. This was very discouraging, so we went across the hills to Clydagh and awaited orders. In the meantime, Michael Collins, the Commander-in-Chief of the Free State forces was killed while visiting troops in West Cork. At this time, on August 22, 1922, four of our men were captured by Free State troops in our area near Kilcummin. They were Capt. William P. Fleming (known locally as Capt. Willpatrick), Con O'Leary, Daniel Mulvihill and Thomas Daly. This was a big loss, as these men were noted for their daring and strategy. Paddy O'Daly, officer in charge of the Dublin Guards, was wounded on this occasion. Our Battalion Adjutant, Francis O'Donoghue, was also captured at some other point, and we never saw him again. The longer the struggle dragged on the more bitter it was inclined to get, and the less chance of compromise.

It was decided at some meeting of our top commanders to pursue the old tactics of guerrilla warfare, which had proved so successful in the past. A complete line of intelligence and communications had to be established. This was more difficult than before as our enemy had set up a whole system of counter intelligence. Many of our contacts (as well as the relatives of some of our men) were arrested and sent to prison camps,. Anybody who had shown sympathy to our side was picked up in raids or in the course of patrols. It became more difficult to distinguish friend from foe. Some former IRA men who had gone to the Curragh Army camp and got their commissions, returned later, and pretended to be neutral. These were the intelligence men of the new army and at the time nobody gave them much attention. But when the towns had been occupied, they joined the garrisons as if it was the most natural thing in the world. Later on they led the raids that proved so disastrous to our side.

Early in September an attack was planned for the town of Kenmare. Our Brigade O.C. was a native of that area and he and the Free State commandant were active opponents. The 5th Battalion was assembled at Loo Bridge, the 3rd at Kilgarvan, and a few grenade men were borrowed from the Ballyvourney Battalion of the Cork command. The town of Kenmare was held by about 125 men and they had been very active. Most of us knew nothing about the plans or the target, but we guessed it in a short time. After being fed, equipped and briefed at Quill's of Kilgarvan we proceeded towards the objective mostly along the railway tracks, with our equipment piled on hand-cars. It was a pitch dark night and all went well until two hand-cars collided while coasting at about thirty miles an hour. Suddenly the lead car was derailed at a spot where some railway track had been torn up. About fifteen men were pitched to the bottom of a steep bank, amid all sorts of gear, but none of them was hurt. This incident evoked more swears than prayers, I can assure you. About a mile from the objective we left the railway track and took to the main road. Here we split up into sections and each was allotted two local men who were acquainted with the geography of the town. Each section leader had a plan of the town and this was passed around to get the rest of us oriented. From here on, all had to be dead silent. At a stop, some scout told us that Brig. Comm. O'Connor and half the garrison had been out on a raid all night to the west of the town. Luckily, we had approached from the east. Our section was led into a golf course along the bank of the Roughty river and took up positions in a rather bleak sand trap, facing the back of a large brick building. My pal, Jerry Daly, was the only one I knew in our section and our leader seemed to know his business. Four or five of the others had grenade cups on their rifles and a few sacks of grenades. It was now about 7 a.m. and day was beginning to break. At length a few rifle shots relieved the tension and the whole town burst into a steady chatter of rifle, Thompson and Lewis gunfire. The garrison was located in three strong buildings; a bank building of cut stone in the middle of town; the Lansdowne Hotel at the fork of two streets; and the Carnegie Library, an isolated brick building on the golf course — already referred to. Several private homes were also occupied near the bank, on both sides of the street. The windows of the library were sand-bagged or had steel shutters. After a few rounds were fired at the building, our leader decided to get closer and said, 'It's only wasting ammunition to be firing at that building, let's try the heavy stuff.' He was concerned, too, about the rising tide in case we got cut off. We left that position and crawled to the road and crouched by a stone wall much nearer the building. Some of the men fired grenades on the roof and around the entrance. We were afforded good protection by the wall when a few bursts of fire came our way.

A messenger arrived about 8 a.m. to request four men to follow him to the railway station. He led us through some gardens and back yards, past another section of our battalion who informed us they had seen no action so far, except a pack of howling dogs that overran them when the firing started. The railway station was our command post and I recognised several officers. They told us Brig. Comm. O'Connor and his brother, Capt. O'Connor, had been killed and a few wounded. We were ordered to scale a high wall and be careful on the other side, to run across a back yard under fire and occupy the house in front of us. This we did safely and entered a house already held by our men, who were firing through the front windows at the bank across the street. The house on our right was occupied by the enemy and they were firing on our communication line. It was decided to rout or capture these as they had control of the back yards. As we entered next door, the body of a man, partly clad in uniform, lay at the bottom of the stairs. At the top of the stairs lay another body, which I recognised as Tom (Scarteen) O'Connor. Both had been killed when the attack started. Our men kept up a steady fire on the bank building, when Gilpin's Lewis gun was knocked out by a sniper from that building. Peter Connaughton was working a Thompson gun on the fellow next door. Meanwhile, the other sections were working closer towards the bank as the firing patterns indicated.

One of these sections was very lucky to capture a sentry post on the opposite side of the town as a prelude to the attack. It was manned by two soldiers, one of whom was trying to ride a motorcycle in front of the pillbox. A few of our men sneaked up on them during an awkward moment and captured them without a shot. That removed a dangerous obstacle and gave the section greater flexibility. Our section removed a fireplace and broke a hole through the wall to the house next door. When the occupants saw us they thought we were some of their men and asked us for ammunition. At first I thought they were our men and I almost gave them some ammunition, as they were dressed in civilian clothes. The mistake was cleared when they fired through the hole and I got hit by a splinter of a bullet as it ricocheted off a stone. Jiles Cooper dressed a wound in my nose and Jerry Daly took me next door to a pub. As he donned the bartender's apron, he asked, 'What will you have?' I answered, 'A drop of wine.' 'Have a bottle of it,' he said. 'As for myself,' he continued, 'I'll have a bottle of some ancient vintage.' He spotted one, covered with cobwebs, of some unfamiliar brand which he brought down. As we drank leisurely, we discussed the prospects of taking the town and we agreed it was favourable. Such comedy in a tight situation provoked a laugh. An observer could feel we were having a quiet toast. During the ten minutes or so we spent in the pub the grocery shelves were being hit by a steady rifle fire, while the bar side of the place was safe, being at an angle to the bank. We returned upstairs to find our men had thrown an incendiary bomb through the hole and the six occupants surrendered. My pal recognised one as the fellow who fired at me previously. He might have shot him there and then, but I suddenly raised the barrel of his rifle and the bullet went through the ceiling. We took these prisoners to the railway station and were greatly relieved as they had been fighting a bit too well. Another one of our sections had got close to the back of the bank and were lobbing hand grenades on the roof and windows.

Pat T. O'Sullivan was in this section and he told me later that they had captured a couple of fellows who had defected from our battalion about six months earlier, including John Singleton. This surrender gave our men a good firing position and the troops holding the bank surrendered about fifteen minutes later. These also were taken to the railway station. In

Pat T. O'Sullivan, Kilquane, Headford, emigrated to Rochester, New York, Never returned.

the bank we found five enemy wounded and a few cases containing forty new Lee Enfield rifles. The situation in O'Connor's house was sad, as a girl and boy relatives were obliged to stay in the place during the day. At one time this girl made tea for us but we had to leave her with her grief. There were still two other posts holding out. Johnny O'Connor collected a dozen of us and said, 'There is a boat in at the pier. Let's get it before the tide rises.' He led us up the street at a trot and one fellow had a Lewis gun. As we went by I saw Pats Healy lying in the middle of the street working a Lewis gun on the windows of the Lansdowne Hotel and some others were firing on the library. In this confusion and cross fire a fellow could easily have been hit. Our section broke into the Southern Hotel grounds as Johnny O'Connor shot the lock off the gate. As we approached the pier we could see the ship moving out into the channel, so we were none too soon. A stone wall provided good cover and we fanned out along it as far as the pier. Nobody knew what to expect from the ship, but after a few bursts from the Lewis and a fusillade of rifle fire they ran up a white flag and tied up again at the pier. This prize would have sailed much earlier in order to evade capture but the tide was too low. Six Free State soldiers were on board as a guard. We recognised Charlie Collins, one of our men who had defected earlier in the year with John Singleton who had already been captured in a house near the bank. Our leader chided him saying, 'You might as well throw yourself overboard, Charlie.' The ship was from Wales with supplies for the garrison — ammunition, food, fuel and general cargo. Six of us were put on guard on the vessel for a few hours until we were relieved. The stokers banked the fires, an engineer played an accordion and the mate borrowed one of our rifles and shot seagulls on the wing.

The town was quiet now as we tried to find something to eat about nightfall. The prisoners, 130 of them, were marched towards Kilgarvan, but we had no means of holding them, so we put them on the road to Killarney and released them to plague us another day. Among them were such widely different individuals as a brother of Kevin O'Higgins, the Minister for Justice of the Irish Free State, and Larry Sullivan from the Quarries Cross. The latter had sore feet so I gave him a pair of clean socks from my haversack, for which he was very grateful. Some of us returned to Kilgarvan and had a good night's sleep after about thirty hours on the move. The next day we rounded up a convoy of horses and carts from Loo Bridge to Clydagh and took them to Kenmare to move the supplies from the ship. Arriving there early in the afternoon we found that another ship, similar to the first, had sailed into the bay and being ignorant of the situation because it had no radio, was also captured. The activity on the pier was like that around a beehive on a sunny day. As fast as the winches could load them, a long line of horsedrawn carts drove away to our haunts. This was just what we needed — a good haul. While we were loading, a case of whiskey (smuggled, no doubt) was uncovered and some officer ordered it thrown overboard, but a wily diver recovered it later.

After some refreshments, our convoy proceeded towards the home area, but we were gone only about two miles when we were ambushed by a few Free State sympathisers. The horses bolted as we returned the fire and one cart almost capsized, but there was no damage. At Artully we pulled into an old castle yard, tethered the horses and slept on the ground as the weather was dry and warm. In the morning, we foraged around for food in the neighbouring farmers' homes. The road bridge was out so the cargo had to be taken across the river over the partly demolished bridge. On arrival at Morley's Bridge we let the drivers find their way home, as we rested for an hour. A huge pile of supplies had no guard and four of us took a hand railway cart loaded with Indian cornmeal towards Loo Bridge. It had to be pushed for a while but as it started to coast Denny Reen and Tom Lyne climbed in front, as Tim Daly and I rode in the back. This was fun until the car ran away and there was no means of braking. Tim Daly jumped off and fired a few shots in the air to warn the gateman ahead. We knew the gates were closed as no trains had run there since the occupation of Kenmare and we had visions of colliding with the gate at high speed. When we rounded a bend the crossing came into view, but our vehicle strangely slowed down and ground to a halt. It was loaded so heavily and without grease that the axles overheated and bent, causing the wheels to rub against the body. We had stopped about two hundred yards short of the gates and it took a pair of good horses and several men to drag the car as far as the crossing where we unloaded it. This war was getting mighty rough and the physical strain was worse than the mental strain of the preceding years.

A similar incident happened on the following day when a boxcar, fully loaded, coasted over the same route, being stopped only when Pat Healy crawled along the side and applied the brake. This car was unloaded and capsized across the tracks at Loo Bridge. For a few weeks we enjoyed a lot of freedom, as we ate well and rested a lot, along the Clydagh valley. There was even no need to post sentries. It was about time to shake up the Rathmore garrison. Troop movements were frequent between the Rathmore post and Millstreet in county Cork. An ambush position was chosen on this route and we mined the road at Inchabeg bridge. Within an hour a patrol came our way, but we were in hostile country and our presence was known. Our force was in two sections, one at the bridge and the other on the high ground to the left. The first section attacked the patrol who, instead of continuing, chose to retreat to the safety of the village. If they had gone ahead our chances of capturing them were good, as they would be caught between two fires. We decided to blow up the bridge anyway but the mine failed to explode. A sow had chewed up the wire leads! I had to remove the mine (a job I didn't relish) as we couldn't afford to waste it. Quoting Jerry Daly, 'at one time the fire was so intense that Francis could not leave.' Francis was a little dog who stuck with us as a pet. The remark was made when a few of our fellows found themselves in a hot corner and were forced to change position, but the dog seemed to sense the danger and refused to move. A number of merchant carts came along the road from which we commandeered some cigarettes and a barrel of stout.

Another attack was planned on the town of Killorglin, so we moved to Scartaglin. A few of our men (among them Paddy Reen) were sent to the attack to handle rifle grenades. This attack was a failure and after some heavy fighting in the town our men were forced to retreat, leaving several dead, including Con Looney of Kenmare. We returned to Rathmore, taking up positions one morning around Shinnagh Cross, in hopes of studying the habits of the garrison, or maybe setting up an ambush, but nothing happened. Although we got within 300 yards of the main post without being observed, we knew little of their defences. Before leaving, just to keep them worried, we sniped at a few spots and picked off a few men. For good measure we fired on the village at random the following night. These were regarded as nuisance attacks but they had the effect of keeping the enemy confined except when he moved out in great strength, and gave us greater freedom to move around and visit our homes. The small secret patrol was the bane of all IRA men. This sniping led to further action in the area.

Some of the men killed in the sniping were connected with the garrison at Killarney and a cycling company from there travelled to Rathmore the next day. It took some nerve to pull off this detail, as they were well aware of our strength by this time, but not our location. We received word of the move after they had passed by about a mile away, around 11 a.m. Since we were near The Bower, it was decided to attack there if they returned. It was thought best to strike a little to the east of the regular site as they might be very cautious about the area.

Preparing for an ambush — the view of Barraduff village from under the arch of the Railway bridge at Kilquane. Three men taking up firing positions. On the left (pointing) is the author, Jeremiah Murphy. In the centre is John McSweeney and on the right is Tim Daly. Note the Six-Mile Bridge over the Owenacree River in the centre of the picture, at the bottom of the hill leading out of Barraduff towards Rathmore.

They were suspicious alright. The leading riders dismounted and scattered into nearby houses. It may have been to pick up some information or a casual search but one of our men fired too soon before all riders were in range. As they were taking cover in different houses and they were spread out, we had little chance of capturing them. McSweeney's house was riddled with bullets but strangely a woman and four children within were not injured. Everything else went wrong in this attack. Only about ten of our men got into action in the first few minutes and then the firing died down.

Dan Courtney came up on our left with some information. He had been home on a short visit and headed towards the action. Timmy Murphy, next to me, lost his magazine in the long grass and as I helped him look for it, a stone, on which my rifle rested a few moments before, was hit squarely. Meanwhile, our men on the other side of the road knocked off a few who were trying to make their way back to the village. Our section leader dropped another fellow he saw peeking over a fence in the wrong direction, and we also took care of the fellow who had hit the stone. Courtney and I moved to our left and engaged a relief column which had come out from the village of Rathmore about three miles away. We crossed the main road at the Cooper's Cross and joined a few others from the south side of the road. Moving east along the fields at Mounthorgan, we made contact with the relief forces and fired on them at Old Chapel. They numbered about a hundred and there were only four of us, so it was impossible to hold them back. As we retired and joined the main body, it was late in the afternoon and starting to get dark.

But the skirmish was not over yet. The local medic, Dr. Collins, was pressed into service by the Free State troops to attend the wounded. Three of our men fired a few parting shots and hit a Capt. Young who was in charge of the relief column. The combined force returned to Rathmore where he died of his wounds a few days later. He was also attended by a local nurse, Mary Reen, who was home from the US on a holiday. The incidents of these two days drew some reprisals. Some of our sympathisers were arrested and held at the courthouse in Rathmore. These included Mick Rahilly, Tim Brosnan and Jeremiah Daly from Shrone. The former two escaped by jumping out the courthouse window during the night and decided to join our column to avoid re-arrest. About this time we were around the Old Chapel. On a very dark night Michael Reen on sentry duty challenged an approaching pedestrian and not receiving a favourable reply, he fired. The challenge was quickly answered and was recognised. The bullet had passed through one of the pedestrian's leggings. The alert sentry had shot at his company captain, Manus Moynihan, who was returning from a visit home to rejoin the column.

There were roughly about 100 men on active service in our battalion area. The problem of supplying this constantly hungry group with food was not easily solved. Apart from the support given by the local farmers and shopkeepers, the supply had to be constantly replenished with contributions from cattle dealers and other sources. One method was to commandeer supplies from those who seemed antagonistic or unsympathetic to our cause. This created more bad feeling, but we had to eat. Our enemy was doing the same thing. We killed and dressed a few bullocks but this did not last very long. The Free State soldiers were sometimes running low in supplies, too, on account of our restrictions on movements on the roads. One day they took some cattle from a dealer as they were being driven through the village of Rathmore. George, a recent recruit from Millstreet, was some sort of a butcher, so he was appointed to perform the ritual of killing and dressing the animals. By all accounts the killing was something like a public execution and was performed in the main street. In order to comply with the accepted humane practice the beast was to be shot in the head. While George held the animal with a short rope, a noble marksman stood a few paces in front and aimed his rifle at the bull's head. When he fired, the bull ran away and George fell. The bullet had ricocheted off the animal's horns and killed the would-be butcher. So they buried George and ate the bull.

We were around Loo Bridge one day when supplies ran low. Jerry Kennedy, Neil O'Leary and I were practising the art of throwing rifle grenades. A couple of others came along and the shortage of meat was discussed. In the afternoon, four of us were ordered to go up on the surrounding hills to get some sheep. One pair took off south of the road, while Dan Hayes headed up the slope of Croghane hill with me. We had been instructed to secure sheep with certain marks. Now all mountain sheep, though not really wild, are really timid and cautious, as their only associations with humans are not very pleasant experiences. They are chased and rounded up by collie dogs, after which they are shorn in spring, dipped in summer, and sent to market in autumn — all very uncomfortable to a docile sheep. Consequently it was very difficult to catch any of them — much less those with a certain mark. We were about to give up when, suddenly on going over a knoll, we spotted about a dozen sheep settling down for the night. It was impossible to distinguish the painted marks as they were all bunched together and some were already lying down. Not having binoculars, we decided to get closer to make sure of the marks and get a clean shot. As if sensing our intentions, the flock suddenly bolted as Dan fired once and missed. They bobbed and weaved about and ran over the rough ground a quarter of a mile ahead, as we followed carefully.

Now they were scared, so we were obliged to stalk them and that delayed the hunt. When we got close enough they bolted again so we both fired at a bobbing bunch of white lumps of wool, in the gloom of twilight. Luckily we hit one. Now, we were miles from camp and faced with a return journey over rough hills carrying a bleeding, dead sheep in the dark. Some places were so steep, we were forced to throw the carcass ahead and climb down trees from one ledge to another. There were some exclamations that do not bear repetition here. We had missed our way and came down by the Robber's Den, over a steep precipice, about a mile from our starting place, but we brought home the mutton. The other pair fared no better. After a futile search, they were returning empty handed when they saw some sheep in a field near a farmer's house. They grabbed one and cut his throat with a reaping hook. We all suffered some discomfort for the next few days from an attack of diarrhoea, probably brought on by the fresh meat or some other unsanitary cause.

One nice, bright morning in October, a large force of the enemy moved out of Killarney, through Glenflesk and up the Loo valley, evidently to reoccupy Kenmare. This move was expected for some time and we were in the right place to prevent it for once. As this force had passed the Robber's Den we opened fire at long range. Its size precluded any chance of overpowering it, but we intended to harass it as much as possible and by making it too costly, force it to retreat. One of our sections, acting as an outpost at Killaha, had engaged it earlier but we had not heard their firing and it was impossible for them to contact us, consequently we had no time to prepare. It looked like a force of 500 to 600 men, with about a dozen trucks and two armoured cars, that extended over half a mile. Only about twenty of our men got into position and the others were scattered out behind us, too far away to be effective. At the first volley, ten men walking ahead of the lead truck fell. The truck also stopped but the others behind it moved up as close as possible. Pats Healy had placed his Lewis gun in a spot covering about a hundred yards of bare road which ran around an outcropping of rock. It seemed strange that the armoured cars remained in the middle of the convoy, but they kept up a steady fire at long range. It was impossible to pass our position, and the trucks could not turn around so they backed up to a convenient place, abandoning the lead truck. The road was narrow, too. One of our men, Denis O'Donoghue, started to play his bagpipes and this really spooked them. We occupied only one side of the road, and on the other side a steep cliff overhung, giving a commanding position to enfilade the enemy. Some of our section, sensing the situation, wished to cross the road beyond the railway station and attack from the other side. Just then, our O.C., Jerry Kennedy, became aware of a body of men about half a mile away on the other side of the road behind the position our men wished to occupy. This complicated matters and all efforts to communicate with them were to no avail. The O.C. said, 'They may be a flank of the main body of the enemy, so positioned as to prevent the same tactic we wished to employ.' We could not understand their movements so our commander decided to play it safe. By this time the convoy was turned around. We had stopped their advance but we learned later that we could have captured the whole outfit. They figured they were trapped between two forces and were afraid to retreat past the other section at Killaha, but they could see none of us. We also learned too late, that the men we had seen on the other side of the road were from the Kenmare battalion and having expected the occupation of their town, had moved out of the danger zone. If both forces had combined, we could have made a real good haul. The captured truck was hidden in the hills. Tim Daly picked up a shoe from the road with a bullet imbedded in the heel. A priest came along on a bicycle and asked to keep the shoe as a souvenir. This shoe figured in a later incident.

Action of this kind took place over Munster and Connacht during the autumn of 1922. The east of Ireland was more or less subdued before the winter. Some of our men, faced with the threat of being captured, were having a rough time and that called for a greater will to resist. The prospect of a long winter campaign was bad, but the prospect of being captured was much worse, so we took each day as it came. In spite of rumours of a truce and peace negotiations, the struggle was increasing in bitterness, but at least it was forming into a certain pattern and it began to be more predictable. After several days of inactivity and thought, the general opinion was that the struggle might last until Christmas or maybe drag along until a few of the leaders got tired of fighting and decided to make peace. Most people were getting tired of feeding hordes of hungry men, and even some IRA men gave us an ugly look if we strayed into what was considered their area. The practice of billeting in houses was becoming increasingly risky, as the enemy intelligence was active. There was an advantage in being in a large body, but this was offset by the problem of food, billeting and secrecy. Likewise, a small body of men was easily fed and billeted but it was next to useless in either attack or defence. Even so, we had a large area to roam through, as no enemy dared enter the secluded valleys among the Kerry hills, but they were raiding many homes in the lowlands and always picking up unwary relatives of active republicans. The prison camps were filling up, and even if there were some innocent ones arrested now and then, they were held as 'insurance'. The local fellows who had joined up with the enemy (Free Staters) were becoming more conspicuous and now leading the raids. The weather was getting increasingly raw and the haybarns were a much sought-after refuge.

One night, Jerry Daly and I were on sentry duty near a farmhouse in Doocarrig. A number of our section were preparing to sleep in the loft of an adjoining hayshed. There was the usual joking and joshing about. Our captain reminded us how lucky we were, as other fellows were not near as well off as we were. Our captain, Jimmy Daly, was a religious man and a few years older than most of us. He had joined the volunteers at their inception and saw things in a different light from the younger fellows. He often said, 'Say your prayers and

Tom McSweeney 'Dundon' from The Bower, Rathmore — First-aid officer for the battalion, nicknamed 'Dundon' after a renowned Cork surgeon, optimistically perhaps! He painted the portrait of Jeremiah in battle dress from memory. He joined the US army after emigrating (seen above in US army uniform). On retirement he returned to Ireland and is buried in Rathmore cemetery, near the front gate on the right-hand side.

go to sleep. You might wake up looking at the muzzle of a rifle and get no time to say them.' He was quite right — many a man got a rude awakening. One of our party, a fellow named 'Dundon' (Tom McSweeney), was particularly slow in lying down and he made an awful noise as he accidentally rubbed his rifle along the ridges of the corrugated roof. He got a real telling-off from Dan Hayes, 'Dundon! Why don't you go out and tell them we're here? I have a good mind to throw you off the bloody barn.' (Followed by subdued laughter which anybody still awake seemed to enjoy.)

It was our turn on guard and we heard footsteps approaching from the road. I roused those asleep by knocking the rifle butt against one of the poles. There was an awful, if silent, scuffle as everyone got his gear and rushed down the ladder. It broke, of course, and a bunch of men piled on the ground amid an avalanche of hay, rifles and curses. We watched a lone pedestrian pass through an adjacent field but didn't challenge him. He didn't seem to be aware of our presence but there was no more sleep that night. It could have been someone who was afraid to sleep at home and had some secret hideout of his own, but it could also be a spy testing the area to find out how alert we were. I often wondered.

One day about this time, being in the comparative safety of my own locality, I called to my home for a change of clothes and a meal. As all visits had to be of short duration, I left immediately after lunch. I walked cross-country for about a mile, carrying my rifle, and then I got on a byroad leading towards the Paps mountain. After about one hundred yards I met a well dressed man, a complete stranger. We exchanged a greeting and he stopped and said his motor car had broken down a short distance down the road. He asked me how he would get to Killarney as he needed a mechanic to repair the car. He explained that he was a commercial traveller (sales representative) and had many outlets to call on.

I suggested that I would take a look at the car. At this stage he seemed to get very uneasy. I believe he did not relish his position — on a back road with a broken down car and an armed man carrying a rifle who was a total stranger to him. I reassured him that he need not be worried — I would help him if I could and I would not do him any harm. We walked a short distance to the car while we discussed the engine trouble he was having. He appeared to relax a little. When we got to the car we opened the bonnet. All the time I kept a firm hold of my rifle. I had a good look at the engine and I was fortunate enough to spot a loose wire. I attached it to its proper connection and had a final look at the other connections to ensure that they were alright. I asked him to sit in and try to start up the car while I gave a few turns of the starting handle. The car started and he seemed very pleased, and I expect relieved, to get going again. He got out of the car and with profuse thanks he handed me a one pound note (a tidy sum of money at that time). I accepted the money, thanked him and wished him 'good luck'.

As he was about to drive off I said to him, 'This pound is worth more than my life if you ever mention to anybody, at any time, anything about our meeting or our conversation; or that you had a breakdown at all — much less that a man carrying a rifle repaired your car.'

He gave me his word of honour that he would not mention the incident and I believed him. We shook hands and parted, each of us going our own separate ways — he driving to Killarney and I heading for the shelter of the hills. It was the first time I was paid for fixing a motor car. I would like to have met that man again years later — but I never did.

Around the end of October, a few of us were in the open country, three or four miles north of Barraduff. With nothing special to do and nowhere in particular to go, we decided to go to church. We had not seen the inside of one in a good while, and a little talk with God might be a good idea. The priests never missed us and seemed to be getting along alright

Portrait of author in battledress by Tom McSweeney 'Dundon' (from memory). Note armoured car in flames at Jeremiah's right arm.
Writing bottom left: "Jerh Murphy First Section Fifth Batt. Kerry No. 2 IRA".
Writing bottom right: "Thomas Myles McSweeney".

without us. We had been in action for four months and some of our battalion had seen a lot of fighting but no one had been killed in our column. A few had been injured in different ways but many had some close calls. To cite a few: Bill DeLacey was cleaning his rifle. It fired accidentally, the bullet going through a fence about a foot from John McSweeney's head. Jerry Kennedy had all the wood cleaned off his rifle, as he held it across his chest, by a well-aimed shot from the enemy at The Bower. I had fired a Lewis gun accidentally in a small open space between ten fellows, a few paces away. But there had been two nasty accidents. A young boy was shot as he examined a revolver belonging to his brother and Denny Reen's new rifle fired when the safety catch broke. That bullet hit a housewife in the leg and she died of the wound. However, these were low casualties when one considers all the lead that had been flying around.

November 1st was a Church holiday and everyone would be at Mass. We reasoned that by going to Confession on October 31st and letting the holiday go by, we would attract less attention by attending Mass on the following day. It was also a good way to test the efficiency of the local intelligence system. So we attended Mass in Barraduff as planned, having left our rifles and equipment with a couple of young scouts in Kilquane. They were posted about a quarter of a mile away on high ground with a good view of the village of Barraduff. As we were about to approach the altar for Communion, one of the scouts walked in behind us and said, 'The Staters are surrounding the village.' Pat T. O'Sullivan and I received Communion and left by a side door as inconspicuously as possible. The troops were already in line with the church and about four hundred yards to the side. We dropped into a shallow stream and followed its course where there was good cover. When the village was searched, particular attention was paid to the church, even the back of the altar and some closets. This procedure was unusual and would not have been resorted to except they expected to find someone. Our mothers attending Mass chided the officers for their behaviour but they only answered, 'Better luck next time.' It was evident that our visit to church had been reported.

Michael O'Sullivan, Cloghane, Headford, killed in action at Knockanes, 2 November 1922.

The patrol travelled south to Headford and our scouts gave them a few blasts, just on general principles. We were very grateful to Pat Daly, John Murphy and a few others for getting us out of that hole. As the patrol turned west towards Killarney, they were fired on by Danny O'Connor and Michael O'Sullivan who happened to be at home. An exchange of gunfire wounded Michael O'Sullivan and both were followed closely. The wounded man sought refuge in a farmhouse as he was bleeding heavily and could not get away. He broke his rifle when his ammunition was exhausted, and he was dragged out by his captors and shot again, at close range. He died in a short time after being refused the rites of his church when he refused to renounce his support of the Republican cause. This was our first casualty and he was buried with full military honours in the Republican plot in Kilquane cemetery. After his burial, his comrades engaged in some reprisals against the families of those they considered responsible for the tragedy. Our area was expected to be raided and we spent several nights and a few days awaiting such a possibility. Even as we relaxed our vigil, our attention was turned to making dumps and dugouts for safety. Our foresight paid off, too, a short time later. Our column was divided into four sections for a while in order to get prepared for winter. We were still a potent force, but the enemy was billeted amid all the comforts of town life, while we ranged the country in secrecy and stealth with the prospects ahead looking none too bright.

One morning, on being awakened by a girl who knew the location of our dugout, we were informed of a large force of the enemy on top of the Tokenfire mountain, and that it was moving downhill in extended order. This was a bad situation, as they must have climbed the hill during the night, and it pointed to the strategy which we expected would be used by some of our former comrades who had changed over to the Free State army earlier in the year. Luckily none of our men were on the hill that day, but the whole search was directed to our company area. Four men, including Dan Hayes and Mick Doherty in a dugout with a dog, could hear the troops talking as they passed within six feet. The faithful dog never barked as his master held him by the muzzle. John McSweeney and I had a close call as a squad of soldiers passed us by, about twenty-five feet away. They had walked into the far end of a

Tokenfire mountain.

field and never saw us, but we had to run for the cover of a few small bushes. In doing so, we had to move fast as I led the way, clearing a low fence in my stride. My pal scrambled over it and later when all was clear he complimented me on my athletic feat. I could hardly believe it, but the evidence was conclusive. I had jumped twenty-one feet. It shows what a fellow can do when he is pushed hard enough. Later that afternoon another squad crossed a different field as we were busy making a dugout. Neither party saw the other but we were plainly seen by two other people a few hundred yards away. What luck!

While John McSweeney and I were congratulating ourselves on our good luck, and on my athletic feat, unknown to us another ally was at work on our behalf. Mothers were, are and will be mothers the world over, and mine was no exception. During this incident both John McSweeney and I, and the enemy, were in full view of my mother as she looked out her front window. She well realised the danger, and as it became more acute, she dropped to her knees in front of a picture of the Sacred Heart and prayed fervently. When the immediate danger had passed, she got off her knees and raising her eyes to heaven she uttered, 'Thank God!' This incident was related to me later by my younger brothers, Patie, John and Michael, who witnessed it.

"Mothers were, are, and always will be mothers the world over — and mine was no exception." (Above — the author's mother, Hannah Murphy)

Our section assembled that night and compared notes. It was decided to leave our own area and stay with the main body in the Clydagh valley. The Staters had lulled us into complacency by not raiding our locality earlier and had even let it be known that they were not particularly interested in capturing us. What perfidy! The truth was, they knew our strength and were reluctant to search for us in such hostile territory except in great numbers, but after the incident in church two weeks before, they had to make some show. However, nobody was captured and better still, the presence of any dugouts was not even suspected. But the chase was too hot and there was safety in numbers, so we crossed the mountains by the Slugadhal pass in pitch darkness — quite a feat in itself. After sleeping all the next day, the whole column was assembled at Tom Fitzgerald's of Derryraig on the Killarney-Macroom road, not far from the Cork-Kerry border. From all accounts, a roundup had been carried out over certain limited areas and it looked like only the beginning. The government was anxious to get the campaign ended before the winter and these small sorties were only a rehearsal for a greater sweep.

We hung around here for a few hours. Some danced a few sets. Our officers were strangely silent and grave, but we thought the events of the past days had made them so. But their troubles and worries were kept to themselves and they were concerned with our lives and our welfare as well as our leadership. So this was nothing new. Suddenly, the lights of an approaching car from the Cork side changed the tension and, strangely, nobody was surprised. It was a small car, containing three men with 'Peter the Painter' pistols and a Vickers machine gun, which taxed the capacity of the car. There was a brief meeting of two of these men and our O.C. and Vice O.C. after which, the whole column was lined up. About forty men were called by name to step forward, close ranks and marched a few hundred feet away. Our O.C., D. Reen and one of the strangers, inspected our equipment and we were marched away in the direction of the 'county bounds', without any explanation. We had begun to recognise these moves as preparatory to an attack or ambush of some importance and as we walked along in broken formation we tried to guess our destination. Our ammunition was low at that moment, and we had been careless about hoarding some after the Kenmare attack, so we vowed to bring about ten slings per man from the next haul. There was a burst of laughter as Dan Hayes reminded us 'to be careful, lest one of us come home slung on a door.'

After walking about five miles we were picked up on side-cars and taken several miles further. There was no inkling of the objective and nobody dared ask. Billeting in farmhouses, we slept during what was left of the night and on into the next afternoon. It had rained all day and we didn't recognise our environment. A messenger directed us to meet down the road a little way and after walking a few more miles we were lined up to receive cigarettes. I always took my share, though I rarely smoked but gave them to my pals instead. Suddenly we were fired on and everyone dropped flat. The muddy condition of the road didn't seem to bother us either. Our guides told us that we were near the village of Reananerree and our scouts must have made contact with an enemy patrol. This proved true, as a messenger came along with the bad news that a couple of scouts had been captured by a cycle patrol which had dashed into the village and left quickly by the same route, at the opposite side from our location. This incident gummed up the works a little but our guides led us across country for about a mile. The journey was tortuous as the ground was rough, full of small bushes and numerous puddles of mud from the rain which had fallen all day.

We stopped on top of a low hill where there was an isolated house on a small farm on a little plateau. In this retreat lived the most unforgettable character we had met so far in all our ranging through the country. A big white mule stood outside, eating from a haystack, and inside the house were a small black cow, a billy goat and several hens roosting on pegs driven into the wall. A large turf fire was burning briskly and it got plenty of attention from some members of our group. Others who could not enjoy the comfort of the fire climbed on the roof and stuffed the chimney with a bag of hay. This trick got the others away from the fire and filled the house with smoke. As our O.C. entered and tried to pierce the smoky atmosphere, I pinched the cow around the flank with the foresight of my rifle and she kicked him across the knees, almost flattening him. Somebody else pulled the goat by the hair and he let out a weird scream. This unusual greeting caused the officers to exit in a hurry, amid the chuckles of those on the inside. This conduct was silently witnessed by the proprietor. The bewhiskered fellow denied he had any 'poteen' (homemade whiskey) but our guides let it be known that he was a well known purveyor of the 'mountain dew.' We could have used some then as we were all wet and cold.

The horseplay came to an end abruptly as the headlights of a car came into view, on a road about a mile away. We were ordered to go towards this car as it approached us. We found it to be a Whippet armoured car of the latest British design, with a revolving turret mounted on a Rolls Royce chassis. The catalogue of our armaments did not include such a weapon, but there were some earlier in the fighting, and some home-made cars, most of which had been captured or lost. This recent acquisition had been made the day before from the courtyard of Bandon barracks by a ruse. Comdt. Gen. Tom Barry and a few others dressed as regular Free State officers entered that town secretly and walked into the barracks yard. They approached the car nonchalantly and ordered the crew to drive to the outskirts of the town, which they did without suspicion. Once inside the car, the IRA men took over the controls and the guard at the gate saluted as it passed through. The amazed crew were disarmed after clearing the outposts and pushed outside, while the car sped into the twilight of the surrounding country, capably operated by the new crew.

This car was to be the spearhead of an attack on the village of Ballyvourney the following morning. The garrison consisted of about two hundred troops, who were very alert, and had an armoured car always ready in front of their headquarters, which was a small hotel in the centre of the village. The remainder were quartered in the houses and stores along the main street. There were some outposts, which were sandbagged huts, by the side of the approaching roads. Our group was assigned to the bridge at Carrigaphuca, to prevent reinforcements from Macroom. Two other roads on our right and left were also guarded. The Ballyvourney battalion carried out the assault, supported by the captured armoured car. It was necessary to get this car into the village to counter the enemy car. It did so by travelling fast and, as it carried the unmistakable identity marks, the challenge was only routine. The sentries were taken by surprise and made prisoners.

In spite of the initial drawbacks, the attack was well planned and brilliantly executed. The attackers' car could not be used in the offensive as it was forced to stand by as a defensive measure to prevent the garrison from using their car. The defenders made several attempts to man our car, especially when the Vickers gun jammed, but the driver of the Whippet held them off with a Thompson sub-machine gun until the gunner cleared the problem with the Vickers gun. If the much heavier Lancia car could have been manned by the defenders, the outcome would not have been so fast or decisive. Our car was under constant grenade attack in front of the enemy H.Q. and only twenty five feet behind the defenders' car. One grenade exploded under the Whippet and blew off a tyre but it stood its ground and the crew dared not move it away. Neither could any of our men board the enemy armoured car. Meanwhile, the men attacking from the back of the houses got another Vickers in position which cut great holes in the walls through which they fired grenades. A fellow named Barrett, whom I knew well, fired these directly from the shoulder, with a bicycle saddle stuffed inside his coat to ease the recoil. The place was a shambles before the defenders gave up. This allowed the attacking car to move around and concentrate on another building at the east end of the town. It enfiladed a hallway at the back of the hotel and all the defenders having been hit, they surrendered. The operation was a great success and a large quantity of supplies was taken, without the loss of a man. The Free State garrison had several men severely wounded.

It was another long walk to Carrigaphuca bridge, but we had some refreshment at the Half Way House. We arrived at the bridge at dawn and immediately started to block the road by felling trees on the far side, while others dug some false mine holes. On the near side of the bridge was a rocky eminence which lent a good, safe resistance position. Mick Dennehy and I were working on the second tree when we were alerted by the sound of an approaching vehicle. We ran across the bridge to the forementioned position and took cover. The vehicle turned out to be an armoured car on its way from the large post at Macroom towards Ballyvourney and it ground to an abrupt halt at the felled tree. That blockade played an important part in the subsequent sorties made by the enemy, and made our day's work a lot easier. If it had not been there, we could not have stopped the armoured car as we had no mines and the outcome might have been quite different. Two occupants of the car, which was a large heavy one, came out and examined the blockade but we held our fire until they were climbing back in. A few bursts of fire from Flor Donoghue on a Lewis gun supplied by a section of Cork fellows caused the crew members to be dragged back into the car as it turned around and sped away towards Macroom. A few minutes later the firing opened at Ballyvourney, four or five miles to our rear. The sound of rifles and machine guns was continuous and interspersed with a great many grenade explosions. In a short time, gunfire on our left attracted our attention and we suspected that the enemy were probing the road on that side. A messenger told us that a scout of theirs had been killed and a little later they showed up in force on our front. The Sullane river separated us at this point and they didn't seem particularly anxious to cross. Some long range exchanges took place and they dropped a few shells short of our position before retiring to the safety of Macroom.

Our section was called back from the bridge and we spent some time looking over the wreckage and helping the wounded. One in particular was a handsome athletic fellow who had taken three bullets in the abdomen. He asked me if I thought he would die, but I lied very ably as I assured him he would not. Another thing that impressed me was Mick Sullivan and Nick Coffey standing near their armoured car, looking at the flat tyre, while someone emptied the car of spent cartridges with a broom and shovel. We took whatever we could use. I needed some clothes and found a good suit which fitted me well. I discarded a pair of pants which was about nine sizes too big for me, and I saw it later on a Free State soldier and it was too big for him, too. When the prisoners were released later that night, they were marched towards Killarney and some of our column on the home area recognised the oversized pants. Some soldiers were given other clothes to wear while their uniforms were taken away, maybe to be used on another occasion as a disguise. We rested that night at Coolea and abandoned most of the excess baggage we had accumulated. The next day was spent on lookout and we heard and saw enemy armoured cars and trucks in the distance but made no contact. These were strong forces searching for the armoured cars so we chose to relax rather than risk a confrontation. This war was already very rough and, at the moment, we seemed to be winning it but fortune could change easily. Next night we moved to a place called Cahernacahac, deep in the west Cork hills.

The local men must have taken care of guard duty as none of our party drew that detail. It was just as well as none of us knew exactly where we were located. A small dance got going in a farmer's house. Out in a large barn, 'poteen' was being distilled, so a few of us who had never seen it before made a short study of this process. John Reen and I accompanied two girls home and stayed at their house that night. Pat Hegarty, one of the scouts who had been captured two nights before, slept there also. We were awakened early next morning by a messenger and marched without breakfast towards the south. No objective was mentioned but after a halt and an hour's wait a rider came along and ordered us back to the place we had left earlier. It transpired that we were to attack the village of Inchigeelagh, but the garrison fled during the night, leaving the sick and wounded behind. This post could have been captured as we had two armoured cars now. We rested during the remainder of the day and John and I helped our host to ring a sow. He was a prosperous farmer, a generous man and better still he had two pretty daughters. There was some talk about bringing the armoured cars to Rathmore to attack that post, so we all returned to the Rathmore area to prepare for our new objective.

It had been an active week and at last we were satisfied with our position. A large area from Kenmare to Macroom had been cleared of enemy garrisons and it was possible to move around there without fear of running into patrols. But not so the rest of the country. Large areas of resistance still held out but there were some counties where a single IRA man of active status could not be found. Nevertheless, we were still a potent force. Even the Free State officials appreciated it to the point of putting out peace feelers in the hope of putting an end to the fighting before Christmas. In fact, some representatives of both sides met, but they failed to agree on anything as the Free Staters demanded our complete surrender. This didn't worry us, as the prospect of more victories was in sight, if not of the eye, then at least of the imagination. It was now about the middle of December and the weather was becoming damp and raw. More and better dumps were made in areas which were considered friendly and safe. We spent a hard night's labour lugging planks from the Quagmire bridge to construct a good dugout. Heavy patrols were moving around searching for our armoured cars which we were expecting to use at any time. All the garrisons in East Kerry and West Cork were very much on the alert.

Moving into the Rathmore district, we carried out a little raid one Sunday as we heard some of the garrison were in the habit of attending Mass, one and a half miles west of the post. Large trees were felled across the road and the priest strongly disapproved of these tactics. We hung around the Forge Cross for a while but on that occasion none of the enemy showed up at church. However, on a later Sunday, when the church was surrounded by Free State troops, who hoped to nab a few unwary IRA men, there was no sermon castigating the raiders. The congregation was exhorted to resist the Republican cause and remove the trees. A large crowd of sympathisers, led by Canon Carmody, tackled the tree removal job and were going along at a great rate chopping the limbs and dragging the trunks off the road when a few of our men fired not too high over their heads. The work came to a sudden stop, as soldiers, horses and woodmen scattered in confusion. For good measure, three or four of the Canon's bullocks were taken away to feed the column. There were reprisals, of course. An equal number of milking cows were seized from Jeremiah Reen of the Old Chapel and driven away to Killarney, to be heard of no more. A small force of the IRA were unsuccessful

A view of the Paps mountain looking south-west from the 'City' pilgrimage site.

in trying to prevent this movement of Reen's cows when they attacked the patrol at The Bower.

We worried the garrison occasionally by sniping or firing a few dozen rounds in the dark, near the outskirts of the village. This tactic had the effect of keeping the game going, as any firing could mean an attack. Sometimes the defenders would get jittery and fire thousands of rounds at the least provocation. Before an effective attack could be planned, one of our two armoured cars sank on a soft road and the other one could not pull it out. The enemy had learned of their location and were concentrating on an effort to capture them, so they had to be destroyed when their loss became imminent. To make matters worse, a large force occupied the village of Barraduff, right in the middle of our battalion area, on the main road between Killarney and Rathmore. This latest occupation was astride a route of communication frequently used by some of our high ranking officers.

We kept clear of this area for a while and spent Christmas and the New Year around Ballyvourney and the Clydagh valley. A group of us went to Confession in Ballyvourney on Christmas Eve. Leaving our equipment outside in the church grounds in the charge of one of our party, we followed another group of hard-bitten rebels into the church. The old priest immediately gave us a lecture about our activities and our defiling of holy ground. Our spokesman, Dan Hayes, reciprocated with a sermon of his own. 'You are supposed to be neutral in this trouble,' he said. 'It was men like us that kept your kind in safety in other troubled times.' The priest stomped out of the church as Dan reminded him of his duty. Emphasising his point by shaking his index finger in the face of the antagonistic cleric, he continued, 'If anything happens to one of us, you are responsible for our souls. Don't forget, we are doing our part.' We enjoyed the dialogue, but not the rebuff. The following morning we went to a small church in Coolea. We went to Confession and Communion and the priest asked us to have breakfast, but we gracefully declined. What a difference between the two men of the cloth.

In the afternoon a little time was spent in target practice with Dan J. Quill at Coolea. While roaming around his farm, I came upon the ruins of a house which was loaded with grenade casings, in various stages of manufacture. On inquiry, I also learned that the house formerly belonged to first cousins of my mother, also named Quill. The family had moved to Cork city after the death of their parents, and were great exponents of the native tongue. Two of this family taught in the Queen's College in the city and were friends of the McSweeney family, the Kents and other Cork patriots.

That night we went again to Cahernachahac and spent the remainder of the week around Gortnascarta with the Moynihan family. From there we returned to Clydagh and found a dance in progress.

7
Dark Deeds and Final Ceasefire (1923-24)

The new year came in with no fanfare and something less than optimism. We knew the enemy were slow to come after us during the winter months, so we made the most of it. Outside of a few sniping operations to keep the garrison worried, there was very little activity. The garrison at Barraduff, after being fired at a few times, let go a couple of bursts at my father one day as he was repairing the roof. It was a thatched house then. Some of the bullets fell harmlessly inside the house. This sort of vigilance kept me from visiting there except in company with several others. My sister sought us out once with a good sized cake, which didn't last long when she found us.

Around the middle of January we moved to Scartaglin, which to us seemed pointless. However, we were assembled there one wet Sunday night at a crossroads. The usual crowd of admirers were hanging around when our Vice O.C. called us to attention. He had something on his mind we guessed, as he told the 'audience' to clear out and 'fight or go home.' We marched away towards the west and after several miles we took to travelling cross-country. It was heavy going in the constant rain, across ploughed fields and many terrains not suitable for parade-ground drill. Just before daybreak we had arrived at some place between Farranfore and Tralee. We recognised the O.C. of another group which joined us. He was Tommy McEllistrim, so we concluded there was going to be some action. We crossed the river Maine over a demolished stone bridge, and the night was still so dark that Pats Healy rammed the stock of his Lewis gun against the forehead of a man who was guiding us across and bowled him over. This guide was called 'Pluggy'. Pats joked about this, remarking, 'I think he got plugged, alright'. At some place further on we were assigned to farmhouses and told to keep out of sight and not to attract attention by putting on lights. The housewife was very kind, even after being awakened unceremoniously at an early hour, and cooked us a breakfast of tea, eggs, bread and jam. I am sure we ate the bread for her family's breakfast as there was only one cake, which one of our boys sliced. As it was passed around by Pats Healy one fellow took the plate and Pats snapped, 'Dundon, you - - - - , one slice to a man.' After eating we slept soundly all day. After nightfall, a large number of men assembled at Daly's house where we were briefed by Tommy Mac and John Joe Sheehy. The target was Castlemaine and the particular role of our company was to prevent reinforcements from leaving Tralee. This location had been chosen, on account of its isolated position, to try out a new weapon — a home-made mortar.

Our position was on a road near the top of a long slope overlooking Ballymac, and after daybreak we could see Tralee a few miles distant. While being led to this position, we travelled across fields. As we were being funnelled through a gate, Dundon missed it and was almost shot as he tried to scramble over the fence. It was pitch dark. Our gunner's No.2 man had some sort of argument and I was assigned to take his place. This responsibility didn't make me feel very happy, but my pal, Tim Daly, was in charge of the crew and had a lot of experience in such matters. The Tralee garrison had an airplane and it was expected it would be used to scout ahead of the reinforcement troops. Pats Healy was an expert gunner and his orders were to shoot down that plane without fail. He certainly was going to try.

The attack opened on Castlemaine as soon as daybreak came. There were some loud explosions, so we figured the mortar was doing its job. Soon after we could see activity in the Tralee garrison with the aid of binoculars. The plane was wheeled onto the field as if preparing to takeoff but, whether the machine was faulty or the pilot plain lucky, it never got into the air. The section was very disappointed, most of all our gunner, as we craved a crack at that plane. He had been an expert gunner with the British army in France, until captured by the Germans, and was demobilised at the start of the civil war. As the morning wore on, the firing died down and we hoped the attack was successful, but a dispatch rider came along and told us it had failed. We got orders to march further west. Being in position all morning with no food and little action made us feel disappointed, to say the least, as this event was expected to be a morale booster. Somebody rustled up food and after that the humour was a little better. The usual question was asked, 'Where are we going from here?' John Reen answered, 'I think we are going to snipe the Blasket Islands.' This got a big laugh. Our orders were a little different as we turned east and crossed the main Killarney-Tralee road. This was very dangerous ground but the local men scouted it well and conveyed us to Currow that night. Some of us were so tired that we almost slept while walking! At Ballyhar, the heels fell off Patie Reen's and Tom 'Dundon' McSweeney's shoes and they were obliged to suffer on until we reached a shoemaker in the morning.

We saw the trench mortar the following day and immediately Ned Bowler christened it 'The Fifth Commandment Gun.' It lacked some refinements according to my limited knowledge of ordnance. The shells were very good, being patterned after the German 'Minnie Wafers', but most of them missed their target or failed to explode at Castlemaine. Actually, only one shell did any damage there, and the exposed surroundings prevented an infantry assault as there would be too great a loss of men. However, in tests, the mortar had been very accurate and effective, and with some slight improvements would be a good assault weapon. Plans always work out well on testing under ideal conditions, better than under the actual stress of practical application.

Another attack was planned on the town of Millstreet. The assault force was to have assembled about two miles north-west of the town on a road bridge over the railway line. It was on a Sunday evening late in January and the weather was very wet and windy. Mick McGlynn came along from the Castleisland area with a Lewis gun and Jack Horan accompanied him towards Millstreet, as the latter was well acquainted with that locality. On the way they were joined by a fellow named Toohig who carried the ammunition pans and who also knew the district well. Our column was instructed to take up a position east of Rathmore to prevent any help going to the relief of the garrison from that point. Other sections blocked the roads leading from Macroom and Mallow.

As the gun crew approached the rendezvous at the bridge along the railway tracks and between two embankments, they were fired on by a body of men from the bridge. This sudden development left Toohig dead on the tracks with the ammunition, while McGlynn and Horan scrambled up the embankment with their arms under a hail of fire. They had been ambushed by a Free State patrol. After returning fire and exhausting their one pan of ammunition, they hid the gun and made their escape as well as they could. We had no way of knowing of this unexpected foul-up of our plans. Our party was divided between Shinnagh Cross and a position close to Rathmore village on the old road where the small by-road leads towards Caherbarnagh. Our presence must have been known to the enemy, as was evident by their tactics. Shortly

Caherbarnagh mountain and uplands — as viewed looking south from Rathmore village.

after dark, we were attacked by two separate patrols at both locations mentioned. Patie Reen and I were just sitting down to eat in one of the adjacent houses when the firing started suddenly. We ran together to our position only to find it deserted, and we were caught between the two fires as our men fired at the patrol from wherever they found cover.

In the few moments of confusion until we had a chance to size up the situation, we ducked under the shelter of a limekiln on the left of our original position. My partner was a veteran soldier having been through the Dardanelles campaign a few years before and was very cool. Suddenly a machine gun opened up on the top of the limekiln, firing at our confused comrades. My first impulse was to get away from there but my pal counselled to wait a while. 'When he changes the pan on the Lewis,' he said, 'we'll run for it.' We knew it was a Lewis and when the expected lull came, we dashed for the shelter of a stone fence across the road. In the darkness we were not seen, but the enemy heard us and directed a few bursts of fire in our direction. Several rounds hit close to us, one going through my overcoat. Patie suggested we fire a couple of rounds at the top of the limekiln, so we fired two shots each. This had the desired effect and the party on the top of the kiln left it in a hurry. In a whirl of shouting and confusion, the enemy patrol scattered and ran for the safety of the village. In the meantime, the other patrol on the main road had been engaged by our other section and fled towards the village also. About half an hour later, both of our sections joined up and fell back to another position at Inchabeg bridge. We had to hold this place. All of our party had some close shaves, but no one was hit.

The Aunaskirtaun river was in flood and lay between us and Rathmore now, so the only places to watch were a road and a railway bridge. This gave us an advantage and the indecisive action earlier left the enemy in doubt as to our strength, our position or our motives. Even having no means to block the road, we still felt confident of holding our new position as there was no armoured car at the post. During the night we took turns at guard-duty between catnaps at Casey's of Inch. I admired one of his daughters as she took care of cooking and feeding us. When morning dawned we were surprised to find an armoured car moving up on our rear from Rathmore. Being completely unaware of what happened at Millstreet, this was a bad omen and we were not prepared to cope with it. So we made the best of a bad situation, and lay low for about fifteen minutes, until the car turned around and went the other way. Some of our scouts who had scattered out to the east brought the bad news that the attack had not come off and that some of our men had been killed or captured. Realising our precarious position, between a deep river and a road patrolled by an armoured car, our officers ordered us out of there in a hurry.

This sort of indecisive action sapped our morale, spent our resources and put us in a worse position to bargain than before. The village of Barraduff was under consideration for attack, but the scattered location of the garrison presented certain problems that were not easily solved. The troops lived in the homes with the people and in case of attack a great many lives of innocent neutrals would be endangered. A lot of small sniping incidents occurred from day to day but these had little or no effect on the course of events. A patrol was usually too large to attack without help from neighbouring battalions and these were so hard pressed themselves that defensive rather than offensive action was found advisable. This left us with no alternative but to be as conservative as possible and move around with stealth from one location to another. We used many deceptive tactics to keep the enemy off balance and prevent him from learning our location, our strength and our attitude. We rarely moved around the open country in daytime except in large numbers to keep up appearances and boost our image.

For this reason the enemy rarely went out from his posts except in large patrols which were easy to spot and avoid. He knew our situation was critical and engaged in reprisals to terrorise our supporters, such as arresting relatives of some of our men. We began to be referred to as 'Diehards' by the enemy and in the press, but the loyalties which bound us together were far stronger than those which tried to rend us apart. The hard core of our organisation were resolute men who had become hardened by the gains and defeats of guerrilla warfare and were not easily intimidated. True, their nerves and physical endurance could not last indefinitely and some became ill from stomach and lung ailments. By far the worst stage of the struggle had to be endured ahead and the decision of the Free State authorities to execute some of our leaders who had been captured early in the fighting was the most unforgivable act indulged in so far. It had been said and written that our side was the first to employ this tactic, but I find it very hard to believe. In Kerry, especially, another tactic was employed by the Free State garrisons — the removal of road barricades by IRA prisoners. In some cases these road blocks were mined to prevent their removal but, if their removal was found necessary, it could have been accomplished by using explosives, not unfortunate prisoners. If we had desired to be that diabolical, it was possible to kill off a great many Free State leaders and officers, but we didn't fight that way. I know of one instance where a few of our side had three officers under their sights at 200 yards range but chose not to shoot them as they were off the post and like sitting ducks.

Tragic examples of using prisoners to remove obstacles occurred in Kerry, at Ballyseedy and Killarney. At Ballyseedy, nine IRA men who were prisoners in Tralee were taken out, tied together with rope. Their captors removed themselves to a safe distance, keeping the prisoners covered with rifles and machine guns. In a short time an explosion occurred, killing some of the men outright and fatally wounding others. Even so, fate has a way of recording such inhuman behaviour. One of the men was blown some distance into a ditch with severe burns to his hands, legs and back. He survived this gruesome ordeal to tell the whole story and make an official report to our top commanders. Of this I write with candour, as his original handwritten report passed through my hands and was read by other members of my company. This man was Stephen Fuller from North Kerry and I believe he was a student at the ecclesiastical seminary in Killarney. Five other prisoners were required to move a blockade on the road near Countess' Bridge at Killarney under similar circumstances, except they were not tied together. When one of them became suspicious of an object in the blockade, he told the others and they all bolted, but a mine exploded and they were fired on as they ran along the road. Four of them were riddled with gunfire, but one escaped without a scratch by scaling a high gate under a hail of fire and running through a park. Years later I knew this man, Tadhg Coffey in New York. He related for me all of the gory details. Again fate had lent a hand in exposing a diabolical system of disposing of prisoners and terrorising the rest of us. On numerous occasions our men fought to the finish rather than surrender with such dubious prospects in store for them if captured.

A dugout had been mined by some of our men in Knocknagoshel near Castleisland. When the location was conveyed to the Free State garrison, an ambitious officer who had been responsible for mistreatment of prisoners, bit on the false information and he and a few others were killed when they explored the dugout. There was another massacre of prisoners near Cahirciveen, but I am not acquainted with the details. Is it any wonder that either side didn't feel like giving up the fight? Our side was afraid of mass murder and the other was fired with ambition and hatred. Our Vice O.C., Jerry Kennedy, had a few close calls around the month of February when his rifle was shattered in his hands during an attack and again when he was surprised in a house, but his pluck and luck brought him through both occasions.

Another incident which passed relatively unnoticed about this time was the transportation of around 300 prisoners from Kerry to Dublin on a small coastal steamer in the middle of winter. This perilous voyage is well known to men of the sea and those who live along the south-west coast of Ireland. This ship had very poor accommodation, with standing room only, and it reached its destination after three rough days at sea. Imagine the state of those unfortunate men, many of whom died after being horribly seasick. The sanitary conditions were also very inadequate. Doubtless, these atrocities never came to the attention of the Geneva Convention, and Britain, in her most brutal moments, would never sanction such treatment. This account of the voyage was related to me by Tom Bowler, one of the men who made it, after his release.

Each raid made by the enemy, while not rounding up many of the fighting men, often resulted in the killing or capture of some unwary fellows. A few men of the Killarney battalion were captured in a couple of dugouts and taken to the Great Southern Hotel in that town where they were tortured over a period of two weeks. One young lad named Moynihan, from Barraduff, who was too young to take part in any military activity, was also taken there and mercilessly beaten to get him to reveal information. The main reason for this was because he was a brother of the IRA company captain of that district. He was thrown down a coal chute and left as dead, but he lived to tell about it. This tactic of arresting relatives of known leaders, and holding them hostage in local posts under threat of execution, put us in an awkward position. If we inflicted losses on the enemy during an attack, it was likely that revenge would be taken by murdering or torturing these unfortunate prisoners.

We made a few dugouts in safer areas and our sentries had to be more alert. Our section occupied a cave on the Tokenfire mountain known as 'Ploosh' (from the Gaelic word 'pluais' meaning 'cave'), which we fortified by building a stone wall across the opening. This place could accommodate fifteen men and was equipped with loopholes. The outside was elaborately camouflaged and there were some outposts to prevent surprise attack. It was warm and dry, had a supply of running water and had been used by wild goats and outlaws for centuries. Before this we had used it occasionally, but it

The house in Shrone where the 'gander' party was being held on the night Michael McSweeney was shot and killed. The original house has been renovated in the intervening years.

snowed one night and I could hear Dan Hayes complaining to himself, 'Holy God, there will be men found dead here in the morning,' as he tried to cover his legs from the accumulating snow. One night, before falling asleep, we heard a stone wall collapse down in the valley. We all sprang up and went outside, expecting to meet an enemy, but it was two of our own men who had failed to cross the hills to the Clydagh valley in bad weather and had returned to the shelter. As for the stone wall, it fell while being crossed by a flock of sheep foraging for food towards the lower ground. This sort of incident was not conducive to sound sleep. Michael McSweeney of our section, who had helped to build the stone wall, never lived to enjoy its safety or the hospitality of its shelter. He was killed a few days later.

In spite of the dangers and all the reverses, our men took many chances attending parties and dances. One of these affairs proved disastrous to our column. A 'gander' party was held at the home of a prospective bride near the base of Paps mountain. We were billeted around the neighbourhood and many of the fellows decided to attend, even though it was possible the place might be raided. Some of us thought it advisable to give the place a wide berth and take no chances, even though sentries were to be placed on all roads. Those of the latter viewpoint camped about a mile away. During the night our sentries heard shots coming from the direction of the party, but there was no communication between the two sections. When the day dawned, we headed in the direction of the last known location of the other section and were told by some of the people who had attended the party that the place was raided — six men were captured and one had been killed. They were not sure of the names of those involved, but they had been taken to Rathmore. It took a while to locate any members of the section as they were scattered and confused. The first man we contacted was Jerry Reen, who told us that he was returning from a sentry post with Michael McSweeney and when close to the party, they were called on to halt and put their 'hands up'. At first they thought it was a joke and they asked who was there, but were answered with a volley. As they turned to run for cover, McSweeney was hit and fell. Reen ran towards a fence but before going over it, he lay down for a few seconds. After firing a couple of shots he ran again and came to the conclusion that the place was surrounded. He laid low for a while, then climbed higher on the hill, but still could not contact any of his section. They had crossed the hill.

Our men had been completely surprised from the rear and the forecast of the night before had come true. Some of the Rathmore garrison, aided by local intelligence men and taking a circuitous route, had eluded the sentries and coming from the hill, or safe side, had surrounded the house and captured those inside it. There was no chance of resistance as the place

On left: Michael McSweeney (The Bower, Rathmore - holding the ammunition pan) who was shot and killed by Free State troops on the night of the Shrone 'gander' party just hours after this photo was taken in 1923. *On the right:* PJ Murphy (cousin of author) with Lewis machine gun. From "Gow's Cross", Rathmore, he emigrated to USA and joined the New York Mounted Police.

was thronged with innocent people. The prisoners were taken to Rathmore and then to Cork. Michael McSweeney's body was given to his father and the members of our section dug his grave in Kilquane cemetery. Later in the day he was buried with military honours as three of us held back a patrol from Barraduff which made an attempt to 'attend' the funeral.

We were at a real disadvantage now as the enemy held five of our men prisoners. They were Con Moynihan, John Reen, Pat Nagle, Pat Duggan and John Crowley. Up to this time we had managed to 'keep our hands out of the dog's mouth', so to speak, but all our previous troubles were insignificant compared to the present situation. Some of the men were captured with arms and their chances of survival were small. It was difficult to get any news about them and we were harried by so many small patrols that we had to keep on the move to save our own hide. A favourite tactic of the enemy was to secrete some troops on our known routes by night and ambush some unsuspecting straggler who came along in the morning. One such spot was the footbridge at Brewsterfield over the river Flesk, as it was often used by the Glenflesk section. Jerry Kennedy had a few close calls on this route, as well as some of his men. On one occasion, John McSweeney and Bill DeLacey were heading for the fort at Lisnagrave for a look around in the morning. As they walked across a field they became aware of a group of the enemy on the opposite side of the fence which they were approaching. Both sides opened fire and only for our two men lying flat and keeping up a spirited fire, they would have been killed or captured. Anyhow, they routed a patrol of twenty or more and saved their necks in the bargain, before we could come to their aid.

A few nights later, Bill DeLacey and I were preparing a place to sleep on the mountain. As the ground was damp we put some heather under our ground sheets to keep dry and soften our couch. I said, 'Bill, what poem does this remind you of?' He quickly answered with a passage from Scott's *Lady of the Lake*. He was educated in Scotland and I guessed he was familiar with 'Rhoderick Dhu', from Scott's *Lady of the Lake*. Having recited:

With that he shook the gathered heath
and spread his plaid upon the wreath,

we slept soundly under a starlit sky on the side of the Paps mountain. Snow had fallen during the day and it was bitterly cold that night, but it was better than being in a hot spot in the Great Southern Hotel in Killarney. As we reflected on our situation, we decided that matters could be a lot worse. At least we were free and tomorrow would be another day. It might even be a little better.

The town of Millstreet was attacked for a second time around March 1st. This date coincided with a large cattle and horse fair which was an annual fixture. I had enjoyed the March Fair at Millstreet on a few occasions as it was an all-night affair of music and dance, but not on that anniversary. The Rathmore column did not participate in this attack. Part of the garrison was subdued but the main post withstood the assault of a very determined body of Corkmen, a few of whom were wounded. Several meetings of our top officers were held about this time to assess the situation with a view towards peace. As these men passed through our area, it was necessary to establish a safe route. Jimmy Daly and Mick Dennehy were responsible for their safety and did a very good escort job under difficult circumstances.

We blew up the bridge over the Beheenagh river near Bealnadeega and this cut the road between Barraduff and Rathmore. It put the enemy at the disadvantage of having to ford the river a quarter of a mile upstream and it stopped the passage of big trucks and armoured cars between these points. It also forced the enemy to travel through country favourable for an ambush. Before I exploded the mine it was necessary to move an old sick man from a nearby house, but he refused to cooperate and came through the shock alright. As we demolished some overhanging remnants of the bridge, Mick Dennehy and Jerry Reen went down with it but were not seriously hurt. A few days later we studied a convoy as they toiled across the ford and got soaked as they did, under a heavy cold rain. We could have given them an awful bad time but did not want to spoil the chance of a successful attack later on. An urgent request from Jerry Kennedy at Loo Bridge for a good mine took our interest in that direction. Jack Horan was taken very sick and we escorted him across the hill at the same time, taking the mine along in a sack. They were both critical cargo as the mine was already primed and the ground was rough. On arrival at Loo Bridge, Kennedy informed us that the Free State forces had rebuilt the bridge over the Flesk river at Killaha. This indicated a move on their part in the near future, so to save ourselves a lot of grief, it would be necessary to demolish the bridge, but it was guarded. We abandoned the sick man at Annies and somebody else took him to Clydagh. He had contracted rheumatic fever and had to be concealed.

The middle of March brought cold hail showers from the north west. The enemy had been very active around the Killorglin and Milltown areas during the preceding weeks. A flying column of picked Free State officers dressed in typical IRA attire had roamed through these areas and were successful in capturing some of our boys. They had enough confidence in their tactics to attend a funeral of an IRA officer whom they had captured and murdered. Accounts of these and other atrocities dribbled towards us and we estimated our turn would come in due course. After a week of vigilance, the guard was withdrawn from the repaired bridge and our scouts informed us of the move immediately. While D. Reen and Jerry Kennedy were discussing this information, an unexpected windfall came our way. About a dozen of us were standing on the road at Poulgorm Bridge when a touring car came along from the direction of Ballyvourney. The occupants, besides the driver, were a man and woman intending to open the Great Southern Hotels in Kenmare and Parknasilla. It also contained several cases of liquor. Our officers decided to use the car to drive us to the bridge at Killaha and destroy it.

Discharging the passengers and luggage temporarily, we loaded the mine and about twelve of us piled on the car and headed for Killaha. Flor Donoghue drove and Neil O'Leary decided to let down the hood in case of a sudden contact with the enemy. Although the road was open to Killarney, Jerry Kennedy sat sedately in the back seat as if we were tourists. About a quarter of a mile from our objective, we stopped and he detailed three men to cover the road with the Lewis gun. He posted a few riflemen up close and gave me two men to dig the hole. We reversed the car onto the bridge, unloaded the mine, reeled out the cable and parked the car around the next bend for a quick getaway; after all, an armoured car could bear down on us at any time from Killarney. It was a stone bridge of five arches and we placed the mine on the arch next to the repaired span. The explosion was very successful as that arch was completely demolished and the repair job of girders and rail ties also fell into the river. We felt a lot safer as we drove back leisurely. This called for a little celebration and we returned the car minus one case of whiskey. Each man was given one drink and the remainder was divided between the company captains, one bottle to each. The original occupants of the car were sent on their way and told to keep quiet.

Two nights later, Tom Lyne and I were sent to check out some information and our route lay over the river near where we had blown up the bridge. Around Glenflesk we were forced to seek shelter in a haybarn until morning as it was raining very heavily. At first light we approached the footbridge at Brewsterfield and drew lots to see who would cross first. It was dangerous country and we studied the opposite bank using binoculars. On the other side was a wheat field, surrounded by a wall about a hundred yards from the river. Lyne crossed first. There was plenty of evidence that our opponents had spent a lot of time there, waiting for fellows like us. We had one bottle of whiskey to deliver, but took a slug each to warm us up a little. A few miles further on, we crossed the main Killarney road at Carrigeen. We had to lie low here for a while to let two lorries of troops go by, as we had no mind to fire at them in our situation. Lyne took a few more slugs out of the bottle, remarking, 'We need it more than Jimmy Daly and if we happened to be captured, I'd hate to see some Free State officer drinking it!' We put in a little water to refill the bottle before delivering it to Jimmy. After breakfast at Annaugh we considered the location for a dugout but could not find a suitable spot. Spending the next night in that area, we checked out information by listening to conversations very quietly. The following night we crossed the Owenacree River into Meentoges and slept in a haybarn after getting wet to the knees. In the morning we were awakened by two girls who were looking for eggs. They recognised us and invited us for breakfast. Remaining there during the day we invited ourselves for lunch and supper and were glad to get back to the comparative safety of the hills the next night.

Jerry Kennedy, Neil O'Leary, Pat Donoghue (who later became a doctor and hearing specialist) and I practised a bit of rifle throwing of grenades. Jerry told us we had good information that a roundup would be attempted as soon as the weather was good and it was already clear and settled. Next day a large contingent of troops rebuilt the bridge at Killaha and remained there a few days guarding it. We needed no further proof of a sweep to be made some day soon. Tom Lyne and I were sent across the hills again by night with orders for our section to fire on the Barraduff garrison during the night. We travelled light, taking only rifles and one sling of ammunition and no overcoats. The night was fair and breezy, but when we reached the plateau on top of the hill we actually stumbled over several sheep in the fog and darkness. When descending on the north side we lost our way and waited for daylight to come. When it came, and we picked up the correct trail, it was 10 a.m. Jimmy already had the section on alert as he had some information of his own. He decided to snipe at the village in the afternoon and cross the hill that night. We did this and slept in haybarns in Clonkeen. Our barn was very drafty and Lyne and I slept on some hay on the ground.

We were rudely awakened in the morning by somebody announcing the progress of a body of troops through Glenflesk along the Loo valley, towards our location. A large sow was lying on the hay across our legs and had to be belted on the snout with a rifle butt before we could get to our feet. Several hundred troops had arrived at Loo Bridge about 9 a.m. and scouts were sent to a low hill overlooking the place to report their movements. Our main body was strung out loosely about a mile long, awaiting developments. When the enemy flank started to climb the hill from the opposite side, it looked like they might nab our scouts, so we were forced to fire before we had intended to. This revealed our position and after a pause, the main body advanced towards us. Our view was restricted to a few hundred yards, so we waited until that part of the road was well crowded before opening fire. They were caught between a steep part of the hill and the river, taking quite a beating. Only one of our sections could engage the enemy and when they located our position more precisely, we were pinned down by heavy machine gun and rifle fire. The day was young, and we had no idea of their plans or objectives, so we stopped firing to conserve ammunition. Besides, there was no telling what the afternoon might bring. When they got as far as Poulgorm Bridge, they decided to turn off and retreat by another road.

In the afternoon another body of troops came over the hill on our extreme right, advancing towards us. This seemed to clear up the mystery of the sound of an airplane heard from that direction earlier in the day. We enticed them downhill by firing a few long range shots. Now they had come under the fire of a section of Rathmore men and were too far downhill to retreat under fire, so they holed up in whatever cover could be found on the bare mountainside. Behind them was a quarter of a mile of the same terrain, all uphill, while in front, more of the same stretched down to a deep river and a road which ran across their line of advance. We lay on the other side of this road, but too far away to be effective. They were pinned down for the remainder of the afternoon and we, being outnumbered ten to one, could not force a surrender. This stalemate ended when night fell and they escaped in the dark. Later that night, Jerry Cahill and Ned Moynihan caught one of them as he was walking along the road while they were on sentry duty. They were as much surprised as he was when he told them he had crossed the river in the dark and was attempting to get back to Killarney. On being questioned further by Kennedy, he told us he was climbing hills all day since dawn. He had started from Barraduff and expected to meet resistance on the north side of the hills. An airplane had scouted ahead but it was not very effective in the fog, and they were late for a rendezvous with the other body. All this made sense and cleared up some of our earlier lack of intelligence. It also proved that it was good strategy to snipe the enemy base the day before.

Our prisoner was in bad shape. He was so exhausted that he had fallen asleep while they were pinned down in the evening and was left behind. We fed him and let him dry his clothes after which he was allowed to sleep in a guarded room. Next morning, Neil O'Leary and I went up to the hill where we found nothing except blood, bandages and spent cartridges. In the afternoon Jerry Kennedy dictated his famous challenge to the Free State command at Killarney. Mike P. wrote it out and it was signed, 'O.C. Robbers Den.' Neil and I escorted him to Glenflesk and turned him loose to make his way to Killarney.

He was scared, but thankful. Who wouldn't be, under the circumstances?

Well, at least there had been some activity during the past days and it made us feel good. We knew our positions could be defended up to a certain limit with a normal strategy, but what we didn't know was the scope of the overall campaign that was being waged against us. 'The wood was invisible on account of the trees.' While we were complimenting ourselves on the success of an empty victory, the enemy had presented us with only one-third of the problem. Fifteen miles at our back they had occupied Ballyvourney again and twenty miles on our left they had also reoccupied Kenmare. These were the other two-thirds. We should have seen the writing on the wall the day we intercepted that car with the officials who were on their way to reopen the hotels. Once again our movements became restricted to the battalion area.

The problem of making more and better dugouts faced us once again. As the days got longer and warmer, we knew the troops would come out in force and camp out, if necessary, making our stay in houses almost impossible. Some of the dugouts were fascinating, constructed with great care and patience. We reasoned that it was better to work at it than spend time as prisoners in precarious custody. Many of our haunts were known to the enemy and it would only be a matter of time until we were surrounded. Since we couldn't hold out in any large engagement, we got orders to scatter out until the hunt cooled off. There was no point in being all together and we stood a better chance of avoiding capture by splitting up into small parties. The same tactics were practised by our neighbouring battalions and the problem of sustenance was less acute. Shoes, clothes and supplies were long since exhausted and the problem of renewal became more of a personal matter. Small raids were carried out to come by these items under dangerous and hostile conditions.

The railways had been out of commission now for about eight months and all supplies had to be hauled by road, across rivers and makeshift bridges, up and down slippery embankments and sometimes under fire. The merchants were in short supply of most staples and some garrisons were nearly as bad. The poor, unfortunate farmers grumbled least of all and oftentimes slaughtered cattle to keep us in food. Two of our column spent a few days studying convoys between Rathmore and Killarney. While in a house on the main road one day, a few lorries of troops stopped and looked around the premises. Our men had to hide upstairs, but the house was not searched. The next day we were sent to make a haul of cigarettes from a passing convoy, when suddenly a couple of enemy lorries bore down on us. We barely missed being seen by jumping inside the fence. After waiting two hours for their return under a small bridge, the suspense got the better of us and we gave up. No smoke, no fire!

While searching for a suitable site for a dugout one day, Dan Hayes found two shotguns that had been hidden since the Headford ambush in 1921. Many men had looked for them before, and now they were found by accident. We spent some time polishing these for relaxation. Having located a likely spot for a dugout, we proceeded to enlarge it by removing several large stones. It was close to a small rivulet of spring water and a large flat rock, weighing several tons, formed a roof. Intending to sleep there one night, we failed to find it, and as it was raining, we decided to sleep in a haybarn, instead. Next day, three of us felt ambitious and decided to go back to the dugout to dress it up a bit. We were surprised to find the rock roof lying on the floor and entry was impossible. Had we slept there the night before we could have been buried alive. Lady Luck had been kind to us again!

The month of March was a bad one for the Kerry IRA. There were no gains and several losses. It became known locally as 'the month of terror'. This was the month when men were killed by their captors at Ballyseedy; when prisoners were gunned down while removing a barricade at Countess Bridge in Killarney; when prisoners were tortured and killed in Cahirciveen and when John Kevins and Jerry Casey were captured and murdered in Beaufort. There were several other outrages committed against IRA prisoners while being detained in various posts throughout the county. A special detail of Free State officers was reported to be engaged in these activities and some of their names became household words. In many parts of County Kerry, certain names — like Col. Dempsey, Capt. Lyons, Col. Nelligan, Capt. Breslin and Lieut. Gaffney — were regarded with fear.

The foregoing record is a sad chapter in the history of Ireland, but all civil wars seem to be fought on a more vicious scale than international ones. The same holds true of the Wars of the Roses and the Stuart era in Britain, the French Revolution, the United States Civil War and many other more recent struggles. What base instinct drives man to hate his brother more than somebody else once his affection is alienated, I'll never understand. Maybe a psychologist would. There was no international tribunal to investigate war crimes then and no agency to which an appeal could be made. To be killed in combat is expected, but to torture or mistreat prisoners is inexcusable by any measure of human civilisation. Dorothy McArdle's *Tragedies of Kerry* gives a fair account of the conduct of the Civil War in our country. Although it is sketchy and incomplete, it does contain the bare facts.

In April, with the approach of fair weather, the IRA position became desperate. There was little or no resistance against Free State authority in Leinster and parts of the lowlands of

Munster and Connacht, so all their attention turned towards bringing the struggle to a quick conclusion in the mountainous districts of the South and West. Several IRA organisers and officers who had gone to Ulster to fight against the Orange mobs and 'B' Specials there, found themselves without support, having to oppose the British, the Orangemen and the Free State. Their lot was a sad one, indeed. Three of those captured and later executed by the Free State authorities on March 14, 1923, were Kerrymen, Charlie Daly, Tim O'Sullivan and Dan Enright. Seán Larkin from County Derry was executed with them. Even sadder was the fate of some Ulster Nationalists who, after opposing the Orange mobs for years, crossed into Free State territory only to be disillusioned and imprisoned. Let history be the judge of the behaviour of those whose conduct was not up to acceptable standards.

Anyway, the patrols in our area had become so numerous and confident, they were getting absolutely careless. This presented a good opportunity for a quick ambush. In spite of the lack of any overall objective or direction, it was still possible to mount a fierce attack in any of the local battalion areas. In view of this, our Vice O.C., tired of being hunted, wanted to explore the possibility of an ambush between Killarney and Barraduff. A few fellows got together and selected the location but it was necessary to get help and some cooperation from the Killarney battalion. The extent of this aid had to be determined before pushing this idea any further. Tom Lyne and I were detailed to go into that area and contact the men. We set out on this mission one fine morning in the middle of April. Near Kilcummin we sighted a few wild geese which we stalked but did not fire on for fear of attracting attention. On our first contact we heard bad news.

We hightailed it back to our own area next night with the news of a large scale roundup. The word was passed around and we didn't have long to wait. The last week in April saw large additions of troops in each post. So it was back to the pick and shovel again, making new dugouts. The old ones were considered safe but not big enough for a long stay. Besides, nobody among us could be sure if the enemy had already known their locations and could net us in one fell swoop. For the next few days we worked night and day. By now we knew the location of every piece of timber and corrugated iron in the battalion area. One farmer was surprised to find the roof of his cowhouse missing and another the ladder from his hayrick. But they said nothing as they guessed where it was being used. The timber from the Quagmire bridge came in handy. A couple of men spent one night burying what was left over, after we had used it to shore up an underground vault. It was hardship, but it paid off.

Four of us had an incomplete dugout when the troops came. By incomplete I mean it didn't have even a good air supply. It was dry, but was too warm, and was fairly well camouflaged. The search troops used the same general plan as the British did in 1921, but did not employ as many men or cover such a large area. It also differed from the former plan by their remaining in the area for a week instead of a day. They also backtracked over the area and criss-crossed over some places several times. So, while avoiding one patrol, it was possible to run into another. All our arms were dumped and we sweated it out in close proximity to the troops who were searching for us. Sometimes they were too close for comfort, the search being so intense that we dared not venture out in daylight. Our retreats were as little known to those we trusted as they were to others, as the slightest clue of our locations meant ultimate capture. The dugouts we had so carefully constructed earlier were our last retreat, and they proved adequate. Very few people knew their exact locations and we made contact

Left: John McSweeney, (The Bower) was jailed in Macroom Castle, escaped and went to New York. He returned later to The Bower. (Brother of Tom McSweeney 'Dundon' and Michael McSweeney who was shot and killed on the night of the Shrone 'gander'. *Right:* Tim Daly, Kilquane, (brother of Capt. Jimmy Daly), emigrated to the USA.

with the trusted few during the hours of darkness only, when we came out for a breath of fresh air.

In one such location, Tim Daly, Dan Hayes, Tom Lyne and I spent six days and a part of the nights in a small unfinished dugout, where the air was so foul that a candle lighted poorly except when it was placed near the entrance. We had to take turns near the door to prevent nasty headaches. When we emerged at night to get news and food, the air smelled so good with the fragrance of growing plants, we were slow to go back inside our hideaway, spending many hours drinking in the cool, fresh air in great yawns and sighs while we listened to the calls of the corncrake and the snipe. It was possible to tell the location of enemy patrols by studying the sounds of night, but sometimes they were in so many locations at once, that it only confused us. It was like playing a game of 'hide and seek'.

On May Day the district was the centre of activity, as many pilgrims came to the 'City' to pray at the site of the old ruins. That evening, Tom Lyne and I left the dugout before it was quite dark to get news and food at a nearby house. We had seen three separate patrols a little earlier, but they seemed to be moving away from us. We stayed only a few minutes. As we left, the owner of the place was out in the yard making strange sounds and motions that needed no explanation. A company of troops was only a few hundred yards away and heading for the house rather briskly. Feeling that we had been seen entering, we proceeded to put as much distance as possible between us and the house. Lyne had a cake of bread and I carried a jug of milk — items that could easily point to our occupation and status. We didn't want to get the owners of the house involved either, so we ran along a fence which gave some cover. Lyne dropped the cake and I kicked it ahead and he picked it up on the fly. We dared not return to the dugout, so we hid the supplies and then hid ourselves in a ditch. Fortunately, we were not seen and the troops, on reaching a road, chose to travel in a direction that led them away from us.

For a few more days we sweated it out and managed to evade capture. The troops moved away and the reports started coming from all parts of the battalion area. Our Quartermaster, Denny Reen, and his brother Jerry, were captured by a body of troops from the midlands under the command of Col. Prout. In this way they were lucky at least for a while, as the name of Reen was not very popular among the local garrisons. As far as I recollect, these were the only active men taken. Jerry Kennedy had a few close shaves but was lucky enough to evade the net. A few days later the news of the ceasefire arrived — it began on 3/4 May 1923. The press carried the text of the order from De Valera through the General H.Q., 'to hide or destroy all arms and elude capture as well as we might.' Our Captain, Jimmy Daly, assembled our company, or what was left of it, and told us the order was official.

We assembled for the last time near Deecarrig Cross under the shadow of the Tokenfire mountain and disbanded with little thought that we would never be all together again. Of course, we often met later on, but all members were never present at any one time. Thus ended, officially, the resistance against implementation of the Treaty which formed the 'Irish Free State.' The fighting was over and the Irish Civil War became history. There were many loose ends and much work to be done before it became acceptable, if it ever did! Many fine men had been killed, much property had been destroyed, but worst of all, the people had been divided right down the middle. The North was lost, while the South fought between themselves. Everybody was disappointed, but at least there was a sort of uneasy peace. The IRA were lauded by De Valera, naming them 'Soldiers of Freedom', and 'Legion of the Rearguard.'

8
The Difficult Post-Ceasefire Days (1923-24)

The strain of the previous week was dismissed lightly in the next few days as we roamed about in the open without arms, hoping for some development or a favourable truce. Our optimism was dispelled by the news that our truce amounted to almost unconditional surrender. We were still being hunted down and, after a few weeks rest, the Free State troops did just that. Our activity consisted of helping the farmers do some work on their farms and it felt good to buckle down to something different. However, our whereabouts soon reached the ears of the troops and they made some early raids to capture us. As we were not carrying arms the Free State forces felt quite confident and did some leisurely searching by being concealed on location before dawn, watching the movements of all the people in the locality during the forenoon. On one of these raids, John McSweeney was nabbed in a house near the base of the Paps mountain. Spurred on by success, they repeated the tactic a few weeks later. Dan Hayes had left our dugout and came right back after a brush with a searching party. He crawled over it, telling us not to come out. By this time, the place had been fitted with a ventilator like a periscope sticking up in the middle of a furze bush. They practically walked over us, but we had become masters of the art of camouflage and evaded detection.

After one of these raids, Tim Daly and I played a very dirty trick on our fellow refugees, Dan Hayes and Tom

McSweeney. About midnight, after the others had retired ahead of us, we walked over the dugout repeatedly, simulating a large number of troops by changing our gait and conversation. We knew from experience that we could be heard, but not distinctly, so we created the impression of a search party which had been led to the place by an informer. After finding the opening, we called out and gave them a chance to surrender, which they decided to do. When we spoke of bombing the place in assumed accents, we could hear them crawling back through a small tunnel. We shouted the names of well known Free State officers to make the plot more realistic and almost exploded at the effect of our successful 'joke'. When Tom McSweeney came out first and gave a wrong name, we burst out laughing and couldn't carry the joke any further. But we never forgave ourselves for that piece of blackguarding, as it could have had serious consequences. I got quite a start, too, one night while making a home visit. Walking silently on the grass by the side of the road near Doherty's fort, there was a sudden scuffle at a gap in the fence, but it was only a fox with a duck on his back. He suddenly reversed direction when he almost ran into me. We had become cunning and foxlike too!

The Free State army and engineers began the task of rebuilding the roads and railways rather leisurely. Our chief problem was to keep out of sight, so Pat T. O'Sullivan and I developed a healthy habit of trout fishing. We even caught an occasional fish. Most of the members of our column whiled away their time in similar fashion, or helping farmers where they stayed. Barraduff village was evacuated, and when the railway was repaired, the troops celebrated the occasion with an awful midnight barrage. I had come home this night and felt too tired to return to the hills, so I filled a sack with hay and used it for a bed in the middle of a corn field.

Unfortunately, the field faced a stretch of the railway about a quarter of a mile long and about the same distance away. I was caught in the middle of this barrage from an armoured train whose occupants kept up a steady fire from all kinds of arms as they travelled between Headford and Rathmore. When I awoke and couldn't figure out what was going on, I soon realised the danger as the lead whined through the oats. It was poor protection, indeed, and I sought refuge in a hurried flight to a safer location in another field. Seldom had I ever been in such a thick field of fire and my escape was next to miraculous. The aimless waste of ammunition was tremendously stupid.

I decided to go and see my pal Jack Horan, but it took me several days to find him where he was hiding out. After a long walk and several reminders of secrecy, I was allowed to go to his hideaway. He was difficult to locate, alright. He had been in this refuge since the big roundup in April and was completely recovered. I stayed with him for a day and exchanged the latest news, leaving there the next night. We discussed our future, if we had any, and learned some fellows were making plans to leave the country. A few lucky ones had already left. Our 'new-found leisure' was proving to be as exasperating as ever and nobody had any better suggestion than farmwork or fishing. More than 11,000 of our men were in prison camps and, while an odd one was being released, the Free State troops were constantly capturing additional unwary ones. We spent some time visiting these discharged prisoners to get news of our former comrades.

During the summer something was added to our curiosity when the first members of the Civic Guard took up duty in the nearby villages. Naturally, we got our first look at the new police force through binoculars, but were not very impressed.

They didn't seem to bother much with anything other than getting acquainted with the young ladies of the area, who seemed to admire them very well. A circus came to Barraduff village one night and Pat T. O'Sullivan and I decided to attend. It was the first time we entered the village since we were almost captured at Mass in November. We had been very close to the village many times, even when it was occupied — much closer than the garrison suspected. In the interim, we had studied every inch of it through binoculars, but were eager to stroll through it again, and we felt sure our presence in the crowd would not be noticed. It was a strange feeling to walk again on ground that had been forbidden to us for so long, except through the sights of a rifle, or the lens of a field glass. We moved through the crowd in semi-darkness, accompanied by a few young scouts, but we dared not enter the circus tent.

After we had enjoyed the treat for half an hour, a cycling patrol entered the village and, as we both carried revolvers, we slipped into the shadows. Entering the field where the big tent was erected we became separated, and I thought Pat had entered the tent, so I looked through a hole in the canvas. Near me were some vacant seats, so I sneaked under the canvas and occupied one. When the lights came on between the acts, I was surprised to find I was sitting among a dozen soldiers who had come in to see the show. One of them complimented me on my sly entry and asked for a match for which he exchanged a cigarette. We enjoyed the show together and they returned to Killarney while we returned home.

It was now the month of July and there was little or no searching in our area. The IRA men seemed to have faded away and we met only a few at a time. I paid another visit to Jack Horan, this time on my own, under cover of darkness. He was asleep and when I awakened him, we talked all night. The next day was hot and we awoke from the heat of the sun under a corrugated iron roof. After lunch we dressed in women's clothes and worked in a field gathering hay near a road where a few soldiers passed by. During the afternoon, a neighbouring farmer came into the field to borrow a part for a mowing machine from our host. He casually saluted us 'womenfolk', but on second glance when he recognised us he was flabbergasted. After my pal's admonition, I doubt if he ever revealed the secret.

The next step to consolidate the Free State was to hold a general election. It had never received a mandate from the electorate and had been operating under a provisional government. The opposition had little or no voice in the decisions; besides, a great part of it was composed of IRA officers, consequently being outlawed. As such a small majority had accepted the Treaty in principle, a slim hope still existed that it might be rejected in a general election. It was entirely possible and could change the whole complexion of the government. The majority party became known as Cumann na nGaedheal and its leaders were W.T. Cosgrave and Kevin O'Higgins, since Arthur Griffith had died and Michael Collins had been killed. De Valera was leader of the minority Sinn Féin party which itself split with the formation of the breakaway Fianna Fáil party in 1926. Both sides engaged in the campaign rather spiritedly but some Sinn Féin candidates were arrested for 'contemptuous utterances or remarks hostile to the established government.' Even De Valera was arrested as he addressed a Sinn Féin election rally at Ennis, and the election could not be called 'free' by any ordinary application of the word.

However, we campaigned as vigorously as the authorities allowed us and we had to be careful to avoid arrest as we were still sought after. This put us at a great disadvantage, but we argued with people whose affiliations were doubtful. We didn't make rosy promises but our chief point was to criticise the conduct of the civil war and the abandonment of our once lofty principles which led to the division of the Irish nation. On one of these trips while distributing election literature and arguing with people, we stayed too late to return to our own area, so we stayed at a place which was considered reasonably safe. Dan Hayes and Pat T. O'Sullivan slept in one house and Tom Lyne and I slept in another, almost across the road in the hamlet of Lisbabe. (We had spent two previous days in a similar way, but not in so friendly a locale.)

Having retired late we slept late, and during breakfast we were startled to see six armed Free State soldiers pass in front of the window. Lyne looked at me and uttered one word, 'Staters'! He immediately ducked into another room as he was wearing army pants and leggings, and might have been recognised. I grabbed all our papers and gave them to an old grandmother who hid them in her clothing as she sat by the fire. The lady of the house, who had been milking the cows, came in and looked very pale and nervous. I addressed her as 'mother' and told her to give the soldiers a drink of milk when they asked for water. Being dressed in ordinary clothes minus the coat, I got up from breakfast and started to sharpen a scythe which the man of the house had prepared for his day's work.

The soldiers engaged in conversation as we joked about the difference between their rifles and mine, meaning the scythe. They inquired if we had seen any strangers about. I assured them we had not, and being satisfied, they thanked my 'mother' for the milk, mounted their bicycles and went on their way. They looked into some other houses but didn't enter the one where our other two companions were hiding. Again the loyalty of the people saved us from capture, but there was someone where we had spent the two previous days who was not so devoted to our cause, I am sure.

The general election was held in August and while our party made a good showing, it failed to elect enough members to turn the tide. All IRA men were prevented from voting, as the polling places were patrolled by soldiers and civic guards, eager to pick up any undesirable who might put in an appearance. As an antidote, all the Sinn Féin members decided to boycott the Dáil (parliament) and refused to take their seats. It was a phony display of democracy from people who had so long craved to exercise it. Cumann na nGaedheal had a majority in the absence of Sinn Féin and now that it had official sanction from the people, it settled down to the business of government.

As a noble gesture, it released a great many prisoners who could not be charged with anything more specific than being in sympathy with the Republican cause, or having a relative in the IRA. But all prominent prisoners were held in captivity and steps were being taken to charge certain individuals with the responsibility for specific deeds and try them in civil courts. In other words, the Free State was intending to set up their own standards after the fighting was over, even though there was no law in their books under which to prosecute. Of course, there were no steps taken to investigate the deaths of prisoners in Kerry at the hands of the Free State army. It looked like one-sided justice to me.

A large scale hunger strike was organised in the prison camps and a few escapes were contrived by various and difficult means. Con O'Leary of our battalion, who had been Director of Operations for 1st Southern Division, was released instead of another man of the same name. The other man cooperated unselfishly in the plot. Rather gallant, I'd say, but somebody's face was red when the mistake was discovered. One individual I heard about, in a prison in Cork, practised running and jumping along a hall under the guise of exercise. When his training had reached a safe stage, he lowered himself from a window onto the top of a wall. He ran along the top of this wall, jumped a gate to gain access to the outer wall and jumped off to his freedom. A tunnel in a camp at Newbridge delivered a few hundred prisoners to open country, many of whom were recaptured. Pat Allman of Firies was prominent in this escape. John McSweeney, a member of our column, who had been caught in the big roundup, got away from Macroom Castle when he discovered a hole in the wall which members of the garrison used to sneak out for drinks in a nearby pub. He told another fellow about it and he also escaped.

The old trick of posing as IRA men was renewed in October, although everything had been very quiet since the election. There was no activity on our part outside of an occasional visit to the released prisoners. Tim Daly and I visited Tom Bowler and he related the account of his trip along the coast, which is described in an earlier chapter. It was no pleasure cruise. It had been quiet now for so long that we enjoyed our freedom even to the extent of attending house parties. We played an occasional game of handball. But no public events such as football matches or sports meetings were held. In Cork, an area noted for the game of bowling, the game was resumed. I bought some cloth to make a suit — and goodness knows, I needed it. After all, we were in circulation again and we tried to look respectable. It would be a welcome change from the 'ensemble' so typical of our situation.

One Sunday afternoon, about the middle of October, I went for a fitting of the suit. While cycling towards Rathmore, my old bike broke down, so I continued on foot. At the Bower,

The crossroads where Jeremiah (author) was arrested while on his way to the tailor for a fitting of his suit.

two men in trench coats approached on a side road from the north. They carried rifles with the muzzles pointing downward and unnoticeable from a distance. Presenting the appearance of typical IRA men, I thought of all sorts of things, such as some new activity or a couple of fellows getting desperate and doing something like a hold-up or robbing a bank. When we met, they saluted, asked for a match and sat on the fence to smoke. I was curious and continued the conversation about the weather and a few other casual remarks. They asked if I had seen any of the 'boys' around and my answer was 'No'. I became suspicious immediately and saw a group of about twenty in similar attire approaching on the side road. I started to move off but one of the two men asked me 'Were you at Mass today?' I answered, 'Yes, at Barraduff.' There was something familiar about this fellow and he asked me my name. As there were seven people of the same name in our townland, I gave the right name, feeling he would not be that familiar. Besides, when he asked which one

I was, I gave him the wrong information like the query about Mass. I underestimated him, and he pulled out a list of names from the back of his bandolier. My name was there all right, among a lot of others I knew well. I didn't know it then, but he told me later that he recognised me. In a few moments the others would join us and I made another attempt to move away, but he took his rifle off his shoulder and ordered me to stay. By this time the group had joined us. They were all strangers except one, he was Bill Sullivan! (The fiddle player I had been friendly with two years earlier.)

He greeted me and we shook hands, while the others inquired if he knew me. Bill answered, 'Yes, he is alright!' One large man tried to put a hand grenade into my pocket and when I objected, Bill told him to leave me alone. I was searched and given a few pokes of a rifle butt around the ribs. They asked if I knew where the 'City' was and told me to accompany them there — and I had no alternative. The 'City' being an ancient ruined city at the base of the Paps mountain, and having nothing to incriminate me, I felt confident but very unlucky for a change. We set out on the side road to the south towards the hills, strung out in broken formation. Before long, I heard someone call the big man 'Tiny', and it dawned on me whom he might be. Bill and I had a little conversation as we walked along together. He told me the big man was none other than Capt. 'Tiny' Lyons, the Free State Army captain who had a fearsome reputation for his dealings with prisoners, and added, 'Don't try any funny business. You are with a bad bunch.' The man in charge was Capt. Harper who had been stationed in Barraduff when it was occupied. We went all the way to the 'City'. They searched a few houses but caught nobody, so we returned by the same route. It being dark by now, they searched some more houses along the way.

When we reached the main road again, we turned west towards Barraduff. It was very dark and many people whom we met were looked over with flashlights and searched. When near my own home, I was walking at the end of the line with Bill. He said he was going up front and also remarked, 'You can take care of yourself around this territory.' I interpreted this as an invitation to escape, and had even given it some thought if the opportunity arose. Unfortunately, the group suddenly came to a halt and they caught Paddy Daly at the spot where I was thinking of making a break. Several people congregated on the road and one woman asked Capt. Harper to release me as the fighting was all over. But he was a bit too smart to be diverted by such soft talk and, knowing his own plans, he felt a few hostages were good insurance, so he took Paddy along too. We made a stop in the village of Barraduff.

Paddy and I were ordered to stand in the middle of the road, right on the cross. It was very familiar ground, and we were left alone while our captors made some social calls and had a few drinks at Murphy's public house. We spoke to each other about the chances of running away — and it looked good, in fact, too good — but we were cautious and looked around long and well. We knew every stone and bush in the neighbourhood, even at night, and Paddy drew my attention to something resembling shrubs near Mike O'Donoghue's house, which he said should not be there. On a longer, more piercing look, we decided it was two men lying down. Our suspicions proved correct, for after a while the two forms left there and went into the public house. Some of the others came out and told us to go into the pub, but Paddy was sent home after wishing me good luck. A cousin of mine in the pub failed to recognise me, although he had known me all my life. I had grown a moustache and it had the effect for which it was intended.

Our party left Barraduff, proceeded to Headford and made another stop at Kelleher's pub. On entering, all the patrons were asked their names and looked over. I was amazed at one who gave this answer, 'Tim Donoghue, sir!' I needed no introduction as he was a member of our column and a companion of mine during the previous eighteen months. His real name was Jerry Daly, a brother to Paddy, who had spent some years in Limerick and was not known to the group. He left the place as inconspicuously as possible without once glancing in my direction. I believe he didn't wish to keep me company on this occasion. Mrs. Kelleher introduced me formally to Capt. Harper and invited me into the living quarters of the establishment, where a meal was being prepared. He sat at a piano and sang and played well. He mentioned that he sang in the choir when stationed in Barraduff. I needed no elucidation on his activities there as we had been well acquainted with them, via the grapevine. Having eaten a hearty meal, we spent some time singing while the Captain played and, for the time being, we forgot our respective circumstances under the influence of wine and song.

It was now approaching midnight and the party decided to move on. I was afraid they might drink too much and give me some rough treatment, but they were too careful, as the next stage of their march was through Kennedy's home ground. I hoped they would not meet up with him for more than one good reason. Without mentioning the first, the second was the possibility of being fired upon, as I knew he was always armed. The party searched some houses in Knockanes and I saw two girls, both of whom had brothers on our side, being questioned. They didn't recognise me, nor did I pretend to notice them, but I knew some of their answers were intended to deceive. Now we had passed Brewsterfield and out of the danger zone, so Capt. Harper gave me his rifle to carry after removing the bolt and magazine, remarking that I should know how to carry one. I was not burdened by this extra load and was well aware of the useless nature of the weapon without its vital parts.

When we were within a few miles of Killarney, something happened that gave me the chills. Although we conversed freely and the fellows were not particularly rough with me, I didn't trust them and took everything they said with the proverbial 'grain of salt'. They were getting tired and so was I. The lead men sat down and waited until the others caught up and the conversation turned to a donkey which was grazing peacefully in the middle of a field. There was good light from a late moon. I was ordered to go into the field and catch the donkey, so I laid the rifle down but they told me to take it along. Knowing the makeup and reputation of my captors, my suspicions flared up and while there was little chance of escape, the alternative of being fired on sent the blood rushing to my temples. I said a few prayers while going on with the job of getting the animal to the road. All the time, several of the men had their rifles trained on me and I heard the familiar sound of putting a round in the breach. Two of the more fatigued men mounted the donkey and rode as far as the railway bridge in the town and abandoned him. I was taken to the Great Southern Hotel and put in a room near the guardroom. I slept very well, too; I was very tired.

In the morning I was awakened early and given breakfast. I was left alone in the guardroom, except during mealtime and an occasional visit from the guard. Some were friendly, some were abusive and all looked suspiciously at me. My mother and some others visited me and seemed surprised to find me alright. I was, too. After two nights in the place, I was escorted to the office of the O.C., one Major Conroy. He questioned me and admonished me for a half hour and I didn't give him any argument. I assured him the fighting was all over since May 2nd. Then he gave me a jolt when he produced a long list of damage to public and private property, roads and railways destroyed and goods commandeered. I was afraid he might associate me with some of these activities, but apparently he was not too clear on my identity. He asked me very pointedly, 'Why did you take up arms against the Free State?' I said, 'We all took up arms for a free Ireland, not a partitioned Ireland.' He told me, rather proudly, that he had been in Seán McKeon's column but I didn't boast of any of my own exploits. He produced a printed form which he asked me to read and sign. It stated that I would not take up arms against the new government, so I signed it. He turned to a sergeant and told him to release me. I was glad to get out of the place and I went home. The hunger strike of the prisoners was already broken and I could see no purpose in staying in prison when everyone in there was trying to get out. I never saw Bill Sullivan again. It was a strange climax to a once great friendship.

We felt free now to go around as we pleased, but the bitterness that the fighting and the atrocities had produced was quite obvious. There was a lot of talk about emigration. Only for the war some would have emigrated long before. Those who had some means of travelling prepared to do so, and others who had no means of scraping up the fare quite openly envied those who had. Those who had farms, or would inherit them, got busy working on them. The future looked very bleak for some of our boys. Then there were a great many college fellows who had to go back and take up where they left off, two years before. Thousands of men were still in prison, not knowing how long they would be detained. Road and rail repairs were being considered but none, except a discharged Free State or British soldier, were being considered for employment.

A spectacular escape was made from the female prison in Cork. Its inmates were not those suggested by the name, but a collection of hardened IRA veterans who were singled out on specific charges and were to be dealt with later, at the convenience of the government. Among other charges, they had been caught boring a tunnel, had been on a hunger strike and were sent to this prison as being the safest place to hold them. John Reen and his brother Denny, who was our Battn. Q.M., were among those who escaped from there. A rope ladder was made to scale the outer wall and bedclothes were used to descend to the ground by night. The success of the break depended on its improbability and the men had feigned illness on the preceding night. After the prisoners had lowered themselves to the ground inside the wall, they had to huddle in the shadow of a wall in sight of a sentry. The position of the moon at a certain hour had to be estimated in order to conceal the movements of the men in the shadows. They went in batches of fourteen as that was the number that fitted in the shadow of the wall, the most wanted men being given preference in the order of the serious nature of their charges. All the men in the first batch were liable to the death penalty and cast lots for the order in line.

When number nine went over the wall some noise attracted the sentry and he made movements which caused the prisoner to baulk. After a few moments silence, the action was resumed, and three batches, amounting to forty-two men, escaped with a lapse of fifteen minutes between each batch. It was a frosty night in December and they had to travel on stockinged feet. Some of them were natives of Cork city and got clear of there before daylight, but others in the later batches were recaptured later in the day. It took two weeks for our men to reach home by easy stages. These escapes touched off another wave of searches but they never caught up with them again.

Our time during December and Christmas was spent visiting released and escaped prisoners. In some cases they were forced to emigrate at short notice and there were some sad and final farewells. But the most unfortunate of all were those who were still being hunted. These were particular fellows whom the authorities wished to get rid of, one way or another, or get even with them by conviction or prison terms. Of course, certain people would feel easier to have them out of the way for reasons of personal safety or revenge. This prejudice was pursued by constant raids on the victims' homes in an effort to eradicate the last vestige of resistance. Our Battalion O.C., Vice O.C. and Quartermaster were constantly hounded.

To go to the United States one needed a passport, and to go anywhere, men were subject to detection, so the wanted ones had to leave in disguise and stealth. They went to England, Canada and Australia. Like the 'Flight of the Earls', history was repeating itself. With the approach of spring in 1924, many trips were made to the railway stations to see the boys off. Many good parties and dances were held during the winter and early spring and it was a last fling for many. In some cases the farewells were for ever, as death and distance separated them from their families. I made one trip to Headford to see Tom Lyne and Pat T. O'Sullivan leave and that was enough for me.

During 'Shrovetime' our family attended a 'gander' party at Caherbarnagh for my cousin, Julia Moynihan. I met my favourite girlfriend there, Nan Casey. My mother complimented me and approved, remarking she had known Nan's father when they were both young. We rode together in the horse and trap to Mass in Rathmore after the party broke up in the early hours of the morning. We were accompanied to the party by my uncle Paddy, an ex-RIC man who had spent the past two years in England. He was looking around to buy a farm but could find nothing suitable right away. A local schoolteacher bought a new car and he needed someone to teach him to drive. Being referred to me, I went along with the idea. It was a change from farming and offered some relaxation when he decided to take a drive. He also needed a garage built near the school and I took on that job, too. A local mason helped me and we finished the job in a short time between trips to Killarney and other neighbouring towns.

Denny Reen, finding it impossible to reside at home, gave up the idea and decided to emigrate. He went to Canada like so many others, and later to New York. With a heavy heart, he said goodbye to his family one night and I accompanied him on foot, part of the way, to a distant railway station in Co. Cork. As we walked along across country, over routes which we had often travelled before, his remarks were distressing. He said, 'When I joined the Volunteers in 1913 I never thought I would have to steal away from home by night.' Yes, he had joined the movement in the beginning, had stuck it out to the end, and the end was bitter. The same evolution had overtaken many other IRA men whose heart and soul had been given to the cause of independence. These were no mere boys, but mature men who had led the life of dedicated patriots. They had planned and fought and suffered only to be reduced to the status of hunted criminals. Fate has a curious way of twisting men's lives. Francis O'Donoghue, our Battalion Adjutant, was released from prison and went to England. I never saw him during the fighting as he was captured early on, and I saw him no more. Our Battalion Officer-in-Command, Vice Officer-in-Command and all the company captains stuck it out in Ireland and were eventually allowed to live in peace.

9
Work, Play and Increasing Restlessness (1924-25)

Human nature took over the direction of our affairs from here on, as they became more personal and selfish. Their aspect was one of survival by other means, and the collective spirit was gradually fading away. Not that the patriotism of anybody had been lost, but the immediate aim seemed to be to survive by the sweat of our brows. Anybody who could find work took it, whether in Ireland or abroad. After all, we had been accustomed to plenty of it and now that the war was over, we could no longer expect to 'commandeer our daily bread'. Some of us were still in our early twenties, but a great many others were over thirty years old and wished to settle down and get married. The work of rebuilding the roads and railways was keeping pace with necessity and gave some relief to the unemployed.

I secured a job with Thomas Cooper in Killarney as a chauffeur and it pleased me well. As his business interests included cars for hire, and he held contracts with the railway and Cooke's Tours, my work took me to many parts of the country, as well as affording me an opportunity to learn something about automobiles. It was very interesting and I met many nice and friendly people in the course of my work. Some were local people, others were cattle dealers, school inspectors, lawyers, police, excursionists and a large variety of 'Yanks' who always advised me to go to the United States.

Dan Griffin sitting at the wheel of one of Thomas G. Cooper's taxis, Kerry Reg. No. IN 1072 — a 1923 Chevrolet 4-cyclinder Superior Series 'B' Touring car weighing 1,880 lbs. It sold for £130 in Ireland and $525 in the USA. It had 4 doors and leather upholstery. Fender-top parking lights were an accessory. The top half of the windscreen folded forward for better ventilation and airflow. Note the right-hand drive. This would be a very valuable car today in a restored condition.

For the next year I lived in Killarney and some very pleasant memories are associated with my stay there. One person whose company I enjoyed very much was a young fellow named Tadhg Sullivan, who was about five years my junior, yet witty and intelligent far beyond his years. He was the link between the town and the country, as his mother was from my townland and all his family were very friendly. I had first met him during the fighting when he visited his mother's people and had grown to like him. He introduced me to many young people in the town and the association was very pleasant. Being a member of the Pipers' Band, he took part in all parades and social events. His curiosity about machinery was unending, and with another fellow named Pat O'Malley, we solved mechanical problems, if only by unorthodox methods.

The town was getting its share of tourists again and sports events, football matches and dances were very exciting. There was always something happening, and on the few occasions when nothing important was taking place, we took long walks through Lord Kenmare's demesne, dreamy strolls on Ross Road, or lively walks along country roads. Occasional dances were held in the Gaelic League Hall on High Street, in the Town Hall on Main Street, and John McCormack gave a concert in the East Avenue Hall. This latter establishment was owned by the Great Southern Railway Company. All the big social events were held here, such as the Commercial Club dance, Golf Club Dance and the Fancy Dress Ball. On Thursday and Sunday nights it served as a cinema. The floor was of boxwood and kept covered except during dances. The patrons were obliged to wear dancing slippers to prevent its surface becoming marred by grit. Of course, most of the affairs held there were a little over my head, but Tadhg and I managed to attend a few wonderful events. There were few tourists during World War I, and owing to the British military occupying all the Railway hotels (including the Great Southern Hotel) from 1914 to 1922, and the Free State forces occupying the same buildings from 1922 to 1924, the town had suffered immensely from the lack of tourist trade. So after a ten year lull since 1914, the return of the tourist trade was a real resurrection.

At the Gaelic League Hall, one could dance on a pine floor one night a week, or listen to the Pipers' Band rehearsing. The Town Hall had a good floor and dances were held there only in the winter. It was there I heard, for the first and only time, the ivy leaf being played. A fellow named Clifford played the accordion very well. He was an ex-Coast Guard, who had been stationed with Peter Wyper, the great Welsh player, and Clifford had acquired some of his talent. When a waltz was played, another fellow whose name I can't recall, accompanied him on the ivy leaf. It sounded like a violin in a high key and was very pleasing to the ear. I have never met another who could play this simple device, but I have been told there were many others.

On summer evenings someone brought along a set of bagpipes, their shrill music fading away into the hills and woods surrounding the lakes. Then there was the Regatta, an event of much importance. The town was surrounded by half a dozen wealthy families, occupying large estates and each sponsored a crew, composed mostly of their employees. They vied for supremacy as keenly as they could and their equipment was imported, modern and expensive. Two other crews in the town were sponsored by the Commercial Club and the Workman's Club. The Regatta was an annual affair, held in August, and attracted crews from other parts to spice the competition. It was there I first heard of the Casey family of Sneem, the renowned oarsmen. Another high point of the day was a tug-of-war held on Innisfallen Island, which sometimes decided the championship of Munster.

Of course there were plenty of nice girls to attract our attention, and they were not lazy to walk or dance. I met a very pretty one named Lily Brady when she visited the house where I lived on College Street, about a week after I started to work. We were pretty good friends until I left there a year later. She had a talent for dancing and once, when I took her to a big dance in the East Avenue Hall, I ran into unexpected competition from other swains who craved to dance with her. Somebody described a dance to me, that was held in this same hall on the occasion of the evacuation of the British forces, as being almost sacrilegious. The hotel became the headquarters of the Kerry No.2 Brigade and the ballroom was used for the revelry. A large crowd of robust IRA men spent a whole night celebrating by dancing in heavy military boots having hob nails and tips. Of course, the floor was ruined and had to be repaired and refinished.

Left: Dan Griffin, Kilcummin. *Right:* Jeremiah Murphy, Kilquane (author). Taken in Killarney studio 1924 when both were driving taxis for Thomas G. Cooper.

Then there was Sheila Flahive who worked in a bookstore on Henn Street (now called Plunkett Street) and she was also a good dancing partner. Another girl whom Tadhg knew was Baby Willis. She was a tall blonde young girl who sold us tickets for a dance at the East Avenue Hall. It was a great occasion and Desmond Dingle's Band from Dublin supplied the music. One member of that band was a redhead who played the violin and, when the dance warmed up, she strapped on an accordion and waltzed around among the dancers. She was most attractive in that particular role. While paying for the tickets, I inadvertently gave Baby Willis the wrong amount and, though I had no intention of deceiving her, she returned later and informed me of the mistake. Tadhg laughed himself sick at the bad impression I had made and chided me for being a country boy. Naturally, I was embarrassed, but I can almost hear him laughing still.

A cousin of mine was the housekeeper for Mr. Maurice McCarthy on New Street. He was a member of the McCarthy family of Headford and a descendant of Daniel O'Connell, whom he resembled very much in features and was a noted lawyer. Among others who kept his place in order was a pretty maid from Kilgarvan named Nellie Gleeson, fresh from the Roughty valley, and pretty as the heather on her native hills. Tadhg had a few nice sisters, too, but they were interested in somebody else. Then there was the gang of boys who assembled at Sullivan's house in the winter evenings to swap yarns. Mrs. Sullivan was a genial host and had a funny way of telling stories. In that house there was never a dull moment and the gaiety would be difficult to equal. Besides Jack Culloty, Dan Griffin and Paddy Sullivan, with whom I worked, there were fellows named Mossy Shea, Jackie Hogan, Denny Sullivan, Timmy O'Connor and Dee O'Connor, all keen to keep a fellow on the move. When there was nothing better to do, we went for long walks out the country roads around Muckross and Ross Castle. In those days there was no regular sportsfield in the town, so all athletic events were held in the old cricket field near Flesk Bridge. Cork and Kerry played a

One of Thomas G. Cooper's taxis from the 1920's. A 6-seater Crossley Hard-top with 4 doors and disc wheels. Note the faded white-wall tyres.Taxi-driver is Jack Culloty.

football match, and a good sports fixture was also held there during the autumn, among keen competitors. I saw Jack Flynn of Farranfore, John Shanahan from Castleisland and J.J. Quill of Ballyvourney throwing the weights on that occasion. They were giants of men.

Dick Fitzgerald of Kerry football fame organised a football tournament among the streets of the town and it was a decided success. I played a few games with College Street and my opponent was a Civic Guard named Carville who was a good soccer player. Killarney had a lot of football talent in those days. Besides some past All-Ireland stars like Denis Doyle and Paddy Dillon, there was Con Brosnan, an army captain; Con Healy, an attorney; and Paul Russell, an 'up-and-coming' college player; Dinso Hurley and Neilus McCarthy. College Street won the tournament and the cup was filled with large contributions of drinks by the pub owners. It was emptied by the team and their admirers.

Thomas Cooper, my employer, was doing a good business that summer and he sold some new cars. I had the job of teaching some of the new owners to drive and it was a pleasant occupation. During one such sojourn in Rathmore, I had an opportunity of renewing my acquaintance with Nan Casey and we spent a few delightful evenings at my cousins, the Cremins of Inches. One evening an English engineer arrived in Killarney by train after going past his transfer point at Headford. He was bound for Kenmare to inspect some machinery and, in his half-sober state, he was in no condition to inspect anything. He hired a car to take him to Kenmare and he didn't mind when I took Dan Griffin, Lily Brady and Margaret O'Leary along to keep me company on the return journey. In fact he slept all the way, was quite generous with a tip, so I treated my friends on the return trip. On the way home we struck a deer on the Muckross road.

One night on another trip to Kenmare, I had four large Civic Guards in an Essex car. The clutch slipped as we were going up a hill around Moll's Gap so we were forced to push. After coasting to Kenmare, Supt. Ryan, Sgt. O'Donnell and a third guard went on in another car leaving the remaining guard with me to take care of the clutch. While awaiting their return, we overhauled the defective parts in Jimmy the Master's garage and drove back to Killarney before daybreak, quite pleased with our accomplishment. Supt. Ryan bought a car later and I accompanied him until he was able to drive by himself. One day, while returning from Kenmare Court, we stopped for petrol at Foley's on the Muckross Road. We were accompanied by Tim Shea, the solicitor, who sat in the back seat. The Supt. was driving and before I could do anything to prevent it, he drove the car up on the footpath, shearing off a light pole and dumping the lamp in the solicitor's lap. There was very little damage to the car except for a hole in the roof where the lamp came through.

The author, Jeremiah Murphy, pumping the tyre of the 1923 Chevrolet with a foot pump. Beside him a colleague holds a wheel brace.

On the last Sunday in July, a few of my aforementioned pals hired a car from my boss, and we took some girls along to Cullen in County Cork for Lateran Day. This was the feast of Saint Lateran and it is celebrated by praying the usual 'rounds', which is actually praying at certain places around where the saint lived. There is a holy well and other places of prayer in Cullen, just as in Ballyvourney, and the people take home some water to sprinkle on any unhealthy thing, whether crops, cattle or people. It is believed that St. Lateran was a sister to St. Abbey of Ballyvourney and the other saint who lived at the 'City' near the Paps mountain. I can't prove it, as research never took me that far back. The usual congregation of 'tinkers' (hawkers and itinerants) thronged the place of pilgrimage. It rained most of the day but we had a good time anyway. We met Free 'the Kid' O'Donoghue, who was a great IRA man and was related to some of our party.

Several trips were made here and there, as monotonous as going to the neighbourhood grocery store. I prefer to remember the pleasant ones, but there were some sad ones, too. There was the night I drove into a flooded road near Castleisland and spent several hours drying out the magneto and carburettor in a farmhouse, after removing them when the car stalled in water up to my knees. Petrol stations and repair shops were not very numerous in those days and when you took a car you were expected to bring it back 'alive' i.e. in working order. My party waited patiently until I got the car going again after the water receded.

My work kept me on irregular hours and I got by with little sleep on many occasions. One morning after spending the night at a great party in Brosna, with two Civic Guards from Killarney who had hired a car for the occasion, we were hurrying back to catch the excursion train to Dublin. It was the day of the football final, Kerry vs. Dublin, and we couldn't afford to miss that train. I drove too fast over one of those small bridges, causing the car to bump and my two passengers got a couple of 'shiners' when they hit their noses against the wooden supports of the car's canvas top. I never had a collision or a bad accident, though some of the roads were narrow, steep and crooked. One night while travelling along the Upper Lake, a large stag with a beautiful rack of antlers jumped clear over the bonnet of the car when I surprised him around a bend. Another night, I counted twenty-four large deer in a herd which forced me to stop as they crossed the road, blinded by the headlights.

While returning from Limerick City, where I had taken some tourists the day before Puck Fair, I happened on a steep, little-used road, north of Castleisland. Before I realised it was the wrong road, the car was gaining speed and my brakes were poor. I failed to stop, so I was obliged to stick with it at a rate of speed entirely too high for the pot holes, puddles and cowdung on the road. It didn't help to hear a young girl shout as she read my face when I went by, "God, he'll be killed!" I emerged on another road after crossing a small stream and making a sharp right turn. The only damage to the car was the straps which held down the open top were broken and the back seat was thrown out. This should give some idea of the rough condition of the road. I was fairly well shaken but I pulled myself together and lay on my back for a few minutes to recover, after which I drove to town and drank two glasses of whiskey to regain my composure. It would never do to miss Puck Fair and I drove a party there later in the afternoon after getting the brakes fixed.

There is only one Puck Fair and it is an occasion of the wildest revelry — no sleep, lots of music and dance, much drinking and a swarm of tinkers alternately cursing and praying. It lasts three days and a large male goat is crowned 'King'. The local lads range through the Kerry hills to find the finest specimen and enthrone him on a platform supported on four high poles in the middle of the town square. It is thought to commemorate a legend which exists around that part of the country regarding the escape of a number of people who were attending Mass in the hills, during the persecution of Catholics under the Penal laws. An alarmed puck goat alerted the worshippers of the approach of some English troops and the event is celebrated ever since, on August 11th. The gentleman goat is gaily decorated and crowned before being hoisted to his lofty throne. As I gazed up from below at his majesty, I felt the sponsors of the affair did well to elevate his abode during the three-day reign as his body odour was a little less offensive at that distance. Apart from the festivities, a very considerable amount of business is transacted in the sale of cattle, horses and livestock. The tinkers could be a great deal more offensive than the Puck, being far more noisy and turbulent. These unfortunate people of no fixed abode, and of little apparent means of livelihood, accost the visitors on all corners, begging and praying, or cursing those who refuse to succumb to their ardent pleas. They come from perhaps fifty miles around on 'gathering' day and wander away over the countryside after 'scattering' day.

One day I drove a party of Yanks, consisting of a man, his wife and daughter and his brother, and a priest, from Killarney to Cork. I had the same party a week previously on a trip to Limerick and they had asked for the same driver. The young lady and I engaged in conversation to the point where she insisted on sitting in the front seat most of the time. The priest remarked that she was monopolising the driver to the detriment of the rest of the party and we all had a big laugh, as I blushed very conspicuously. After passing through the tunnel between Kenmare and Glengarriff, the broad vista of Bantry Bay came into view and a pretty sight it was. The priest asked me to stop and, after they had feasted their eyes on the beautiful scenery, we had a fine lunch from one of those baskets they supply in the Irish hotels. It was laid out on the top of a flat rock above the Hairpin Bend and left little to be desired. When we had finished, the man stood on top of the rock and sighed, 'Bantry Bay, famed in song and story.' He turned to me and asked, 'Do you know that song, *Bantry Bay*?' and I answered, 'Yes'. Whereupon the priest interposed, saying he was sure I could sing it as he had heard me humming while driving along.

I realised the man was sentimental and appreciated one of Malley's great songs. He said his mother had told him about Bantry Bay when he was young, and that he was the son of Irish emigrants. They had settled in Kansas and owned a large ranch, but he had enough respect for his mother's country to know the history of the beautiful bay he was looking on for the first, and perhaps the last, time. Anyhow, I sang the song after a little coaxing, in the best tenor voice and with as much feeling as I could muster. The party listened attentively to my effort and, at the conclusion, the man grabbed my hand, saying in an emotional tone, 'I had hoped to see it and now I do, thank God, under such pleasant circumstances.' It was, indeed, an unusual sight to see me perched on top of a rock singing an Irish song for a party of Kansans at high noon, but I cannot remember even one car passing by to mar the delicacy of the occasion. We proceeded to Cork city along by the river Lee. I told them some stories about the recent fighting as we passed the scene of Tom Barry's escapades. The party was most generous and the man gave me an extra pound for singing the song. This is the only time, as far as I recall, that anybody paid to hear me sing. As usual, he reminded me to look him up if I ever decided to go to the United States.

One night the Civic Guards hired a car to make a trip to Killorglin on what seemed to be a routine inspection. As we left Killorglin on the return journey, another man, in civilian attire, accompanied the Superintendent, a sergeant and a guard, who were my original passengers. I reckoned the stranger was an official of the Guards as there was a noticeable absence of the usual light conversation. On arriving at Killarney, I was informed to be ready to make another trip to Castleisland with the same party, so I waited. The Superintendent, the sergeant and the stranger, who sat beside me, were all in civilian attire now and I noticed the stranger was carrying a pistol in a belt under his trench coat. I followed their directions by an unusual route to our destination, Castleisland. Before reaching there they ordered me to stop and turn off the lights. On alighting from the car I noticed they all carried pistols, so I wondered what strange mission they were involved in. They said they would be back in about an hour. Curiosity kept me awake for a while and by the sound of barking dogs I estimated they had visited several houses. When they returned, several hours later at dawn, I couldn't start the car as the battery had gone dead. We had to be towed back to Killarney by a truck and, after attending Mass, I went to bed. My boss, who thought I was in bed all night, awakened me about an hour later and sent me on another trip.

This was a comparatively short trip to Glengarriff, where a regatta was in progress and my fares were a group of young men, all bank clerks, whom I knew slightly. We stopped for lunch at the Eccles Hotel and were requested to leave after some unruly behaviour. They were about my age and took me along on all their adventures that afternoon. Later in the afternoon I met Danny Dwyer, from Muckross, who invited me for a ride out to Garnish Island in a motor boat. This place was a small paradise with beautiful lawns, strange shrubs and flowers and a gorgeous fish pond. Some baroque statues were located around the house and garden. We were reluctant to leave this little Eden. When I got back to the car I had to repair a flat tyre instead of having a sleep as I intended. On the way home, we stopped off in Kenmare long enough to discover a dance, so a few hours slipped by very fast to midnight. On returning to Killarney, we noticed a car in a ditch on the Muckross Road. When I had finished with my party, I started driving towards the garage. I was hailed by Charlie Foley of New Street and he asked me to drive some friends of his to Milltown. Their car had run off the road after hitting a deer. I said we had seen the car, but that it was my second night with little sleep, but he pleaded so hard I relented and drove the party to their home. I was so sleepy that I missed a road where it turned off to the town. The party was very generous and one lady insisted on giving me a glass of wine. This only made me more sleepy and I ran off the road on the return trip.

The car landed on its side after clearing a low sod fence onto a soft, grassy field. After getting it back on its wheels, the ground was too soft to drive on, so I curled up on a seat and slept soundly until dawn. My plight was noticed by a passing postman who telephoned my boss and Dan Griffin came to my aid, pulling me out with another car. I slept until late in the afternoon and my first concern was the trip with the Civic Guards. It seems they were searching for someone who was suspected of killing one of their members and an army officer some time previously.

At the risk of boring the reader, I feel compelled to mention a few more trips. Since this was the way of life I led, and being constantly on the move, hither and thither and yonder, the time passed quickly, yet each trip made was a new experience for me. One day it might be a group of cattle dealers who were a hard-headed, yet generous, lot of business men. Next day it could be a very serious school inspector and the next, it might be a few clerics. One day I had a middle-aged American couple who quarrelled all day about anything and everything. To make matters worse, the day rained and that did not help the situation.

Once I drove a party to a seaside resort. The man got drunk and the kids cried. On the way home, the car collided with a donkey. He was badly injured and I had to jack up the car to release him. During this operation one of the people got kicked by the donkey so we had to put him out of his suffering before proceeding on our journey. I mean the animal not the passenger!

During the Christmas and New Year holidays I made some trips home and enjoyed the respite from work, but there was a strange air of emptiness around the place. Although my family had remained intact, there seemed to be a lack of excitement and the whole neighbourhood was very quiet.

Gone were the familiar faces from the village and the list of those who had departed for other parts of the world was a long one. However, many letters had been received indicating that the exiles were doing pretty well and seemed to have no regrets. During one of these visits to home, I got the first, real idea of emigrating. Some letters contained references to dances and gatherings which smacked of the gaiety of the past and were very influential in nourishing the idea in my head. Very little of the new year had gone by when I applied for a visa to the United States.

An event which was observed by many of the young people in most of the rural districts around Killarney was the 'Biddy's Night'. It seems to have some connection with the feast of Saint Brigid, early in February, but my belief is that the participants couldn't care less as long as it included the usual dance. A collection of young people around Muckross decided to celebrate. They were led by Patie Lynch and Matt Leahy, whom I knew, so I was invited to take part. The procedure consisted of visiting the homes in the area while being masked and disguised, singing or playing a few numbers, or maybe dancing a few steps or part of a set and asking for a contribution. We were courteously received by some wealthy and dignified people who seemed to enjoy our capers. Patie Lynch was dressed as Santa Claus, another fellow in the silks of Lord Carnarvon's jockey, while I was clad in an RAF uniform. The resources from these antics were pooled and a big shindig was held at Alice O'Connor's house in Muckross. The proceeds were spent lavishly on an all-night affair of music and dance. It was a memorable night of mirth and happiness for the young people present.

There were many weddings during Shrove and the people were beginning to break away from the traditional horse-drawn vehicles for such ceremonies. Consequently, I drove a few parties attending weddings. They invariably lacked the excitement such a proceeding held in the past, as the banquet was held in a hotel, the number of guests was smaller, and the affair was of a more sophisticated nature. Only one wedding at Kilcummin produced enough entertainment to give any degree of satisfaction. My employer sent three cars to that wedding and had to come looking for us at 5 a.m. when we failed to return at a reasonable hour. It had all the trimmings — strawboys, intoxication, music and dancing, weeping and laughter.

In February 1925 I was called to Cobh for a passport visa. While in Cobh I made the acquaintance of Paddy Mahony, a retired RIC man living there. He was a native of Mounthorgan in Rathmore but had not made a return visit there in many years on account of the fighting. We sat up late and I had to bring him up to date on all the happenings of the past couple of years. Next day I met his wife and daughter as well as several IRA men who were there on the same passport business as myself. After returning to Killarney I didn't seem to be as interested in the place as before.

By the beginning of 1925 things had returned to normal. A great many fellows had found some kind of employment, but the stream of emigration continued to flow. Presently, a new horde of workers appeared. They were British and Irish ex-servicemen who gobbled up the jobs pretty fast. Some idea prevailed that they were the only ones entitled to public work on the roads and railways. There was a lot of resentment among the ex-IRA men. During these labour disputes a few noteworthy incidents occurred, which caused those responsible to examine the situation and distribute the employment on a more reasonable basis. North-west of Killarney in the Farranfore area, there was some trouble on the railway and after the local labour force issued a warning (which was ignored), a train was derailed. The engineer noted a red light on the tracks as he piloted a freight train towards Tralee before dawn. Before he could come to a stop, the engine and several cars had hurtled over the ties where the rails had been removed. Fortunately, the engine and a few cars got on the rails on the other side of the cut, but the following cars were hurled about in all directions. Several members of the Civic Guard visited the scene, under the command of Inspector Ryan whom I drove there from Killarney. It was an awful sight. Some freight cars were laying at crazy angles at the bottom of an embankment, others were catapulted into adjoining fields, but there was no loss of life. Many cars were burst open and their contents scattered about. These included farm machinery, seeds and fertilisers. At night time, seagulls which had gorged themselves with food, stayed after dark and roosted on top of the cars, an unusual sight, indeed.

On another occasion some weeks later, there was a dispute over railway work around Glenflesk. Those in charge of the work ignored similar warnings and followed up by importing a trainload of workmen the next day. As these alighted from the train in an unpopulated area, they were fired on from the hill at Curreal and scattered in confusion. It was rather obvious who was doing the protesting, but nobody was charged with the disturbances. After a compromise, and a more realistic attitude towards the distribution of work, both sides seemed appeased and the project was completed satisfactorily. In fact, working together seemed to dispel some of their differences and animosity began to wane. The Free State troops were withdrawn from the smaller posts and concentrated in the bigger installations. The Civic Guards, after a somewhat shaky start, took over the enforcement of law and order.

The tourist season was a few months away yet, but St. Patrick's Day brought a big influx of travellers to Killarney. One beggar I noticed was a blind man who played the dulcimer very well, as he accompanied his mother — a singer. My old pal, Tim Daly, visited me and we talked long and seriously about emigration. He had been stationed at the Brigade H.Q. in the town and was now in Kanturk, serving an apprenticeship as a motor mechanic with Bill Moylan. That night, as he started on his way home, I conveyed him about a mile outside the town. He intended to emigrate also but had to finish his apprenticeship first. I had the misfortune of betting on an 'also ran' in the Grand National which depleted my savings so that slowed me down too. This forced me to write to my cousin Mike Reen in the U.S. for money to pay my passage fare. We attended the funeral of Charlie Daly whose remains were brought back to his native parish from the North during the civil war. Jiles Cooper, a member of the 5th Battalion Flying Column, passed away also and was buried in Kilquane cemetery with full military honours. He was laid to rest in the Republican Plot beside Michael O'Sullivan and Michael McSweeney.

During the summer of 1924 I had driven the Killarney football team to Tralee in their quest for the county championship. The Tralee boys were far too good for them. This, and other associations already mentioned, gave me an opportunity of getting to know many of the Kerry football players, and in the autumn of that year I went to Dublin to see my first All-Ireland Final. It was a great game but the Kerry team lost. Now, as the same teams were to meet again at the same venue for the championship (played in April, 1925, due to upset schedules during the fighting), there was considerable interest in the affair and the team trained very hard to reverse the defeat of the previous year.

Republican plot in Kilquane Cemetery. Killed in action — Michael O'Sullivan and Michael McSweeney. Lieut. Jiles Cooper died later as a result of active service. Patrick McCarthy shot in 1921 by Black and Tan forces, was buried in Kilquane originally but later re-interred in the family plot, Killarney, during the Truce.

While waiting for a haircut one Saturday night in Wade's barber shop in New Street, Killarney, this match and the recent Grand National race were the chief topics of conversation. The discussion got so heated at one stage that the barber sliced one of the dimples from Dan Culloty's chin as he turned aside quickly to emphasise a point. The place was a great haunt of sports lovers and horse and dog lovers. It was in great contrast to another barber's shop in New Street where the proprietor sometimes asked for his fee before shaving you, 'in order to steady his hand.'

Sometime in early spring, I drove Mr. Lyne — who was farm steward for Lord Kenmare — to Mount Melleray in the County Waterford. His purpose was to purchase a prize boar and the price ran into a considerable figure. This was a remarkable specimen, one of the many prize animals the monks were noted for raising. In fact, the whole place was remarkable and unique. Its occupants were monks whose predecessors were banished from France during the Revolution and settled in this part of Ireland in the early 1800's. Mount Melleray is situated on a southern slope of one of the foothills of the Galtee Mountains. Apart from the Abbot, only one of the community was allowed to speak each day, and he was the doorman or receptionist, whose selection was rotated. On my first visit there in the summer of 1924, I was amazed at some of the practices and observances. On that occasion I had driven a party there, one of whom was trying to shake the old 'Demon Rum' by taking 'the cure'. On that memorable trip I collided with a policeman who was riding a bicycle near the bridge at Lismore. He was knocked over a wall and fell about twenty-five feet down into the Blackwater river. Our 'alcoholic patient' was the only one of our party who could swim. I gave him a little help to rescue the victim when he got him out in shallow water. We were able to dry our clothes at the monastery, but the victim was badly hurt and died a few days later. I was questioned about the unfortunate occurrence and deemed faultless. The accident was witnessed by another Guard who said the victim was intoxicated, was riding unsteadily around a bend on the wrong side of the road, giving me no chance to avoid the collision.

One of my many trips took me to Middleton when I drove Sir Maurice and Lady O'Connell to an agricultural, livestock and flower show. They had some entries and I enjoyed the trip, as well as the exhibits, as it was a beautiful, sunny day.

While walking around the town, I was pleasantly surprised to meet a girl who had been in my class in school many years before. She invited me to her uncle's house for tea and the conversation was pleasant but too brief. I had to return with my party and some dogs they had shown.

But the trip I enjoyed the most, and remember best, also started out with a dog. It is not a 'shaggy dog' story, either. Some people who lived near Killarney hired a car to drive to Cork city one wet Sunday afternoon. The party was a young man and his mother and they brought along a beautiful greyhound, probably to exhibit or take part in a coursing match. As I drove through Killarney, I was hailed by Dan Griffin, one of the men with whom I worked. Dan had the day off and he was just curious about the performance of the car, as we had done some work on it the night before. The lady suggested he come along for the ride and keep me company on the return trip, to which he agreed as he had nothing better to do. After arriving at the Imperial Hotel in Cork, the lady paid me, gave me a generous tip and invited Dan and me to dinner in the hotel. It was a bit over our heads, but we got through it without too much embarrassment and left there highly satisfied with the experience. As long as we were living high, I decided to drive fast to give the car a trial run out on the Western Road. When we hit 57 mph — all it could do — it was difficult to hold the road, as it was pockmarked with mine holes from the recent campaign. We decided that the car was performing well enough and I eased off as Dan didn't relish any more speed tests.

When we reached Macroom I took a road towards Millstreet. Before long we came to a river running right across the road and Dan realised we were on a different route from the one taken on the outward trip. An adjacent bridge had been demolished during the fighting and the only passage was to ford the river, which was in flood. My companion implored

Dan Griffin driving one of Cooper's open-top Touring taxis in 1923.

me to turn around but he had no idea of my incentive to cross the river, not yet anyway. I had crossed that stream during the fighting and later in a car, so with the aid of the headlights I judged it was not too deep to drive through. Removing my raincoat and having wrapped it around the carburettor and wires, I gave the car a good racing in second gear and crossed the river with only a few spits near the end. Dan decided I was mad and became furious when I refused to tell him where I was going.

On arriving at Millstreet, my pal was so confused that he failed to recognise the town, though he had been there several times. A few miles further west I disclosed to him that we were going to a dance at Rathduane Hall. This prospect soothed him somewhat, but he remarked, 'We won't know anybody there.' I said, 'Wait and see.' As we entered the hall I was greeted by several people and my eyes swept the crowd for a certain familiar face. A girl beside me interpreted my actions and informed me that Nan Casey was not at the dance. I enquired further about my girlfriend, pretending not to be too anxious, though it was doubtful if I could conceal my concern. On learning she was probably at home, I decided to call there, but got cold feet at the thought of how ridiculous this untimely visit might appear to her parents. Not that I would be an unwelcome guest, but the idea seemed to 'slow me down.' I sat in the car for a while, planning the approach, and decided to use my companion as a pawn in the game of love. In the first place, it had to be established if she was at home, and if not, the whole trip was wasted and no further plans were necessary. But if she was sitting idly around at home, it would be a pity to lose such an opportunity. I said so to Dan, but he was no help and thought the whole idea absurd.

I decided to pose as an ordinary business man whom Dan was driving to Killarney. Then we drained some of the water from the radiator of the car. He was to go to Casey's house, about two hundred yards off the main road, for a bucket of water. Having a description of the members of the family, he reluctantly approached the house. In fact, he was so hesitant, that I followed to make sure he didn't baulk and return with a phoney story. When he knocked, two girls came to the door and I can see him, to this day, trying to decide to whom he would deliver my message. He had only to say that I was up at the road, yet it took him some time to get the message across as he was a total stranger to the family.

Nan's father, Willie Casey, being a friendly man, was very willing to help a traveller in distress. He fetched a pail of water from a pump while the girls got a lantern to light the way. Somewhere about this point, Dan delivered the message, so I ran back to the car and sat in the back seat to await developments. While Casey helped Dan put the water in the car radiator, Nan slipped around to the back of the car and thrust her hand under the side curtain and in a familiar whisper, assured me she understood. When the car was running again, I asked in a strange voice if everything was alright and Dan answered, 'We are OK now, sir!' I chuckled at our performance as Willie Casey said 'I was just going to play cards at a house further along the road.' We were only too eager to oblige our unwary guest and dropped him at his destination, after receiving profuse thanks. We continued ahead and around the next bend, Dan turned the car around and we joined the girls to explain the unusual situation. We could not take advantage of their offer of tea under the circumstances and waited in the car instead, while they dressed for the dance. During the interval we laughed heartily at the success of the plan and Dan thought I was an awful fellow. But his romantic urge was less than mine and besides, it was a challenge for young love. After a merry time, we escorted our fair ladies home from the dance, quite satisfied with our activity for one wet Sunday evening, and we arrived back in Killarney in the small hours.

The All-Ireland Final was played in Croke Park in April and anybody who could scrape up the fare attended the classic. A large contingent boarded the train at Killarney and the chief cheerleader was Jerry O'Leary. He held a large umbrella, on the sectors of which were painted the years that Kerry had won the football championship, a large question mark being on one sector. The match was a great tussle of powerful, robust football. I believe no Kerryman sat down during the game and there was wild excitement during the closing stages as Kerry won.

On another trip to Mount Melleray I attended religious services in the evening. The choir and organ music was delightful and provided the proper atmosphere for celestial thought and reflection. Wandering through the monastery buildings, under the guidance of the receptionist, we saw extraordinary prize cattle, horses and other farm animals.

Some of the monks, returning from the fields with teams of Shires and Clydesdales, unharnessed their noble animals without a word or a glance in our direction. This seemed not unusual to us when we were shown their cemetery where each monk scooped out a little earth each day from his own grave. No doubt it is a great place and the same conclusion was reached by an English atheist and industrialist who visited the place. He heard of its hospitality and enjoyed it, getting no bill for his sojourn. He bequeathed a substantial sum to the community in his will. I don't know if this is true, but that is how someone related the story to me.

It was now only a month away from the time I was supposed to leave the scenes of my boyhood and emigrate to the United States. For once, the pattern days at the 'City' or Ballyvourney didn't seem very important anymore. My spare time was taken up in planning for my departure. I bought some suit length and got it tailored by Denis O'Donoghue on Henn Street (now Plunkett Street), Killarney, along the style fashionable in the United States. I also disposed of some army equipment which had been hidden since the ceasefire agreement. Otherwise, my daily work was routine, repairing cars and driving when necessary. People were beginning to say goodbye to me and as the time for my departure came closer, I had a strange desire to reverse my plans and stay at home. Only recently had I discovered that my father had some idea of leasing a farm and setting me up at cattle dealing. Many people gave me presents, among them a gold watch from my employer and co-workers which I prized very much and had for many years.

My grand uncle, John Houlihan, with his son Fr. Michael, arrived in Ireland for a vacation in May, from Haverhill, Massachusetts. They had visited about twenty five years

Left to right: Patrick J Murphy (author's uncle), Johnny Houlihan (author's granduncle from Stagmount, home from Haverhill, Massachusetts, USA), Hannah M Murphy (author's mother), Michael J Murphy (author's father). Photo taken by Father Michael Houlihan, son of Johnny Houlihan from USA.

previously, when the priest had graduated from high school. I made a trip to Muckross with Tadhg Sullivan one night, to say goodbye to its fine people, among whom I had spent many delightful hours. We stopped to buy cigarettes at a store near the post office and we were surprised to find Julianne Fitzgerald and Agnes Donoghue in the store. They were natives of Loo Bridge and I had been acquainted with them during the fighting. Mr. Fitzgerald had recently bought the premises but we had not heard about it. We spent some time chatting and drinking tea while the girls entertained us and I said the usual goodbye. An 'American Wake' (going away party) had been planned at my home and Patie Lynch and Matt Leahy were invited. It was now Saturday morning, my last day at work, and in the evening I said a sad farewell to the boys and girls who accompanied me to the railway station in Killarney. So after a few final arrangements for the following day — which was to be a very busy one — I slept for the last time in my own home as soundly as when I was a child.

I attended eleven o'clock Mass at Rathmore on Sunday, after a three mile cycle ride, after which I went to Caherbarnagh to say goodbye to my relatives there. On the return journey, stops were made at the Forge Cross and the Old Chapel for some more farewells. Father Houlihan took photos of the relatives and my cousin, Mary Reen, went with us to Kilquane. It was about sunset and some of the early guests were there already. In about an hour the party was going full swing, without a thought but reeling off one set after another. The dancing was interspersed by singing, to give uncle Paddy, Patie Lynch and Mike Carroll — who were doing the playing on the fiddles — a bit of a breather. Around midnight, John Houlihan, moved by some old favourite hornpipe, called for a round of step dancing. He was then seventy-three years old, but straight and loose as a man of forty, and he did justice to the occasion. He was joined by Matt Leahy, my mother and others. It was a moment I will always remember. We danced until dawn, in blissful disregard of the morrow.

But to part is the lot of everybody at some stage of life and daybreak brought some more sad farewells to the guests at the dance. Many of them lived in the locality and I had known them all my life. I walked as far as Barraduff village with the last of the guests and gazed on the empty street, the handball court, the shops and the school, all of which I knew so well. On returning to the house, somebody suggested we go to sleep but that was beyond my ability at a time like this. So Tadhg and I took a camera along to get some pictures of a few more old haunts and say a few more goodbyes. We found a rifle and a shotgun in an old dump, shot a crow and a rabbit

The Day before Jeremiah left – 23rd May 1925
Rear from left: Jeremiah Murphy (author), Mary Joe Reen (cousin — Old Chapel, Rathmore), Michael J Murphy (author's father), John M Houlihan (Haverhill, Massachusetts, USA, formerly of Stagmount); Patrick J Murphy (author's uncle — ex R.I.C. Head Constable who passed 'vetting test' of I.R.A. Intelligence); Jeremiah Reen (Old Chapel, Rathmore).
Front from left: Mrs Mary O'Donoghue, Kilquane (author's aunt); Mrs Elizabeth Reen with teapot (author's aunt); Mrs Hannah Moynihan Murphy (author's mother).

near Doocarrig and returned home around noon. The train was due at Headford at 3:00 p.m. and the next few hours were very depressing. My mother took me for a walk in one of the nearby fields and gave me some good advice as she had experienced my feelings many years before. I returned to the house and decided I felt like the central figure at an impending execution, so I braced myself for the final moments with a good draught of whiskey from a bottle I found lying around. Such a thing was very unusual for me but I imagined it helped. Next, I played a few favourite records and Fr. Michael took some photos of the family. It was to be the last time we were all together. I said goodbye to my brothers and sisters and I walked away from the house without looking back. Passing through a nearby field, I threw myself on the green sward and burst out crying. In a few seconds it was over. I had left home! I had left there many times before, but this time was vastly different. It could be for ever.

The die was cast now, and soon I walked to the railway station accompanied by my parents, my uncle Paddy, uncle Johnny Houlihan and Fr. Michael and my pal, Tadhg Sullivan. I said a final farewell to my father and mother as the train began to move and I never saw my father again, except in a home-made movie. As the train passed my house, I knew how all the other emigrants felt, those I had seen depart over the same route. At Rathmore my uncle Patie ran towards the train and it was the last time I saw him also. Four girls boarded the train to say goodbye, my cousins Mary Reen, Margaret and Liz Murphy, and alone, looking sad but loyal, my affectionate friend Nan Casey. I didn't expect her, yet I felt happy at her gesture. I was tempted to ask her to stay on the train as far as Millstreet or Mallow, but I appreciated her friendship too much to cause her any inconvenience or embarrassment. She said her wish would be to go with me and I was sorry afterwards that our last meeting was cut short so abruptly. It was only a small measure of our regret and interest in each other, but fate had taken the matter in hand and we were destined to end a pleasant romance which I have never forgotten.

As the train sped through Duhallow my composure returned and I had a few words with another passenger to get my mind off my misery. We reached Cork and took another train to Cobh. On arriving at Paddy Mahony's, he told me Dan Hayes was already there and we had booked passage on the same ship. This was a pleasant announcement, as nothing served to dispel my forebodings in the past better than some of Dan's dour remarks. I slept like a log that night, and the following day we had an appointment with the American

Consul. We learned that we could not travel together as the ship was full, so I had to wait for the next sailing. The following morning, Pat and Mrs. Mahony and Kathleen and I went down to the pier to see Dan off. Our host remarked, as he said goodbye to my pal, that he felt he would do well in America and added he would see him back in about ten years. Dan answered, 'When my foot leaves this pier, it has stood for the last time in Ireland!' He had served his country, backed up his ideals with action and was leaving it in the same frame of mind as many others like him — disappointed.

Next day I had a long chat with Kathleen and discovered she was very unhappy and wished to go to America. She looked forward to joining some relatives in Boston. The *S.S. President Harding* was due to sail two days later and I whiled away my time reading and chatting with the guests at Mahony's. After attending Mass in the cathedral in Cobh, we walked to the pier at the base of a steep hill. It was a beautiful, sunny morning, while a fresh breeze brought us the sound of the carillon from the church steeple, played by a Belgian organist. As we boarded the tender I could see the big liner steaming into the harbour. (The bay is shallow, so the liners cannot dock but are served by a tender from the pier.)

My mind dwelt for a moment on the endless line of Irish emigrants who had sailed from this very spot. But I also reflected on John Locke's poem, *The Exile's Return*, and I hoped that I, too, some day, would survive to return to my native land. These thoughts soon got lost in the bustle and excitement, and before long, we were on the tender. The Mahony couple, whom I knew only slightly, were my going-away party and I never saw them again. I watched others, unemotionally, in the final tearful farewells to their relatives. As the tender went out to meet the liner, a band played appropriate music and I gazed around the deck on the solemn crowd of Irish boys and girls. Few were acquainted, as most were lone individuals like me. There were a few brothers and sisters among the throng, plenty of beauty and brawn but very little brains — at least not the cultivated kind.

It bothered me quite a bit when I realised we were deserting our native land, just as thousands of our race had done before us. The Flight of the Earls, The Wild Geese and Sarsfield's Irish Brigade all came to mind and I couldn't help thinking how little Ireland had benefited from anyone who had ever left her shores. They may have been wealthy or famous in other climes, but how many of them ever returned to help the land of their birth? Not many! And here was the paradox — I was now joining the same movement, to which my knowledge of history made me opposed. My uncle Paddy had said to me once, 'If the tears of Irish emigrants could be collected in one spot, it would form a pool many feet wide and many feet deep, and would float a good sized ship.' I didn't need to be an economist to know that not all the people born in Ireland could be supported there without some emigration. I had also seen some very fine people return there, so I consoled myself with those thoughts.

In a short time we were alongside the big ship. It was the largest movable object I had ever seen, though I learned later that it did not exceed 15,000 tons. We were hustled aboard through an opening in its side and our passports and other belongings examined. It was noon. The odour of cooking was strong, but not appetising. A few sat down to lunch in the dining saloon, but the majority of the new people on board preferred to stay on deck. The day had grown cloudy and a fresh breeze whipped the bay into white caps as the liner sounded its whistle and got under way. As we walked around on deck, I was amazed at the different races and languages,

The author *(rear right)* with a group of fellow emigrants on board the *S.S. President Harding,* May 1925.

none of which I could understand, or even identify. It was a motley crowd of people from Egypt, Asia Minor, Greece, Italy, France, Germany and the Lowlands. There were a few from Britain, and as it was an American ship, we were able to find our way about. As the afternoon wore on, most of the Irish folks huddled in little groups as the wind increased in velocity. This, of course, produced the inevitable result of seasickness and the most susceptible went below when their misery became too great to endure. But some of us, mostly boys, stayed at the rail until we saw the last little spot of the coast of Ireland fade away from sight. It was starting to get dark and we were getting sick, too, as the ship began to roll.

Thus, I said adieu to my native land and started out on a journey that would change my whole life and make me an American. The happy state of a carefree existence could have gone along for quite a while, or at least until I got married, but the wanderlust of the Gael brought it to a close. If I could have foreseen the future I probably would never have emigrated, for I had to wait thirty years before I got a real opportunity to return to the scenes of my youth. This was entirely too long and another generation had grown up in place of the one I had known. Some of those who remained behind have to be commended for their loyalty, as they stuck by the ship while others sought the security of greener pastures. Nevertheless, I can never forget my native country and hope to visit it once more when opportunity calls, and stroll again amid the places I loved so well — *when youth was mine*.

Appendix I
Letter from America

The author landed "a free man" on Battery Pier, New York, at 10.30 a.m. on the morning of Friday 30th May 1925 — 6 days after setting sail from Ireland. The day after arriving in New York he wrote the following letter to his mother.

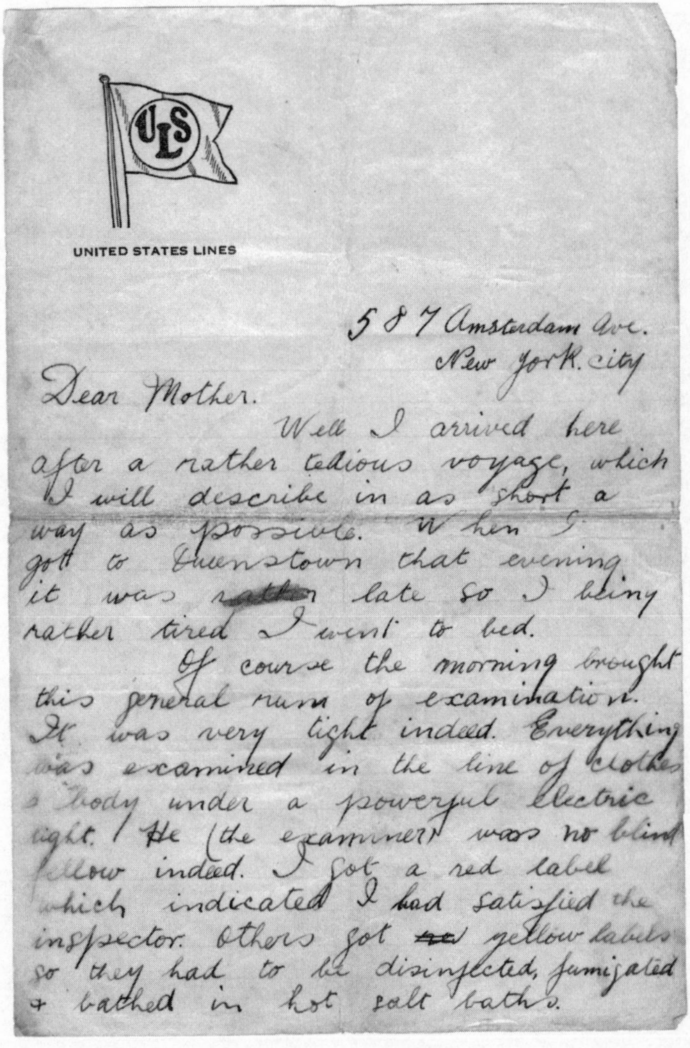

ULS

UNITED STATES LINES

587 Amsterdam Ave.
New York. city

Dear Mother.

Well I arrived here after a rather tedious voyage, which I will describe in as short a way as possible. When I got to Queenstown that evening it was ~~rather~~ late so I being rather tired I went to bed.

Of course the morning brought this general run of examination. It was very tight indeed. Everything was examined in the line of clothes & body under a powerful electric light. He (the examiner) was no blind fellow indeed. I got a red label which indicated I had satisfied the inspector. Others got ~~a~~ yellow labels so they had to be disinfected, fumigated + bathed in hot salt baths.

UNITED STATES LINES

I had a few nice days in Queenstown at Magorys. He has a nice house, wife & girl. They came to the wharf with me when I went on the tender. There were about 85 Irish emigrating none of whom I knew though of course I made many acquaintances. I will send you a few snaps of my associates on board. We sailed on the liner about 11.45 a.m. Of course we had a big feed about 12.30 but that was the feed that done us. We were hardly two hours on board when we all got sick. I was sick that evening & the following day. The weather continued rough & got worse on Sunday night so we were kept down till Tuesday afternoon when the sea got as smooth as an ice-pond.

UNITED STATES LINES

We sailed up New York harbour on Thursday evening. The band played up to the wharf. Indeed we had several bouts of music even Irish selections. It shows you how much the United States lines appreciate their passengers.

We were kept on the boat till Friday morning while the citizens were left off. We disembarked on the tender for Ellis Island. about 6 in the morning after dancing until 1.30 the night before in the 1st. class apartments. We were closely examined in Ellis Island in reading, writing heart. lungs. eyesight & general. I landed a free man on the Battery pier N. Y. about 10 30 a.m. & had no one to claim me. I remained there until 12.30 & then decided to make out the Ben's home. I visited a

Travellers Aid Society Hall + consulted a map etc. So I got instructions how to travel there.
you see there are offices all over the city for this business + they never charge for their services. I thought some one of the Reens would meet me as I wired when the boat landed. Nell went to the pier + missed me some way so I came by train (elevated) to 65th St. + 'twas only 3 minutes walk from there. I saw the no. on the door + walked in. Michl was in + he told me about Nell so we laughed until Nell came. All the lads were home for tea so we "blackened" till midnight.
They have a lovely home + very happy. Paddy Gough came to see me last night + I had a chat with Liz on the phone. This is an awful place far beyond my imagination. Fred has made suits for all the Reens so we are to see him to night. dont be expecting a letter every minute I'll have nothing to say I'm in some fierce form Jerh

587 Amsterdam Ave.
New York City

Dear Mother

Well I arrived here after a rather tedious voyage, which I will describe in as short a way as possible. When I got to Queenstown that evening it was late so I being rather tired I went to bed.

Of course the morning brought this general run of examination. It was very tight indeed. Everything was examined in the line of clothes & body under a powerful electric light. He (the examiner) was no blind fellow indeed. I got a red label which indicated I had satisfied the inspector. Others got yellow labels so they had to be disinfected, fumigated & bathed in hot salt baths.

I had a few nice days in Queenstown at Mahony's. He has a nice house, wife & girl. They came to the wharf with me when I went on the tender. There were about 85 Irish emigrating none of whom I knew though of course I made many acquaintances. I will send you a few snaps of my associates on board. We sailed on the liner about 11.45 a.m. Of course we had a big feed about 12.30 but that was the feed that done us. We were hardly two hours on board when we all got sick. I was sick that evening & the following day. The weather continued rough & got worse on Sunday night so we were kept down till Tuesday afternoon when the sea got as smooth as an ice-pond.

We sailed up New York harbour on Thursday evening. The band played up to the wharf. Indeed we had several bouts of music even Irish selections. It shows you how much the United States Lines appreciate their passengers.

We were kept on the boat till Friday morning while the citizens were left off. We disembarked on the tender for Ellis Island about 6 in the morning after dancing till 1.30 the night before in the 1st class apartments. We were closely examined in Ellis Island in reading, writing, heart, lungs, eyesight & general. I landed a free man on the Battery Pier N.Y. about 10.30 a.m. & had no one to claim me. I remained there until 12.30 & then decided to make out the Reen's home. I visited a Travellers And Society Hall & consulted a map etc. so I got instructions how to travel there.

You see there are offices all over the city for this business & they never charge for their services. I thought some one of the Reens would meet me as I wired when the boat landed. Nell went to the pier & missed me some way so I came by train (elevated) to 65th St. & 'twas only 3 minutes walk from there. I saw the no. on the door & walked in. Michael was in & he told me about Nell so we laughed until Nell came. All the lads were home for tea so we "blackened" till midnight.

They have a lovely home & very happy. Paddy Gough came to see me last night & I had a chat with Liz on the phone. This is an awful place far beyond my imagination. Fred has made suits for all the Reens so we are to see him tonight. Don't be expecting a letter every minute. I'll have nothing to say. I'm in some fierce form.

Jerh.

Appendix II
Page of Original Manuscript

1

"When Youth was Mine"

Chap 1 1900 to 1907

In the Spring of 1902 two women were talking about the outlook for the current year. One about 25 yrs old, the other about 60 were discussing farm business because that was their way of living. The younger woman, a returned yank had gone to the U.S. seven years before—and having saved enough money to pay the dowry or "fortune" as it was referred to in that part of the country—had been married to a small farmer the previous year. Owing to the peculiar marriage arrangements which were the custom and the law, the older people could retain the ownership of the "farm" by agreement for a year or two after the young couple got married. The purpose was to try to save some money to tide them over their declining years. Old age pensions and social security as we know them now, did not even exist in those days and people, especially the elders, were forced to make their own arrangements.

A Grandchild's Eulogy

Grandpa came from a time when a 'pusher' wasn't a drug dealer, but a piece of bread that you used to get your vegetables onto your fork. And woe to the man, woman or child who ate their pusher before dinner was through.

Grandpa left Ireland and all the people he loved, to come to America and start a new life and a family. But he never forgot all the people he loved, his friends and family from the Old Country. He talked about them all the time. Of course, some of us were better listeners than others.

Grandpa met our beautiful Grandma and married. He started a family and became King of the Castle but he always knew that the Queen Bee made all the rules. A more loyal and devoted wife couldn't be found. They went on to have five children and he was very proud of all of them; seeing them finish school, marry and start families of their own. For the last thirty years he was busy being a Grandfather and a Great-Grandfather, and we couldn't have asked for better. I can still remember on cold winter mornings in Amawalk, climbing into bed with Grandma and Grandpa to listen to his songs and stories. We all remember the 'Horsey Going to Cork.'

He was a very smart man. He taught all of us something; how to fish, how to garden, how to fix a motor, how to clean our plates. We all learned that easily. None of us wanted to spend any time in 'the chicken coop'.

I think my Grandpa had a very happy life. He loved God and his church, his family, his friends and a good joke.

He instilled in all of us a sense of our roots. Last year some of our family went to spend time with Michael and John, Grandpa's family, and see the Old Country. The people were just as wonderful and the country just as beautiful as Grandpa always told us. He forgot a lot of things, but he never forgot Ireland.

The last few years were difficult for my grandparents. Many of their friends helped them through this tough time. We would like to thank people like Bea and the Collella family. Words cannot express our family's gratitude.

We're all going to miss Grandpa. But he left precious memories with each of us which we will carry in our hearts always. As we go on, there will be someone up there that loves us, and his Irish eyes will be smiling.

Those we love are with the Lord.
And the Lord has promised to be with us.
If they are with Him and He is with us,
Then they cannot be far away.

Jeremiah Murphy February 17, 1902 to July 29, 1990

Maureen Doran
Granddaughter

The author
Jeremiah Murphy
(1902-1990)

Index of People
mentioned in the book

Name	Details	Chp.
Allman, Dan	IRA leader, killed in action at Headford station.	4
Allman, Fr.	brother of Dan Allman, later P.P. Glenflesk parish.	6
Allman, Pat	of Firies, died 1927.	8
Ashe, Thomas	died in Mountjoy prison	3
Bailey, Jim	fiddle & accordion player, killed in action at Headford station.	4
Barrett	friend of author, particular aptitude for firing mortar gun.	6
Barry, Tom	commandant of West Cork Brigade	4, 6
Batt	a dead man — a very tall man for whom a special coffin was needed.	2
Billy, Tom	blind fiddle player, surname Murphy, blind and incapacitated from youth.	2 ,3
Bishop, Capt.	suspected of ill-treating IRA prisoners	7
Bowler, Tom	from Shronedarragh, brother of Edward, active IRA man.	7,8
Bowsey	police sergeant, Headford.	1
Brady, Lily	author's friend	9
Brosnan, Con	Free State army captain, captain of Kerry football team.	9
Brosnan, Tadg	Castlegregory area, prominent IRA man	3
Brosnan, Tim	captured at Shrone 'gander' party.	6
Browne, Peter	from Scartaglin, fought at Headford.	4
Browne, Fr. John	parish priest, Glenflesk	1
Buckley, Jim	from Killorglin area, joined Civic Guards in 1922	6
Burns	two girls, one from Australia, connections with Glenflesk area	4
Cahill, Jerry	active IRA man	7
Carmody, Canon	P.P. Rathmore	6
Carmody, Mossy	from North Kerry, fought at Headford.	4
Carrol, Patsy	non-qualified, competent and practical "veterinarian"	2
Carroll, Mike		9
Carson, Sir Edward	Ulster Volunteers Leader	3
Carville, Mr	Civic Guard	9
Casement, Roger	executed 1916	3
Casey, Jerry	captured and killed at Beaufort	7
Casey, Nan	author's friend from Rathmore area, later lived in Cork.	8
Casey, Willie	father of Nan Casey, author's friend.	9
Cleaver	former dancing master, surname O'Donoghue, grandfather of the 'Kid'.	2
Clifford	accordion player	9

Coffey, Jim	from Beaufort, ex-British army	4
Coffey, Nick		6
Coffey, Tadhg	escaped from the Free Staters, native of Barleymount, emigrated to US.	7
Collins, Charlie	defected from IRA to join Free State side	6
Collins, Dr.	local medic	6
Collins, Michael	IRA leader	4
Connor, Johnny	Pub owner, Barraduff, returned 'Yank'.	2
Connoughton, Peter	Thompson machine gunner	6
Conroy, Major	O.C.- Free State army HQ, Great Southern Hotel, Killarney	8
Cooper, Jiles	fine physique, athlete and footballer, died 1924.	3,6,9
Cooper, Thomas G.	"Cars for Hire" in Killarney, later made film *The Dawn*, 1935	9
Cosby, Sir Francis	English massacre "host".	2
Courtney, Dan	Agricultural School attendee, later active IRA man.	6,9
Cremin Family	author's cousins from Rathduane	9
Cronin, Con		2
Cronin, Den Bat	Reaboy, Gneevegullia, went to USA, returned later.	4
Cronin, Jerh	teacher, excellent fisherman, native Irish-speaker.	1, 2
Cronin, Mrs.	teacher, maiden name Murphy, taught in Raheen later.	3
Crowley, Dave	instructor (engineering/munitions), brother to Fred, later became T.D.	5
Crowley, John	from Rathmore, held prisoner after Shrone party.	7
Culloty, Jack & Dan	brothers, worked in Cooper's Garage with author.	9
Cummins, Maj. Gen.	Commander of British troops, killed in Clonfanin ambush.	4
Daly, Charlie	shot by firing squad at Drombac Castle 14/3/'23 during civil war	7,9
Daly, Jerh.	from Shrone	6
Daly, Jerry	author's pal, active IRA man in Limerick and later in Kerry	3 ,6,8
Daly, Jimmy	tug-of-war team member, local IRA Officer	3,4,7
Daly, Paddy	friend of author, good scout.	8
Daly, Pat	killed while a prisoner	6
Daly, Tim	Kilquane, author's comrade, Lewis gunner, active IRA man	4,5,6,8
DeLacey, Bill	from Rathmore, emigrated to US	6,7
Dempsey, Col.	suspected of ill-treating IRA prisoners	7
Dennehy, Fr. Jerry	football player, missionary in China	3
Dennehy, Mick	active IRA man from early age to Ceasefire.	6,7
Derby, Lord	in charge of conscription scheme	3
Dillon, Paddy	from Killarney, All-Ireland football star	9
Dineen, Joe	intellectual, pub frequenter, brother of famous Dictionary compiler	2

Doherty, Matt	became a priest	2
Doherty, Mick	from Lisnagrave, tug-of-war team member, active IRA man.	3,6
Donnelly family	victims of the 'Moving Bog' disaster	2
Donoghue, Agnes	of Muckross, later emigrated to USA	9
Donoghue, Dan		2
Donoghue, Flor	Lewis gunner, member of Kerry football team, later emigrated to USA	6,7
Donoghue, Micky	Author's friend	3
Donoghue, Patrick	later Dr. Donoghue, practice in Killarney, very popular.	7
Dooner, Tom	groom on Hutch farm, Buttevant.	3
Doyle, Denis	All-Ireland football star	9
Duggan, Pat	held prisoner following Shrone party, later emigrated to USA.	7
Dundon	(see Tom McSweeney 'Dundon')	6
Dwyer, Denny	from Muckross	9
Fitzgerald, Dick	Kerry footballer, Fitzgerald Stadium, Killarney named after him.	9
Fitzgerald, Julianne	of Muckross, owner of Muckross P.O.	9
Fitzgerald, Mr.	of Muckross, owner of Muckross P.O.	9
Fitzgerald, Tom	of Derryraig	6
Flahive, Sheila	author's friend	9
Fleming, 'Small' Jack	band leader from Toormoor, IRA man.	3
Fleming, Jack	captured and killed by Free Staters	7
Flynn, Jack	of Farranfore	9
Foley, Charlie	of New Street	9
Foley, John	from Goulane, cousin of author's mother, killed in France.	3
Forde, Ned	fiddle player	2
Fuller, Stephen	from North Kerry, survived Ballyseedy explosion, later a T.D.	7
Gaffney, Lieut.	suspected of ill-treating IRA prisoners	7
Galvin, Mossy	singer from Farmer's Bridge, well-known IRA family, later emigrated to USA	4,6
George	trainee butcher	6
Gilpin	from Cahirciveen, Lewis gunner, active IRA man.	6
Gleeson, Nellie	from Kilgarvan	9
Gows, The	two families of blacksmiths, surname Murphy.	2
Griffin, Dan	from Kilcummin, worked with author in Coopers, later emigrated to UK	9
Harper, Capt.	Free State officer, stationed in Barraduff.	8
Harrington, Denis	young tinker, flu victim	3
Hastings, Sgt. Jack	of Headford	3
Hayes, Dan	from The Bower, fearless IRA man, later emigrated to USA.	2,4,6,8,9

Name	Description	Chapter
Healy, Buck	active in agrarian struggle 1880/90	2
Healy, Con	attorney, popular Killarney and Kerry footballer.	9
Healy, Fred	ex-British Army	6
Healy, Paddy	athlete, All-Ireland football player	2,3
Healy, Pats	ex-British Army, Fred's brother, Lewis gunner.	6
Hegarty, Pat	scout who had been captured	6
Hickey, Ned	author's comrade, apprentice blacksmith, Kilquane.	4
Hogan, Seán	Rescued from British at Knocklong by his comrade	4
Horgan, Jackie	friend of author in Killarney 1924/25	9
Horan, Jack	active IRA man, emigrated to USA.	7, 8
Houlihan, Fr. Michael	author's cousin from North Dakota, son of John Houlihan	3,9
Houlihan, John	of Haverhill, Mass., U.S.A., author's granduncle, visited Ireland 1925	9
Houlihan, Mike	member of author's company, cousin/friend of author.	5
Hurley, Dinso	Killarney, Kerry footballer.	9
Hutch, Mr.	farmer and veterinarian, Buttevant	3
Jerry the Cock	surname O'Sullivan, owned fighting cocks, Kenmare area.	6
Jimmy the Master	surname O'Sullivan, garage, auto repairs, Kenmare area.	9
Kelleher's Pub	in Headford, now Spillane's	8
Kennedy, Jerry	from Headford, Vice O.C., fearless leader.	6, 7
Kent Family	Cork patriots	6
Kevins, John	IRA man captured and killed at Beaufort, ex R.I.C. man.	7
Kirby, Rev.	parish curate, Glenflesk.	2
Leahy, Matt	from the Muckross area, friend of author while working in Killarney.	9
Looney, Con	of Kenmare, killed at Killorglin	6
Lucey Brothers	fiddle players, cousins of author, from Cummeenavrick, Clonkeen.	2
Lynch, Con		2
Lynch, Denny	of Clydagh, active in agrarian struggle 1880, obliged to go to USA, buried Newbury Port, Massachusetts.	1,2
Lynch, Jack		1
Lynch, Margaret	from Headford, native Clydagh, later Sr. Martha.	1
Lynch, Paddy	accordion player from Kenmare.	4
Lynch, Patie	gamekeeper at Muckross Estate for many years. Lived at Killegy.	5,9
Lyne, Mr.	farm steward for Lord Kenmare.	9
Lyne, Tom	from Annaghmore, active IRA man, emigrated to USA.	2,6,7,8,9
Lyons, Capt. Tiny	Free State officer, suspected of ill-treating IRA prisoners	7,8

MacEllistrim, Tommy	a Group O.C. took command at Headford when Dan Allman was killed, later T.D. for Kerry.	5,7
Mahony, Kathleen	of Cobh	9
Mahony, Paddy	of Cobh, retired RIC man, native of The Bower, guesthouse owner.	9
Malone, Tom	suspected spy	4
McCarthy, Maurice	on New St., Killarney, attorney, formerly of Headford.	9
McCarthy, Neilus		9
McCarthy, Patrick	accidentally killed with own gun, buried Kilquane, later Killarney.	4
McCarthy family	of Headford, owners of large estate, later divided.	9
McCurtain, Thomas	Mayor of Cork.	4
McGlynn, Mick	from the Castleisland area, active IRA member.	7
McLeod, Angus	steward of Sir Arthur Vincent	5
McLeon, Sean		8
McSweeney John	The Bower, Rathmore, companion of author, captured near Paps mountain, escaped from Macroom Castle, emigrated to USA, returned later to live in Cork.	6 ,7,8
McSweeney Michael	The Bower, Rathmore, brother of John/Tom, killed at Shrone party, buried in Kilquane.	7
McSweeney Tom	The Bower, Rathmore, companion of author, alias 'Dundon', First-Aid man, good artist, fearless IRA man.	6
McSweeney, Terence	Mayor of Cork	4
McSweeney Family	Cork patriots	6
Mor, Jerh		2
Moynihan, Manus	Agricultural School attendee, O.C. IRA at Rathmore Bog Road ambush	3,6
Montieth, Capt.	Irish rebel leader	3
Moriarty	family of masons and builders	2
Morley, Dan	old man	2
Morley, Johnny	old man's son, active in agrarian struggle 1880	2
Moylan, Bill	auto mechanic, active IRA man, brother of Seán.	9
Moylan, Seán	member of North Cork Column	4
Moynihan	from Barraduff	7
Moynihan, Con	held prisoner, arrested at Shrone party, later emigrated USA.	6,7
Moynihan, Johnny	blind fiddle player	1
Moynihan, Julia	author's cousin from Caherbarnagh	8
Moynihan, Madge	became Mrs. Cronin, P.J.'s cousin, taught in Raheen school.	1
Moynihan, Malachy	dancer, tug-of-war team member, Agricultural School attendee, home burned down after Bog Road ambush	3
Moynihan, Ned	Shronedarragh, active IRA member	7
Moynihan, P.J.	author's uncle, Caherbarnagh, Gaelic speaker, musician, dancer, player of war pipes.	1,2
Moynihan, Tady Ned	carpenter, lived near Beheenagh Bridge.	2

Moynihan Family	of Gortnascarta, James was IRA leader, Gaelic speaker.	6
Murphy, Eugene	pub owner and blacksmith.	2
Murphy, Fred	nicknamed "Free Gow", Kilquane, good fiddle player.	1
Murphy, Free	Castleisland, North Kerry Brigade Commander, teacher, footballer.	5
Murphy, Jack	author's friend, Kilquane, IRA man, emigrated to USA.	4
Murphy, John	author's next-door neighbour, singer of old patriotic songs.	2,3
Murphy, John	killed while a prisoner.	6
Murphy, Liz	author's cousin, sister of Margaret, IRA supporter, emigrated to USA.	9
Murphy, Margaret	author's cousin, sister of Liz, IRA supporter, emigrated to USA.	9
Murphy, Mike	carpenter, native of Barraduff.	2
Murphy, Mike	author's neighbour, farmer, later lived near Knocknagree.	5
Murphy, Ml.		6
Murphy, Paddy	author's cousin, Rathmore, Lewis gunner, later policeman in USA.	1
Murphy, Timmy	Headford, active IRA man.	6
Nagle, Pat	held prisoner	7
Nelligan, Col.	suspected of ill-treating IRA prisoners	7
O' , John	fisherman	2
O'Carroll, Mike	violin player, neighbour and farmer.	3
O'Connell, Daniel	lawyer, Irish Party leader.	2
O'Connell, Phil	local farmer from Beheenagh Bridge.	4
O'Connor	owner of a fine cow.	6
O'Connor, Alice	of Muckross	9
O'Connor, Brig. Comm.	Free State officer, killed.	6
O'Connor, Capt.	Free State officer, killed.	6
O'Connor, Danny	wounded while a prisoner but escaped, later emigrated to the USA	6
O'Connor, Dee	from Kilcummin, footballer, IRA man.	9
O'Connor, Johnny	IRA man, Lewis gunner, fearless, emigrated to USA, returned later	4,6
O'Connor, Timmy		9
O'Connor, Tom	Scarteen, killed in Kenmare attack 1922, former member of Kerry No.2 Flying Column.	4,6
O'Donnell, Sergt.	Civic Guard	9
O'Donoghue, Denis	played bagpipes, tailor on Henn Street, Killarney, went to USA.	6,9
O'Donoghue, Francis	author's Battn. Adjutant, captured, later emigrated to England.	5,6,8
O'Donoghue, Free	"The Kid", farmer, native of Cullen, IRA man.	9
O'Donoghue, Mike	teacher in Barraduff	8

O'Donoghue, Mrs.	teacher in Barraduff	2
O'Donoghue, Pat	boy, 15 years old, first cousin of author, emigrated USA.	4
O'Higgins Kevin	Free State Minister for Justice	6
O'Keeffe, Eugene	Meentogues' School Principal	5
O'Keeffe, Pádraig	outstanding fiddle player from Sliabh Luachra	2
O'Leary Con	former school teacher, high ranking IRA officer, emigrated to UK	5,8,9
O'Leary, Jerh.	local owner	3
O'Leary, Margaret		9
O'Leary, Neil	native of Headford, Kerry footballer, IRA man.	6,7
O'Leary, Tom	native of Kerry, resigned from RIC and joined IRA.	4
O'Malley, Pat	author's friend, motor car driver, emigrated to England.	9
O'Shea, Ellen		1
O'Shea, John		2
O'Sullivan	family of carpenters	1
O'Sullivan, Denis	intrepid Barraduff youth, later joined Free State side.	3
O'Sullivan Michael	native Cloghane, shot and killed at Knockanes, buried Kilquane.	6,9
O'Sullivan, Ml.	Agricultural School attendee, Rathmore farmer.	3
O'Sullivan, Owen	Kerry poet	2
O'Sullivan, Pat T.	in author's Company, went to Canada and USA.	5
O'Sullivan, Tim		4
Paddy, Uncle	P.J.Murphy, ex R.I.C., later a farmer near Tralee.	9
Prout, Col.	Free State officer	7
P., Mike	Mike O'Donoghue, Glenflesk IRA man.	7
Quill, Dan		6
Quill, J.J.	Ballyvourney	9
Quill, Mike	Kilgarvan, IRA man, later Trade Union boss in New York.	6
Rahilly, Mick	captured at Shrone party	6
Reen, Dan		6
Reen, Denis "D"	5th Battn. O.C., native of Rathbeg, emigrated to Australia.	5
Reen, Denny	Battalion Quartermaster, cousin of author, one of five brothers active in IRA, captured, interned in Cork jail, escaped, went to Canada, later to USA.	5 ,6,8
Reen, Jerh	of the Old Chapel, father of Reen brothers.	6,7
Reen, John	Denny's brother, captured at Shrone party, held in Macroom Castle jail and later Cork, escaped to Canada, then USA.	6,7,8
Reen, John		8
Reen, Mary	nurse, home from U.S.	6
Reen, Mary Joe	author's cousin, went to USA, married IRA man.	9
Reen, Mike	author's cousin, IRA man, fought in Waterford/Kerry, signaller	6,9

Reen, Paty	Rathbeg, veteran of Dardanelles campaign, brother of Denis 'D'.	6,7
Reen Michl.	Agricultural School attendee	3
Rice, John Joe	Brigade, O.C., native of Kenmare, outstanding officer.	5
Riordan, Jerry	No.3 Brigade O.C., Castlegregory area, fought in Limerick/Kerry	6
Russell, Paul	college player, from Killarney, later Civic Guard.	9
Ryan, Jerh.	Agricultural School attendee	3
Ryan, Supt.	Civic Guard	9
Shanahan, John	from Castleisland	9
Shea, Mossy	Killarney, joined Civic Guards.	9
Shea, Tim	Kenmare Battn., fought at Headford.	6
Shea, Tim	solicitor, Kerry footballer, IRA man.	9
Sheehy, J.J.		7
Singleton, John	local owner	3
Singleton, John	native of Gneevegullia, school friend of author.	6
Slattery, David		2
Smyth, Col.	RIC officer, shot in Cork.	4
Spillane, Ned	athlete, Kerry footballer, IRA man.	2
Stack, Austin	Irish rebel leader from Tralee.	3
Sullivan, Bill	fiddle player from Gneevegullia area, one-time comrade of author, later joined Free State army.	5,8
Sullivan, Denis	captain of Barraduff Co., later joined Free state army, friend of author	4
Sullivan, Larry	from the Quarries Cross	6
Sullivan, Paddy		9
Sullivan, Pat	captured and shot	6
Sullivan, Pat	IRA man, later joined Free State side.	6
Sullivan, Pat	of Headford	8
Sullivan, Thady	nicknamed the "Clerk", parish clerk.	1
Sullivan, Thady	Carpenter	2
Sullivan, Tadhg	from Muckross, author's friend, later cameraman on *The Dawn* film.	9
Toohig	native Ballydaly.	7
Twiss, John	of Northeast Kerry near Co. Limerick.	1
Vincent, Sir Arthur	owner of Muckross and adjoining lands.	5
Wade's	Barber Shop in New Street, Killarney.	9
Williams, George	fiddle Player	2
Willis, Baby	author's friend	9
Willpatrick, Capt.	captured Div. Officer (real name William P. Fleming)	6
Woodcock, Sgt.	Killed in action at Bog Road ambush	4
Young, Capt.	in charge of Relief Column, killed at The Bower ambush 1923.	6